CUT YOUR BILLS IN HALF

CUT YOUR BILLS IN HALF

THOUSANDS OF TIPS
TO SAVE THOUSANDS OF DOLLARS

By the Editors of Rodale Press

Rodale Press, Emmaus, Pennsylvania

The information in this book has been carefully researched, and all efforts have been made to ensure accuracy. Rodale Press, Inc., assumes no responsibility for any injuries suffered or damages or losses incurred during or as a result of following this information. All information should be carefully studied and clearly understood before taking any action based on the information and advice presented in this book.

Printed in the United States of America

Managing Editor: Margaret Lydic Balitas
Editor: Cheryl Winters Tetreau
Writers: Donald Best (chapter 6); Kathi Kull (chapter 4); Gary Mayk (chapters 2, 13, 14, 15, 16); Vicki Jarmulowski Mayk (chapter 5); Carol Munson (chapters 1 and 3); Suzanne Nelson (chapter 7); Connie Nesteruk (chapters 8, 9, 10, 11); Kerry H. Pechter (chapter 12)
Book design by Sandy Freeman
Illustrations by John Carlance, Kathi Ember, and Paul Harvey

Library of Congress Cataloging-in-Publication Data

Cut your bills in half : thousands of tips to save thousands of dollars / by the editors of Rodale Press.
   p. cm.
  Includes index.
  ISBN 0–87857–818–8 hardcover
  1. Consumer education. I. Rodale Press.
TX335.C87 1989
640.73—dc19   89–5943
                                                CIP

Distributed in the book trade by St. Martin's Press

4 6 8 10 9 7 5 3   hardcover

CONTENTS

Introduction 1

1 *Eating Better for Less* 3
2 *Making Deals on Wheels* 46
3 *Dressing on a Shoestring* 71
4 *Great Furniture You Can Afford* 90
5 *Putting a Ceiling on Home Expenses* 107
6 *Save Energy, Save Money* 142
7 *Prune the Price of Garden and Lawn Care* 194
8 *Cutting Costs on Kids* 246
9 *Higher Education, Lower Tuition* 256
10 *Take Off to Travel Bargains* 271
11 *"Twofers" and Other Entertainment Treats* 283
12 *In Sickness and in Health* 297
13 *Telephones: Dialing for Dollars* 329
14 *Taking the Bite out of Taxes* 341
15 *Beating High Insurance Rates* 354
16 *Estate Planning: A Will to Save* 370

Index 380

INTRODUCTION

If you're like most people, you want your money to go further than just making ends meet. But there are always bills to pay. Short of choosing to pay only half your balance each month, are there really ways to cut your bills in half? You bet—and they're all right here.

We've asked experts in home economics, health, consumer affairs, gardening, and other fields to give us their very best advice on cutting costs. They let us in on the secrets to savings—and we're passing these secrets on to you.

Did you know:

- There's a limit on the amount of time you should spend in the supermarket if you want to check out cheaply.
- Your car will last longer if you *don't* follow the owner's manual timetable for oil changes.
- You can trade in your old wardrobe for a new look—and it may not cost you a cent.
- You can have a lush, productive garden by using *free* fertilizers and other soil amendments.
- You can take advantage of free home decorating advice to beautify your home.
- A more expensive refrigerator may still be the better buy—use our formula for figuring appliance life-cycle costs to find out why.
- You *can* fight city hall—and reduce your property taxes.

These are just some of the thousands of money-saving tips you'll find inside. Enjoy and use this book. You'll find yourself counting your savings from the very first page!

EATING BETTER
FOR LESS

Do you spend $100 a week on groceries, or perhaps closer to $200? This translates into big bucks on an annual basis—anywhere from $5,200 to $10,400. A cut of as little as 10 percent each time you go shopping could mean a savings of $520 in a year. What follows are dozens of suggestions for trimming your grocery and food bills by 10 to 50 percent. These tips will help you save money each time you go to the grocery store, plus you'll learn how to be a smarter shopper and how to make the most of your food dollars.

Supermarket Savvy

Check Out Food Ads

Careful scrutiny of advertising claims can help you save money by buying the specials listed in food ads and circulars. One word of caution: Real savings depend on recognizing which specials are real bargains, so it's to your advantage to keep track of what the everyday prices are on the products you buy.

Ad Lingo:
Two-for-One Sales

These are also known as "Buy one, get one free" sales. These can be excellent buys if you know the prices have not been raised to compensate for the sale.

Ad Lingo:
Manufacturers' Promotions

In this case, a manufacturer runs a special promotion to make its products most appealing. Check prices before making your selection—another manufacturer's everyday price may be lower for the type of product you want.

Ad Lingo:
Loss Leaders

These are exceptionally good buys designed to lure you into the store. Marketers are willing to take a loss on the product—hence, the term *loss leader*—just to get you into the store. The hope is, of course, that you'll buy additional items while there.

Don't See Red

Cast a wary eye on color ads. Shoppers have become conditioned to recognize red as meaning *bargain, sale, reduced;* so some advertisers make liberal use of red, hot pink, and orange in their ads. Yellow and black are other attention getters. Full-color ads are also meant to trigger your appetite. Read these ads carefully—there may not be any bargains involved.

Conditional Bargains

Sometimes the fine print states, "Tuesday only" or "Saturday only." Other limiting features include: "With $5 purchase"; "With coupon"; "We have the right to substitute"; "No rain checks." Be on the lookout for the fine print.

"Drastic Reduction" Ads

Have the prices really been slashed? To decide, you must be familiar with regular prices.

"New" and "Improved" Tags

These are powerful selling words, so you'll see "new" and "improved" whenever the manufacturer can justify using them. What's not clear is just how big, small, or advantageous the improvement may be. Is it a new perfume in the facial tissue? Is it a few noodles in the vegetable soup? Is it a new seasoning in the tomato sauce? To the smart-money shopper, "new" and "improved" signals caution.

What to Compare
When Comparing

When comparison shopping, consider the price of food items in all forms: fresh, frozen, canned, and dried. And check several variations: whole, sliced, chopped, pitted, and so forth.

Most of the year, you'll find that canned or frozen will vie for the least expensive. But come a food's peak season, fresh is where the bargains will most likely be. Among the variations, whole and pitted are often most expensive, while chopped or crushed are the least expensive. But packaging and promotions can influence all this, so stay alert for exceptions.

No Time to Comparison-Shop?

It takes time to comparison-shop. And if you run from store to store, it takes more time (and gas for your car). Your best bet is to settle on two or three stores that consistently have competitive prices. Then save time and travel by reading their newspaper ads closely before you leave home.

Nonfoods Cost Big Bucks

How many of these nonfood items do you usually buy at the supermarket?

brushes	paper napkins
cigarettes	shampoo
dish detergents	tissues
garbage bags	toilet paper
laundry detergents	toothpaste

The more of these items that you buy at the grocery store, the more you're wasting your money. Grocery stores put high markups on nonfood items to help compensate for the low markups on fresh food. But you can tally big savings by purchasing these nonfood items at discount stores, such as discount pharmacies and department stores.

Nix Impulse Buying

When you walk into a grocery store, you are the captive audience of what *Consumer Reports* magazine calls a selling machine. And every part of the store—from the arrangement of the shelves to the placement of the packages on those shelves—is designed to sell something, *anything,* to you. What the marketers hope to capture are your impulse decisions—the ones made right in the store.

How can you resist the pressure to impulse-buy? Your first line of defense is a good, detailed shopping list. But for the list to work, you must stick to it closely. Your reward? Savings that can check out at around 50 percent. Here are some strategies:

- Prepare an ongoing list and jot down items as you run low.
- Before shopping, check your freezer, refrigerator, and pantry for staples on hand—flour, honey, coffee, tea, canned tomatoes. Add any items you're low on to your ongoing list.
- Review recipes for the coming week and include missing items on your list.
- Study supermarket advertised specials. If you see any items you regularly use and you have room to stockpile them, put them on the list. Note: You should do this only with items that have a fairly long shelf life.
- Arrange your shopping list according to the general layout of your supermarket. You'll save steps as well as unwanted exposure to impulse items.

Refunding Revelations

Generally speaking, refunding is not a recommended way to save on food purchases. Using coupons gives you a discount at the time of purchase, but refunding requires that you purchase the product at full price to get reimbursed later. And if you think clipping coupons is a laborious chore, just look at these not-so-easy three steps to refunding:

1. Find the offers. This means searching through newspapers and magazines, checking at supermarkets and on products, and even subscribing to expensive "refunding" newsletters.

2. Collect proofs of purchase. Manufacturers often require a seal, label, boxtop, lid, ingredient panel, and even the entire package. And they don't stop with one; some may request proofs of purchase (POPs) from two, three, even five of their products. Add to this the requirement that many manufacturers now make—store receipts with the purchase price circled for that particular item—and you're talking about having to stockpile quite a bit of paper, cardboard, plastic, or what-have-you before you can cash in.

3. Mail in POPs with refund request form. These forms are in such demand that it's sometimes difficult to get them, even from the manufacturers. To counter this, some refunders exchange forms at parties, club meetings, conventions, and through the mail. Some enterprising refunders collect extra forms to sell. Of course, don't forget that it costs you $.25 for each mailing, so a $1 refund actually nets you only $.75—an amount you could more easily save by double couponing and/or shopping wisely.

The outcome of all this collecting and clipping? Once you've deducted your expenses and have taken into account the top prices you've paid for national brands, your savings through refunding are less than if you had employed savvy shopping techniques, used coupons wisely, and were on the lookout for bargains.

Calculate Unit Prices

Take full advantage of unit pricing. It's the easiest and most accurate way to compare prices across brands and sizes. Some stores have already done the calculations for you and have the unit prices posted on the shelf. *Read them carefully and save.* If your store doesn't unit-price, you can easily do so yourself. Using a pocket calculator, divide the cost of the product by the number of ounces in the can or package. This will give you the price per ounce. (For example, a 12-ounce can of peas selling at $.51 would cost $.043 an ounce. A 7-ounce can at $.37 would cost $.053 an ounce.) Then, compare. In this example the 12-ounce can of peas is the better buy.

Buy in Bulk

When the price is right, buy in large quantities. That's good advice—most of the time. But if you're not crazy about the product, can't use it up before it spoils, or don't have room to store it properly, buying in bulk doesn't spell economy. If your freezer will hold a case of frozen orange juice cans, go ahead and stock up while the price is right. But if the family doesn't like canned peas, there's no point in buying a caseful. By the same token, don't get two or three bushels of grapefruit if they'll rot before you can eat them all.

The same advice goes for buying the large economy-size package of various items. If you do decide to buy, double-check the price. Sometimes you'll find that it's cheaper to buy two smaller packages than one economy size, yet you'll get the same quantity.

Coupons Can Save Cents

Clipping coupons is a habit that saves cents—sometimes. Manufacturers often give away coupons as advertising for some of their most expensive products. So comparative shopping will often net a better buy—even if you can get double the coupon off at the supermarket.

If you decide to use coupons, use them effectively. Clip and file manufacturers' coupons only for products your family likes and will use. Then keep track of the expiration date and toss any that are over-the-hill. When you're in the supermarket, check the in-store flyer for coupons to use then and there. Sometimes you can get terrific buys, such as one dozen large eggs free with a $10 purchase.

Shopping Strategies That Save

Good Enough to Eat

Eat before you shop. Studies show that hungry shoppers buy more goodies. Everything looks so-o-o good when you're hungry.

Skip the Singles

Avoid packages with individual servings. Extra packaging almost always boosts the price.

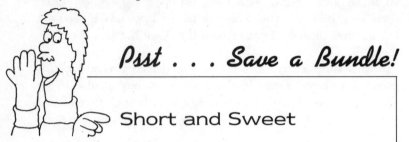

Psst . . . Save a Bundle!

Short and Sweet

Keep your visit to the grocery store short. If possible, stay under 30 minutes. If you linger longer, remember this: Market surveys indicate that shoppers spend an extra 50 cents a minute for every minute over 30 in a supermarket.

Running a Tab

Bring a calculator. You can use it to keep a running total of what you're spending. That way, you can put back whatever exceeds your food budget, and you won't be surprised at the checkout counter.

Look High and Low

Usually you'll find the less expensive generic items and store brands on the very bottom and very top shelves. The higher-priced name brands are "conveniently" located at eye level.

On the Outside Looking In

Stick to the perimeter aisles. That's where you'll find food with the least processing—produce, meats, dairy—and, therefore, the lowest prices.

Go Alone

Whenever you can, shop alone, because it's easier to stick to your list. Your baby will distract you, and older children will want everything they see—especially if it has been advertised on television!

The Best Time to Buy

Shop at midweek and at off hours. The sales and double couponing are most likely to be on during midweek. Also, there's less distracting hustle and bustle early or late in the day or at mealtime. Keep your mind clear for the job at hand.

Once a Week Is Enough

Do your shopping only once a week. Or, better yet, once every two to three weeks, except for perishables such as milk and produce. Shoppers who frequently run to the store buy more impulse items.

Check Your Register Tape

Research shows that unintentional mistakes are commonplace, especially on large purchases.

Know Where to Go

Supermarkets

These medium- to large-size grocery stores carry about 10,000 items and do $2 million or more in business a year. Usually owned by large corporations with numerous stores in a geographic area, supermarkets can buy in volume and get price breaks for doing so. As a result, they can pass reasonable prices on to customers. Most also carry house brands, which sell at competitive prices. Closely related to the supermarkets are the "independents." These individually owned markets have joined the Associated

Grocers or the Independent Grocers Association (IGA) in order to buy in volume and pass on savings to customers. Most independents also carry IGA or similarly named house brands.(Barbara Salsbury lists and describes supermarkets and their alternatives in her book *Cut Your Grocery Bills in Half!* [Acropolis Books, 1982].)

Corner Grocery Stores

These are often dubbed mom-and-pop stores because they're small, independent, and family owned. Because of their low volume, they usually must pay high prices for their stock, so what they sell is almost always priced on the high side. Occasionally you can find one that carries fresh local breads or produce at bargain prices, and some have competitively priced fresh deli foods.

Box Stores

Also called limited assortment stores, these carry fewer than 1,000 items. Here you'll see little variety in either brands or sizes. To keep overhead costs down, these stores don't stock the perishables: meat, dairy, or produce. And customers must do their own bagging since the number of employees is lean. Cash is the only way to pay and store hours are short. No coupons are accepted. What kind of prices can you expect? Generally speaking, savings of 20 to 30 percent are possible.

Warehouse Stores

Although these stores have a low overhead and carry only 1,000 to 7,000 items (a reduced selection of brands and sizes), they *do* offer meat, produce, dairy, and other perishables. If you shop at warehouse stores, you'll quickly notice that the stock varies from week to week. That's because these stores operate on "deals." That is, they carry whatever they can obtain cheaply from wholesalers. You can pay for your order with cash or a check for the exact amount. You must bring your own bags and do the bagging yourself.

Discount Stores

Coupons and specials are rarely evident at discount stores. Instead, they offer consistently low prices. Unfortunately, the choice of brands is generally limited.

Specialty Stores

These small markets include health food stores; gourmet shops; shops that carry one item such as cheese, meat, or fish; and shops that emphasize foods from a particular cuisine such as Italian, French, or Oriental. Items here are generally quite expensive, although you can occasionally find a decent buy.

Thrift Stores

Here's where you can consistently save about 40 percent, even though the store volume is low. Their secret to cheap prices? Leftovers—better known as day-old breads, cookies, buns, doughnuts, and English muffins. Many thrift stores carry only one commercial baker's products, such as Pepperidge Farm or Entenmann's.

Psst . . . Save a Bundle!

Watch That Scanner

If your grocery store uses price scanners at the checkout counter, watch the display screen carefully. Many grocery stores will give you an item *free* if its price scans for more than what the sticker or shelf label indicates. This little-known freebie isn't advertised, although if you look carefully you may see a tiny sign posted on the side of the cash register that explains the store's policy. So stay alert at the checkout line, and you could take home some free groceries.

Convenience Stores

No matter how often you check the prices, convenience stores are outrageously expensive. What they offer instead of competitive prices is convenience—in the form of round-the-clock (or almost so) service. Located mainly in areas that are densely populated, convenience stores stock staples, such as milk and bread, plus snack food and high-impulse items packaged in individual serving sizes.

Membership Stores

Generally competitive with chain supermarkets, these stores sell exclusively to customers who purchase a membership. You'll get good buys if you watch for sales. In this category, too, are the commissary stores, run for families of United States military personnel. You can often, but not always, save up to 30 percent on items at the commissary. Check around for bargains.

Another type of membership store is the store-front co-op. Although anyone can buy here, only members who volunteer to help stock and run the store are eligible for a discount.

Superstores

The latest trend in supermarkets is the superstore, which offers not only food and nonfood products but also customer services, such as camera counters, optical centers, and restaurants. Prices in these stores can be highly competitive—food bargains always attract customers—but you must be careful not to succumb to impulse buying.

Combo or combination stores fall somewhere between the supermarkets and the superstores. Once again, the markup on nonfood items is extremely profitable—for the store owner.

Groceries on the Side

Drugstores, gas stations, discount chains, and department stores all try luring customers with food. The department stores tend to have the most elaborate setups, often offering top quality—and expensive—goods in a bakery, deli, or coffee shop. Some also carry expensive candies, top-of-the-line canned goods, and other gourmet foods. Drugstores and discount chains occasionally have good deals in the form of loss leaders.

Direct from the Source

Most of us know these as farmers' markets and roadside produce stands. In large cities, the farmers' markets are often located in the docking or trucking district where the produce is sold in bulk between 2:00 A.M. and 6:00 A.M. each day. Be ready to haggle and compete with grocers.

Some smaller towns have scaled-down versions of the traditional farmers' markets. In most instances, the markets are open for a limited number of hours each week. During the summer, small produce stands dot the roadsides in many communities. At any of these sources, you can get superb bargains—if you know prices well. Contact your local extension service for the farmers' market nearest you.

Manufacturers' Outlets

Is there a cannery, dairy, factory, egg ranch, mill, or other processing plant in your area? If so, check to see if it runs an outlet store. At manufacturers' outlets, you can get terrific bargains on overruns or products with minor defects.

Wholesale Outlets

If you can buy in bulk, consider contacting a wholesaler who supplies small groceries, restaurants, schools, and hospitals. Some will sell directly to individuals. Savings of 20 to 40 percent are possible.

Buying Clubs and Co-ops

Big savings—more than 50 percent on some items—can be had through a buying club or a co-op. How's that possible? You and other members of the group do the ordering, telephoning, picking up, repackaging of bulk orders, and delivering. So, instead of dealing with middlemen, you work directly with manufacturers and wholesalers. For information on setting up a co-op, write the Cooperative League of the U.S.A. (CLUSA), 1828 L Street NW, Suite 1100, Washington, DC 20036.

Salvage Stores

Prices at salvage stores are phenomenally *low*, but the health risks can be *very high*. Here's why: Salvage stores sell products damaged in shipping, salvaged from train or truck wrecks, or stored too long at a grocery store or warehouse. We suggest that you stay away from salvaged food items. Because of the rough handling, cans can be dented or split at the seams (opening the way for bacteria to enter the food), and packages holding cereals or pasta may be torn or dirty. It's not worth risking your health, no matter how good the savings may be. On the other hand, you can get great deals on some nonfood items at salvage stores, particularly paper products. Just check to be sure the packages are intact and that you're not buying boxes of water-damaged tissues or dirt-smudged toilet paper.

All about Food

Convenience by the Dollar

With our busy lives, it's easy to see why convenience foods are so popular. But convenience comes in a mixed bag of prices. On the low side, there are the simple foods: frozen orange juice, peas, green beans, corn, and other vegetables. Most often, you can save time *and* money by buying such convenience items instead of squeezing juice and shucking peas. But the more convenience you buy, the more you spend. On the high side, there are the fully prepared entries: lasagna, chicken divan, and other oven-to-table meals. When buying these products, you can expect to pay 300 percent more than you'd pay if you prepared the foods yourself. To save money, set aside a night or weekend when you'll have some free time, enlist the help of other family members, and make several meals that can be frozen for later use.

Are Brand Names Best?

Not necessarily. Whenever you're tempted to try a store brand or generic, go ahead. You have nothing to lose but up to 40 percent of your grocery bill. In many cases, you'll find the less expensive brands suit your needs and tastes just as well as the brand-name product does.

Why are the store brands cheaper? They don't have huge advertising tabs to pass along to you, even though they are produced by the same reputable manufacturer as the name brands. For example, Hap Hatton and Laura Torbet, authors of *Helpful Hints for Better Living: How to Live Better for Less* (Facts on File Publications, 1984), report that Heinz makes soup for Grand Union, Pantry Pride, and Giant; Morton, Diamond, and International supply salt, and Borden and Sealtest produce ice cream for the supermarket chains.

As for the generics, try these items, which have the same chemical makeup no matter what the label:

baking soda	nonfat powdered milk
cooking oils (except olive)	orange juice
cornstarch	peanuts
dried fruits	salt
extracts and flavorings	spices
herbs	sugar
honey	unbleached flour
lemon juice	vinegar
lime juice	walnuts
molasses	

The Dating Game

To maximize the food dollars you spend, go for the freshest products possible. For fruits and vegetables, this means choosing from the bins rather than buying in bags or cellophane-wrapped trays, so you can see what you're getting. (A 20-pound bargain bag of potatoes, for example, will contain many cracked and decayed potatoes that are unusable—not a very good bargain at all!) Avoid fruits and vegetables that are badly bruised, too soft, discolored, or have wilted leaves or stalks. For packaged foods, look for the freshness date.

Packaged Food Lingo I:
Use By

This is the date after which the product is no longer at peak freshness.

Packaged Food Lingo II:
Sell By

This is the last day the product can be sold in the market. It's also called the pull date. Remember that the sell-by date does not indicate when the item must be used. Most food products will still be usable about a week beyond the sell-by date.

Packaged Food Lingo III:
Expiration

This is the last day the product should be used.

Safeguard Your Investment

There's nothing worse than spending $100 or more on food only to find it rotting in the back of your refrigerator a week or so later. Storing food properly is akin to saving at a secure bank—you'll have your investment for another day. To make sure you get to use what you paid for, see the tables "Keeping Meats and Fish Fresh," "Keeping Fruits Fresh," and "Keeping Vegetables Fresh."

Cheaper Moo Juice

If your household has growing children and teens who down milk almost faster than you can bring it home, you can noticeably cut the cost of milk these ways:

- Buy fresh milk in multiquart containers. Usually, milk in $\frac{1}{2}$- and 1-gallon containers costs less per quart than milk in single quarts.
- Buy nonfat dry milk in 20-quart boxes.
- Use nonfat dry milk in cooking and baking and as a beverage. For a beverage, mix equal amounts of reconstituted nonfat milk and fresh whole (or lowfat) milk.
- Use evaporated milk in cooking.

Keeping Meats and Fish Fresh

FOOD	STORAGE
Bacon, ham, hot dogs, luncheon meats, smoked sausage	Wrap in waxed paper or plastic wrap and refrigerate; will keep 1 week (bacon, hot dogs, whole ham, smoked sausage), 5 days (half ham), 3 days (ham slices), 3–5 days (luncheon meats)
Beef, lamb, pork, and veal roasts; beef steaks; lamb and pork chops	Wrap loosely in waxed paper or foil; store in coldest part of refrigerator; will keep 3–5 days. To freeze, rewrap in freezer wrap or bags; will keep 6–8 months (roasts), 6–12 months (steaks), 3–4 months (chops)
Chicken and turkey, duck and goose	Wrap loosely in waxed paper and refrigerate; if whole, remove giblets and package separately; never stuff before storing. Will keep 1–2 days. To freeze, rewrap in freezer wrap or bags; will keep 12 months (whole birds), 6 months (parts), 3 months (giblets)
Fin fish	Wrap in waxed paper and refrigerate; will keep 1–2 days. To freeze, rewrap in freezer wrap or bags; will keep 6–9 months
Ground and stew meats; variety meats (liver, kidney, etc.); pork sausage	Wrap for refrigeration as above; will keep 1–2 days. Rewrap for freezer as above; will keep 3–4 months (ground, stew, and variety meats), 1–2 months (sausage)

(continued)

Keeping Meats and Fish Fresh— Continued

Shellfish	Refrigerate live in shallow dish covered with damp towels; will keep 1–2 days. Refrigerate peeled shrimp and shucked shellfish in covered jar; will keep 2–3 days. Refrigerate lobster and crabs; use immediately

Keeping Fruits Fresh

FOOD	STORAGE
Apples, cranberries, lemons, limes, oranges	Refrigerate unwashed; will keep 2 weeks
Apricots, nectarines, peaches, pears, plums, rhubarb	Refrigerate when ripe; will keep 3–5 days
Bananas, melons	Refrigerate when ripe; will keep 2–3 days
Berries, cherries, pineapples	Refrigerate unwashed; will keep 1–2 days
Grapefruit, mandarin oranges, tangelos, tangerines	Refrigerate; will keep 1–2 weeks
Grapes	Refrigerate; will keep 4–6 days
Watermelon	Refrigerate; wrap exposed surface; will keep 1 week

Keeping Vegetables Fresh

FOOD	STORAGE
Asparagus	Wrap in moist toweling, refrigerate in plastic bags or covered container; will keep 2–3 days
Beets, cabbage, carrots	Refrigerate in plastic bags (cut off beet and carrot tops); will keep 1–2 weeks
Broccoli, cauliflower, cucumber, greens, leeks and scallions, peppers, summer squash	Refrigerate in plastic bags; will keep 3–5 days
Brussels sprouts	Refrigerate in plastic bags; will keep 2–4 days
Corn	Refrigerate in husks; will keep 1–2 days
Eggplant	Store in cool place or refrigerate in plastic bags; will keep 2–4 days
Green, string, and wax beans	Refrigerate in plastic bags; will keep 2–5 days
Lima beans	Refrigerate in shells; will keep 2–5 days
Mushrooms	Refrigerate in closed paper bag; will keep 1 week
Onions, potatoes, winter squash	Store in cool, dark, dry place; will keep 1–2 months
Radishes	Refrigerate in plastic bags; will keep 2 weeks
Snow and sugar snap peas	Refrigerate in plastic bags; will keep 1–2 days
Sweet peas	Refrigerate uncovered in pods; will last 2–4 days
Sweet potatoes	Store in cool, dry place; will keep 1–2 months
Tomatoes	Refrigerate ripe; will keep 1 week

Thrifty Substitutes

Sometimes a new recipe calls for a small amount of an ingredient you seldom use. Instead of rejecting the recipe—or running out and buying an ingredient you'll never use up—why not try one of the substitutes found in the tables "Ingredient Substitutes" and "Herb and Spice Substitutes"?

Quality Saves

Buying top-quality fresh food can really stretch your food dollars. The reason you save? There's little or no waste, and when you buy fresh foods, you're not paying for fancy packaging. But not all fresh foods are equal; know what you should look for to get the most for your money.

Marvelous Meat

Check the label for the wholesale and retail names of the cut, the price per pound, the grade of the meat, a suggested cooking method, and a sell-by date. A uniform, bright, light to deep red color is characteristic of good beef. Red, porous bones also indicate good-quality beef. Since the color of beef fat varies with age, feed, and breed, fat color is not a reliable clue to the quality of the beef.

The meat of good, young lamb is pink to light red in color, and it is firm and fine textured. Bones are slender, red, moist, and porous. Again, color of fat varies and is not a good indicator of quality.

Good-quality fresh pork has a high proportion of meat to fat and bone. The meat is firm, fine textured, and grayish pink to light red in color. A deep pink color is typical of the meat of cured pork. The meat of very young veal is pale pink to grayish pink; that of somewhat older veal is slightly red. All veal should have a smooth texture and practically no fat.

Prime Poultry

The skin on fresh birds is soft, smooth, cream colored, moist but not wet, and tears easily. You'll want a minimum of pinfeathers. In a sniff test, the bird should not smell foul. If you are buying a

Ingredient Substitutes

INGREDIENT	AMOUNT	SUBSTITUTE
Arrowroot	$1\frac{1}{2}$ tsp 2 tsp	1 Tbsp flour 1 Tbsp cornstarch
Baking powder	1 tsp	$\frac{1}{4}$ tsp baking soda plus $\frac{5}{8}$ tsp cream of tartar; or $\frac{1}{4}$ tsp baking soda plus $\frac{1}{2}$ cup buttermilk or plain yogurt; or $\frac{1}{4}$ tsp baking soda plus $\frac{1}{4}$ cup molasses
Butter	1 cup	$\frac{7}{8}$ cup vegetable oil
Buttermilk	1 cup	1 cup plain yogurt; or 1 cup skim milk plus 1 Tbsp lemon juice
Catsup	1 cup	8 oz tomato sauce plus $\frac{1}{2}$ cup brown sugar and 2 Tbsp vinegar
Cayenne pepper	$\frac{1}{8}$ tsp	3–4 drops liquid hot pepper
Chocolate	1 oz	3 Tbsp carob plus 2 Tbsp water
Corn syrup	1 cup	$1\frac{1}{4}$ cups sugar plus $\frac{1}{4}$ cup liquid; or 1 cup honey
Cracker crumbs	$\frac{3}{4}$ cup	1 cup whole grain bread crumbs
Cream, heavy	1 cup	$\frac{1}{3}$ cup butter plus $\frac{3}{4}$ cup milk
Cream, sour	1 cup	1 cup plain yogurt
Egg yolks	2	1 whole egg
Flour	1 Tbsp	$1\frac{1}{2}$ tsp cornstarch; or 1 Tbsp quick-cooking tapioca; or 1 Tbsp corn flour; or 1 Tbsp potato flour
Lemon juice	1 tsp	$\frac{1}{2}$ tsp vinegar
Milk, whole	1 cup	1 cup reconstituted nonfat dry milk plus $2\frac{1}{2}$ tsp butter
Mustard, prepared	1 Tbsp	1 tsp dry mustard
Onion	1 cup, chopped	1 Tbsp instant minced onion, rehydrated

(continued)

Ingredient Substitutes—Continued

INGREDIENT	AMOUNT	SUBSTITUTE
Prunes, pitted and minced	$\frac{1}{2}$ cup	$\frac{1}{2}$ cup raisins
Tomatoes, chopped	1 cup	$\frac{1}{2}$ cup tomato sauce plus $\frac{1}{2}$ cup water
Tomato sauce	2 cups	$\frac{3}{4}$ cup tomato paste plus 1 cup water

Herb and Spice Substitutes

HERB OR SPICE	SUBSTITUTE WITH
Allspice	Cinnamon, cloves, nutmeg
Basil	Marjoram, oregano, thyme
Bay leaf	Mint
Caraway	Anise
Cardamom	Coriander, ginger
Celery seed	Finely chopped celery leaves
Chives	Scallions
Cilantro	Italian parsley
Cumin	Turmeric
Dill	Caraway
Fennel	Anise
Mace	Nutmeg
Mustard	Prepared mustard
Oregano	Basil, marjoram, thyme
Paprika	Cayenne pepper
Parsley	Basil
Rosemary	Mint, sage
Saffron	Turmeric
Sage	Rosemary, savory
Tarragon	Chervil

whole bird (or breasts), the breasts should look plump and meaty. Check the breastbone and wings: In young birds, the breastbone is flexible and its color light; the wings offer little resistance when bent upright.

Fabulous Fish

Whichever fish is in season will be your best buy. Fresh fish has firm flesh that clings to the bones, a stiff body, and tight scales. If you poke the flesh, it'll spring back. The gills are reddish pink— they'll fade to pink, gray, then brownish green as the fish ages. Bright, clear, bulging eyes and a mild briny smell are two other characteristics to look for. All shellfish should have a mild, sea-breeze odor. Crabs, lobsters, oysters, mussels, and clams should be alive with tightly closed shells when you buy them. Look for leg movement on lobsters and crabs; a lobster's tail should curl under when the lobster is picked up. Fresh shrimp is firm; bay scallops are light tan to pinkish to creamy white; sea scallops are white with some pink or light orange.

First-Rate Fruits

Check the table "Best Buys by the Month" to see when you can expect the lowest prices. Quality fresh fruit should be free of insect damage and show no signs of bruising or mold. Whenever you can, buy loose fruit. That way, you can inspect all pieces and all sides.

Blue Ribbon Vegetables

The best buys can be had during the peak of the harvest. (See the table "Best Buys by the Month.") Quality vegetables are always free of soft spots and insect damage. Whenever possible, get loose instead of prepackaged vegetables. Loose vegetables let you inspect all pieces and sides.

Best Buys by the Month

JANUARY

Apples	Chicken	Pork
Beef	Eggs	Rhubarb
Broccoli	Grapefruit	Turnips
Brussels sprouts	Oranges	

FEBRUARY

Apples	Fish	Rhubarb
Broccoli	Oranges	Scallops
Chicken	Oysters	Turnips

MARCH

Apples	Eggs	Pineapple
Artichokes	Fish	Rhubarb
Beef	Grapefruit	Scallops
Broccoli	Lamb	Turnips
Chicken	Oranges	

APRIL

Artichokes	Fish	Pork
Asparagus	Grapefruit	Rhubarb
Broccoli	Lamb	Summer squash
Chicken	Lemons	Turkey
Eggs	Pineapple	

MAY

Asparagus	Eggs	Pork
Beans	Fish	Rhubarb
Beef	Lamb	Strawberries
Broccoli	Lemons	Summer squash
Corn	Peas	Tomatoes
Cucumbers	Pineapple	

JUNE

Apricots	Corn	Plums
Asparagus	Cucumbers	Radishes
Beans	Eggs	Rhubarb
Beef	Fish	Salmon
Beets	Lemons	Summer squash
Berries	Melons	Tomatoes
Cherries	Peas	

JULY

Apricots	Fish	Peas
Beans	Grapes	Peppers
Beets	Lemons	Plums
Berries	Limes	Salmon
Cherries	Melons	Summer squash
Corn	Nectarines	Tomatoes
Cucumbers	Peaches	Watermelon

AUGUST

Beans	Grapes	Peppers
Beets	Lemons	Plums
Chicken	Melons	Salmon
Corn	Nectarines	Summer squash
Eggplant	Peaches	Tomatoes
Fish	Pears	Watermelon

SEPTEMBER

Beans	Clams	Pears
Beef	Corn	Peppers
Beets	Eggplant	Plums
Broccoli	Fish	Scallops
Cauliflower	Grapes	Tomatoes
Chicken	Peaches	

(continued)

Best Buys by the Month—Continued

OCTOBER

Apples	Cauliflower	Pumpkin
Beans	Chestnuts	Scallops
Beef	Cranberries	Sweet potatoes
Beets	Parsnips	Turkey
Broccoli	Pears	Turnips
Brussels sprouts	Pork	Winter squash

NOVEMBER

Apples	Fish	Tangelos
Beef	Lamb	Tangerines
Broccoli	Oranges	Turkey
Brussels sprouts	Oysters	Turnips
Cauliflower	Pears	Winter squash
Chestnuts	Pumpkin	
Cranberries	Sweet potatoes	

DECEMBER

Apples	Lamb	Tangerines
Broccoli	Oranges	Turkey
Brussels sprouts	Oysters	Turnips
Chicken	Pork	Winter squash
Cranberries	Sweet potatoes	
Grapefruit	Tangelos	

NOTE: Carrots, celery, onions, and potatoes are good buys throughout the year.

Eat, Drink, and Be Thrifty

Bag It

A Saturday lunch for four at the zoo can reach well over $10, even for the most meager fast-food or vendor meal. Weekday lunches from the company cafeteria can average $3 to $5 a day. Wouldn't it be nice to reduce the cost of eating lunch out?

You probably know you can save money—50 percent or more—just by packing your own lunch every day, but brown-bag lunches are so *boring.* The key is to make your brown-bag treat more than just the typical cold meat sandwich. Try some of these tempting ideas:

barbecued chicken legs and wings
casseroles of all types—if you have access to a microwave
chicken, barley, and pecan salad
deviled eggs
homemade soups and stews
poached chicken and pasta salad
poached fish
rice or noodle pudding
salmon and rice salad
tossed greens salad with cheese or turkey cubes
tuna and pasta salad
vegetable soup
yogurt with fruit salad and walnuts

To make lunch preparation easier, keep a stockpile of take-out fixings on hand: napkins, sandwich bags, foil, plastic wrap, small plastic dishes with lids, a thermos and other handy-size thermal containers, and plastic utensils. A good time to think about tomorrow's lunch is right after tonight's dinner—you can pack up the leftovers for lunch as you're cleaning up.

Baby Food for Less

The best and easiest way to save on baby's food is to breast-feed while your child is young. La Leche League, a support organization for nursing mothers, estimates that mothers who nurse their babies save more than $1,000 in the first year alone. The savings are on formula, baby food, feeding equipment, and vitamins.

When you introduce baby's first foods, look for alternatives to the manufactured baby foods. Instead of baby apple juice, buy regular apple juice and dilute it with water. Instead of baby orange juice, squeeze your own or prepare from frozen concentrate. If your baby is just starting to drink orange juice, strain the juice before serving.

For fruits and vegetables, serve what you're giving the rest of the family, but leave out salt, sugar, and other flavorings. Puree the food in a food processor, blender, or baby food grinder. If your baby is just starting solid foods, strain the puree. You can do the same thing with meats, poultry, and fish.

Home-cooked tapioca pudding, cornstarch pudding, custards, and junket are also fine for baby and cost much less than manufactured equivalents.

Leftovers: Twice As Nice

Money-smart food shoppers make their dollars go a long way by planning the use of leftovers. Besides being thrifty, the use of leftovers may lead you to discover that some foods taste even better the second time around. So, why not experiment with some of the ideas for savory leftover creations in the table "Encore Presentations"?

The Right Amount

There are times when you don't want leftovers. But you don't want any waste, either. Use the table "How Many Servings Will You Get?" to estimate the amount of foods to buy.

Cut Costs
with the Right Cut

To save money buy the less-tender cuts of meat (such as chuck, short ribs, and stewing meat, and cuts from the foreshank, brisket, tip, and hind shank). In beef, lamb, and pork, these are also usually the least expensive. High in flavor, they make an excellent choice for moist, slow-cooking stews, casseroles, and soups (especially when made in a slow-cooker like the Crockpot).

Encore Presentations

LEFTOVER	NEW CREATION
Beef roast	Beef and vegetable soup, stew, chili
Beef slices	Beef sandwiches
Broccoli	Cream of broccoli soup
Carrots	Marinate for salad
Cauliflower	Cream of cauliflower soup
Cooked pasta	Vegetable soup, chicken soup
Cooked rice	Rice pudding, pilaf, Spanish rice
Corn on the cob	Corn fritters, creamed corn, corn chowder
Meatballs	Vegetable and meatball soup
Poached chicken	Pot pie, turnovers, soup, salad
Steamed shrimp	Shrimp stir-fry, salad
Turkey pickings	Salad, soup, tetrazzini
Turkey slices	Turkey sandwiches

How Many Servings Will You Get?

FOOD	SERVINGS PER UNIT
Meat	
Little or no bone	3 or 4 per lb
Medium amounts of bone	2 or 3 per lb
Much bone or gristle	1 or 2 per lb
Poultry	
Chicken, turkey	2 or 3 per lb
Duck, goose	2 per lb
Fish	
Whole	1 or 2 per lb
Dressed or pan-dressed	2 or 3 per lb

(continued)

FOOD	SERVINGS PER UNIT
Fish—*continued*	
Portions or steaks	3 per lb
Fillets	3 or 4 per lb
Clams	2 per dozen
Crabs	1 or 2 per lb
Lobsters	1 per lb
Oysters	2 per dozen
Scallops; shrimp	3 per lb
Fresh Vegetables	
Asparagus	3 or 4 per lb
Beans, green	5 or 6 per lb
Beans, lima	2 per lb
Beets, diced; broccoli	3 or 4 per lb
Brussels sprouts	4 or 5 per lb
Cabbage	
Raw, shredded	9 or 10 per lb
Cooked	4 or 5 per lb
Carrots	
Raw, diced or shredded	5 or 6 per lb
Cooked	4 per lb
Cauliflower	3 per lb
Celery	
Raw, chopped or diced	5 or 6 per lb
Cooked	4 per lb
Kale	5 or 6 per lb
Okra	4 or 5 per lb
Onions, cooked	3 or 4 per lb
Parsnips	4 per lb
Peas	2 per lb
Potatoes, spinach	4 per lb
Squash, summer; sweet potatoes	3 or 4 per lb
Squash, winter	2 or 3 per lb
Tomatoes, raw, sliced, or diced	4 per lb
Frozen Vegetables	
Asparagus	2 or 3 per pkg (9–10 oz)
Beans, green or lima	3 or 4 per pkg (9–10 oz)

FOOD	SERVINGS PER UNIT
Broccoli, brussels sprouts, cauliflower; corn, whole kernel	3 per pkg (9–10 oz)
Kale, spinach	2 or 3 per pkg (9–10 oz)
Peas	3 per pkg (9–10 oz)
Canned Vegetables	
Greens, such as kale or spinach	2 or 3 per 16-oz can
Most vegetables	3 or 4 per 16-oz can
Dried Vegetables	
Beans	11 per lb
Peas, lentils	10 or 11 per lb
Fresh Fruit	
Apples, bananas, peaches, pears, plums	3 or 4 per lb
Apricots, cherries, grapes	5 or 6 per lb
Blueberries, raspberries	4 or 5 per pt
Strawberries	8 or 9 per qt
Frozen Fruit	
Blueberries	3 or 4 per pkg (10–12 oz)
Peaches, raspberries, strawberries	2 or 3 per pkg (10–12 oz)
Canned Fruit	
Drained	2 or 3 per 16-oz can
Served with liquid	4 per 16-oz can
Dried Fruit	
Apples	8 per 8-oz pkg
Apricots, mixed fruits	6 per 8-oz pkg
Peaches	7 per 8-oz pkg
Pears	4 per 8-oz pkg
Prunes	4 or 5 per 8-oz pkg
Dried Pasta	
Macaroni, noodles, shells, spaghetti	8 per lb
Grains	
Barley	11 per pkg (11 oz)
Oatmeal	18 per pkg (18 oz)
Rice	16 per pkg (16 oz)

SOURCE: U.S. Department of Agriculture.

Buy Boneless

Before you turn away from more expensive boneless, trimmed cuts of meat, consider this: While the price per pound may be cheaper for bonier cuts with more fat, you will need to buy more pounds per serving to get the same amount of meat. You'll need only ¼ to ⅓ pound of boneless beef tenderloin per serving, but ⅓ to ½ pound of T-bone steak per serving. And if you plan on cooking up some short ribs, you'll need a whopping ¾ to 1 pound per serving. To really get your money's worth, calculate price per serving, not price per pound.

Become Your Own Butcher

How many times have you noticed that poultry quarters or beef chuck cubes cost more per pound than the whole bird or roast? Learn to quarter your own chicken or cut cubes from chuck roasts; then pocket the change. Remember to put the bones aside for soup stock.

One Man's Fish
Is Another Man's Lobster

Monkfish, sometimes called poor man's lobster because of its firm white flesh, can be interchanged with lobster in many dishes. You'll savor the savings! And several of the lean fish, such as orange roughy, haddock, sole, and flounder, are so much alike that you can use whichever one happens to be the best catch—buy—of the day.

A Little Goes a Long Way

Stretch meat, poultry, and fish. You can do this simply by adding bread crumbs, oatmeal, or rice to meatloaves, fish cakes, or meatballs. Beans, pastas, and potatoes in casseroles, salads, chowders, and soups guarantee hearty satisfaction—even when meat, poultry, or fish portions are small.

Waste Not, Want Not

Estimate portions. To do this you'll have to judge how much lean and how much waste is in a cut of meat, poultry, or fish. Then

Quartering a Chicken

To cut up poultry: (1) place the bird breast-side up and cut the skin between the thighs and body; (2) lift the bird by the legs and bend the legs back until the bones break at the hip joints; (3) turn the bird to one side and remove the leg and thigh by cutting from tail to shoulder; repeat on the other side; (4) separate the thighs and legs by cutting through the knee joints; (5) with the bird on its back, remove the wings by cutting inside the wing from the top down; (6) cut through the joints on either side of the rib cage to separate the breast from the back; (7) split the breast by cutting the wishbone at the V.

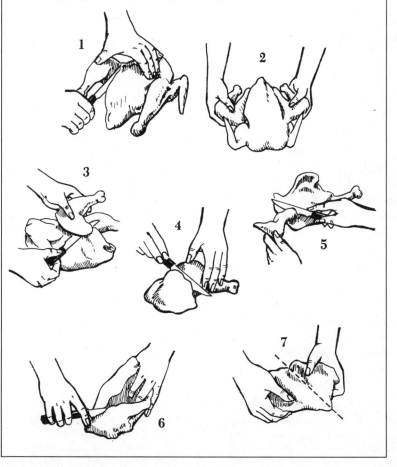

compare the servings and price per pound with another cut. Often, a slightly higher-priced cut will yield more edible servings to the pound because there's less waste (fat, gristle, and bone).

Declare a Vegetarian Day

Several times a week, serve meals based on less expensive sources of protein:

dry beans, peas, or lentils　　pasta with cheese
　with rice　　　　　　　　　rice with nuts
eggs

Grow Your Own

Remember the victory gardens of World War II and President Gerald Ford's inflation gardens? Both serve as reminders that gardening is a terrific way to save money and get wonderful fresh produce.

For down-to-earth information on growing your own, check out Rodale's *Organic Gardening* magazine, *High-Yield Gardening* by Marjorie B. Hunt and Brenda Bortz (Rodale Press, 1986), *Jeff Ball's 60 Minute Garden* (Rodale Press, 1985), and *Backyard Fruits and Berries: How to Grow Them Better Than Ever* by Diane E. Bilderback and Dorothy Hinshaw Patent (Rodale Press, 1984).

Freeze It Yourself

Don't spend big bucks on frozen prepared meals. For the price of two one-serving packages of frozen lasagna, you can make enough lasagna to feed six or eight people. A potful of stew, or any other casserole, portioned out into small containers and frozen, will provide your family with meals at far lower cost than frozen commercial entrées. And you don't have to make the time for a special cooking session; when you cook up a casserole, simply double the recipe and freeze one batch for later use.

Store It Right and Save

Cubical containers are best for freezer storage because they conserve space and stack better than cylindrical ones. You can buy plastic freezer containers, or save money and use heavily waxed cartons, such as milk cartons (folded over and sealed at the top) or the boxes that frozen vegetables come in. They can be used over again. Simply wash them in soapy *cold* water (to keep the wax firm) and dry thoroughly before reusing. Be sure to seal them tight and wrap with aluminum foil after filling. Cool hot foods before putting them into any kind of waxed container. Aluminum foil cartons (such as roasting pans fitted with aluminum foil lids) are especially useful. They chill rapidly and can go from freezer to oven and can be reused if they are not pierced or split. To keep foil from being pierced, carefully scoop out the contents with a plastic spatula or spoon. Do not use metal utensils, and do not slice the food while it's in the container. Meats and irregularly shaped foods should be wrapped in heavy aluminum foil.

Label and date everything you put in your freezer. The quickest way to lose money with frozen foods is to keep eating the recent additions while the older foods languish in the deep freeze, inedible and fit only for the garbage can by the time you take them out. Always put new foods in the back or bottom and move older foods forward or to the top so you use them first.

Do It Yourself for Less

For just minutes spent in the kitchen doing something yourself, you can save pennies to dollars in the supermarket. That's because you pay for the convenience when you have someone else do the slicing, mixing, grinding, or cooking. Here are a few do-it-yourself-for-less suggestions:

add sweetener to cereal
chill tea, add lemon for iced tea
cook an easy spaghetti sauce (crushed tomatoes, oregano,
    onions, basil, and garlic)
dice and mince onions
form and freeze hamburger patties
grind dried bread for bread crumbs
grind walnuts

make croutons (see the directions below)
make macaroni and cheese
make mushroom soup (basic white sauce with a little chicken
    broth and sautéed mushrooms)
mince garlic
mix a variety of seasoning blends (see page 43)
mix hot vegetable combos
mix orange juice with seltzer water for orange soda
pop popcorn
prepare a simple salad dressing (see page 42)
prepare celery powder (dried celery leaves pressed through a
    sieve)
sauce apples for applesauce
shell roasted peanuts
slice and grate cheeses
slice fresh mushrooms
sliver almonds
squeeze lemons, add honey and ice for lemonade
whip up a simple barbecue sauce (catsup, onions, honey,
    vinegar, and mustard)

Make Your Own Croutons

Have you bought a box of croutons lately? For the price that's
being charged, it's hard to believe that all you're getting is some
dried bread and spices. Don't throw your money away on store-
bought croutons—make your own. It's easy. Start by cutting
crusts and pieces of dry bread into small cubes. Then sprinkle the
cubes with garlic powder and toast them under the broiler, or
sauté them in a tablespoon of butter or olive oil in a moderately
hot skillet. Note: Toasted croutons have fewer calories and less fat
than sautéed ones.

Money-Saving Mixes

No doubt about it. Muffin and pudding mixes *are* a boon to the
busy cook. But are they worth the expense? After all, they can
cost about twice what home cooked costs. The next time you are
in the grocery store, check the price per unit. You will find that
many pudding mixes, for example, are well over $11 per pound.
So, whip up your own quick mixes for double savings of time and
money.

PUDDING MIX

5½ cups nonfat dry milk
1½ cups cornstarch

Combine ingredients; stir until well blended. Store in a tightly covered container. *Yield: about 7 cups*
    To prepare pudding: Combine 1¼ cups mix, ¼ cup honey, and 2½ cups water in a heavy 2-quart saucepan or double boiler. Cook over medium heat, stirring constantly, until thickened. Add 1 tablespoon butter and remove from heat. Beat two eggs slightly; add some of the hot pudding to beaten eggs. Blend egg mixture into the rest of the pudding and cook 1 minute.
    Remove from heat and add 1 teaspoon vanilla. Chill in individual dessert dishes at least 30 minutes before serving. *Makes 4 to 6 servings*

VARIATIONS
Tapioca Pudding Mix: Substitute 1¼ cups tapioca for the cornstarch in the mix.
Rice Pudding Mix: Substitute 3 cups brown rice for the cornstarch. Cook over low heat without stirring for 30 to 40 minutes. Finish with the butter and eggs, as in the original recipe.

BASIC MUFFIN MIX

2½ pounds whole wheat flour
2½ pounds unbleached all-purpose flour
5 Tbsp baking powder
1 Tbsp baking soda
3¾ cups nonfat dry milk

Combine all ingredients in a large bowl and mix until thoroughly blended. Store in a covered airtight container. *Yield: about 26 cups.*

PUMPKIN MUFFINS

1 egg
½ cup water
½ cup mashed cooked or canned pumpkin
¼ cup corn oil
¼ cup honey
1½ cups Basic Muffin Mix (see page 39)
½ tsp cinnamon
½ cup golden raisins

Preheat oven to 400°F. Spray muffin cups with nonstick vegetable spray or line with paper baking cups. In a medium bowl, beat egg slightly. Stir in water, pumpkin, oil, and honey. Add muffin mix and cinnamon; stir until just moistened. Fold in raisins.

Fill muffin cups ⅔ full. Bake until done, 15 to 20 minutes. *Yield: 12 muffins*

CRANBERRY–ORANGE MUFFINS

1 cup cranberries, halved
¼ cup honey
1 egg
1 cup water
2 Tbsp corn oil
2 Tbsp honey
1 Tbsp grated orange rind
2 cups Basic Muffin Mix (see page 39)

Combine cranberries and the ¼ cup honey. Set aside. Preheat oven to 400°F. Spray muffin cups with nonstick vegetable spray or line with paper baking cups. In a medium bowl, beat egg slightly. Stir in water, oil, and the 2 tablespoons honey. Add rind and muffin mix; stir until just combined. Fold in cranberry mixture.

Fill muffin cups ⅔ full. Bake until golden brown, 15 to 20 minutes. *Yield: 12 muffins*

VARIATION
Raspberry–Orange Muffins: Substitute fresh or frozen raspberries for the cranberries. (The raspberries should be dry, not in syrup.)

Be Your Own Baker

Today the price of a loaf of bread starts at 89 cents—that's for white bread on sale—and goes up from there. But homemade bread costs about half that, even when you factor in the cost of the energy required to bake it. This basic bread recipe is designed to save you some dough.

BASIC BREAD

2 cups hot water, milk, buttermilk, or leftover
  potato water (heated to 110°F)
1 Tbsp honey, brown sugar, or molasses
1 Tbsp dry yeast
1 tsp salt
2 Tbsp melted butter or oil
5½ to 6½ cups all-purpose unbleached flour, or substitute half
  whole wheat flour or half rye flour

Pour hot liquid into a large mixing bowl. Add sweetener and stir to dissolve; sprinkle yeast over water and stir until dissolved. After yeast has become bubbly, add salt and butter.

Gradually add flour. As mixture begins to hold together and pull away from the sides of the bowl, turn out onto a floured kneading surface. Knead for 10 minutes until smooth and elastic, adding flour as necessary to keep dough from sticking. Form dough into a ball and place in a large, greased bowl. Turn dough to grease all sides. Cover bowl with plastic wrap and leave dough to rise in a warm (about 90°F) place. This will take about an hour.

When dough has doubled in bulk, punch down and knead to remove bubbles. Let dough rest for about 10 minutes. Shape dough into two loaves. Coat two 9 × 5-inch bread pans with nonstick spray. Place loaves in pans and let rise for about 45 minutes. Bake in a 400°F oven for 35 to 40 minutes. *Yield: 2 loaves*

Do-It-Yourself Dressings and Seasonings

It's easy to save lots of money by making your own salad dressings and seasonings. This is obvious by a quick check of the prices of these items at the grocery store. Another advantage is that *you* control the ingredients. This means you can make low-calorie dressings or ones that are not full of preservatives. Here are some of our favorites.

HERB DRESSING

½ cup vegetable oil
3 Tbsp wine vinegar
¼ tsp dried thyme
¼ tsp dried marjoram
1 tsp chopped fresh tarragon or ¼ teaspoon dried basil
1 Tbsp chopped fresh parsley

Combine all ingredients in a jar with a tight-fitting lid and shake vigorously. Allow to stand for 15 minutes before serving. Shake well before adding to crisp greens. *Yield: ⅔ cup*

RUSSIAN DRESSING

½ cup plain yogurt
1 cup mayonnaise
½ cup catsup
1 tsp horseradish, drained

Combine yogurt and mayonnaise with a wire whisk, then mix in catsup and horseradish. *Yield: 2 cups*

ZESTY ITALIAN HERB DRESSING

1½ cups vegetable oil
½ cup wine vinegar
2 cloves garlic, crushed
½ tsp dried basil
½ tsp dried oregano
¼ to ½ cup grated Parmesan cheese (optional)
    freshly ground pepper, to taste

Combine ingredients in a quart jar and shake well. Refrigerate overnight before serving. *Yield: 2 cups*

ALL-PURPOSE SEASONING BLEND

1 Tbsp dried parsley
1½ tsp celery flakes
1 tsp ground toasted sesame seeds
½ tsp onion powder
½ tsp paprika
½ tsp dried thyme
½ tsp dried marjoram
¼ tsp garlic powder
⅛ tsp cayenne pepper

Combine all ingredients and store in an airtight jar. *Yield: about 3 Tbsp*

POULTRY SEASONING

3½ tsp ground white pepper
1½ tsp dried sage
1 tsp dried thyme
1 tsp dried marjoram
1 tsp dried savory
1 tsp powdered ginger
½ tsp ground allspice
½ tsp grated nutmeg

Combine all ingredients and store in an airtight jar. *Yield: about 3 Tbsp*

PUMPKIN SPICE

4 tsp ground cinnamon
2 tsp powdered ginger
2 tsp grated nutmeg
1 tsp ground allspice
1 tsp ground cloves

Combine all ingredients and store in an airtight jar. *Yield: about 3 Tbsp*

Take Advantage of Government Food Programs

Federal Nutrition Education Program (FNEP)

Available through your local extension service, this educational program can help you maximize nutrition and food dollars. You're eligible to participate if you qualify for food stamps.

WIC's a Winner

Would you like to get free milk, eggs, cereal, juice, and peanut butter? Of course you would. That's why you should know about WIC, a nationwide program for Women, Infants, and Children. This government-sponsored program provides free nutrition information for pregnant women, nursing women, and their children. What's more, qualified families receive vouchers for important dietary staples like milk and eggs.

It's easier to qualify than you might think. Although WIC serves many people on public assistance, financial eligibility is generous. In 1988, guidelines called for a family of four to earn no more than $21,553 before taxes. You may well find yourself within the limits.

To join WIC, submit proof of income to the program, which is operated under government contract by such agencies as county health departments or hospitals. (To find your local program, check the Guide to Human Services section of the blue pages in the phone book.) A nurse or nutritionist then determines medical or nutritional need. The specialists will go over your diet, take a quick blood test to check for iron levels, and measure and weigh children for growth. Reviews take place every six months. You graduate from the program when you no longer need the help.

The clientele in Bucks County, Pennsylvania, is typical. "We have many single parents, working mothers, who really need the service," says a supervisor. "WIC is not just for people on welfare."

Food Stamps

The federal food stamp program provides coupons that are exchanged for eligible food items in grocery stores. You can obtain food stamps through your local department of human services (public assistance or welfare) office. The coupons can be exchanged for most foods and food products in the supermarket, with the exception of alcoholic beverages, tobacco, and hot foods prepared for immediate consumption. The coupons may also be used to purchase seeds and plants to grow foods for personal consumption; meals prepared and delivered by an authorized meal delivery service; meals served in a communal dining facility for the elderly; and meals prepared and served by personnel in authorized drug addiction or alcoholic treatment and rehabilitation centers. To be eligible for food stamps, you must meet certain financial and residency requirements, which vary from state to state. The amount of food coupons received is based on household size and net income.

2

MAKING DEALS
ON WHEELS

Cars cost a lot to run. You don't have to drive a luxury land yacht to know that. "Economy" cars cost a lot, too. And even that first hand-me-down car from parents can eat up thousands of dollars in maintenance, repairs, gasoline, and insurance in just a year's time. You can, however, cut your bills by thousands of dollars over the life of a car. Some of your savings will come from old-fashioned know-how—learning to do simple or, if you're so inclined, complicated repairs yourself. Other savings will come from making wise decisions—choosing services that cost less and/or prolong the life of your car. You may be able to save hundreds in a year on gasoline alone. And smart buying can save you $1,000 in just an hour.

You don't need advanced technical aptitude or a Ph.D. in high finance to learn how to save on car costs—just the help of this chapter and some common sense. We'll show you how to save by buying fewer cars and fewer replacement parts, and by paying the lowest amount possible when you do buy cars, parts, and service.

Safety First

The Ins and Outs of Air Bags

Don't buy air bags to cut your insurance bill; the discount, which is applied only to medical coverage premiums, isn't big enough to pay for the cost of the air bags over the life of the car. But air bags do cut the risks of serious injury or death in violent crashes, and to you, that may be worth the $800 or more that they cost.

According to Diane K. Steed, administrator of the National Highway Traffic and Safety Administration (NHTSA), "Air bags alone can reduce the chances of fatality in an accident by 20 to 40 percent and, combined with a lap belt, can reduce the risk by 40 to 50 percent. Even more effective is the air bag in combination with lap and shoulder belt, which can reduce the chance of fatality by 45 to 55 percent."

By 1990, every American automaker will install air bags on at least some cars. Only Chrysler has decided to install air bags at no additional cost to the customer on the driver's side of some cars.

Air Bags Mean Lower Premiums

According to the National Highway Traffic Safety Administration (NHTSA), these major auto insurance carriers offer the following discounts on medical coverage premiums when your car is equipped with air bags or automatic seat belts:

| | AIR BAG DISCOUNT | | AUTOMATIC BELT |
| | | | |
COMPANY	DRIVER ONLY (%)	FULL FRONT (%)	DISCOUNT (%)
Aetna Casualty	30	30	30
Allstate	20	30	30
AMICA	30	30	30
Continental Casualty	30	30	30
GEICO	30	30	30
Hartford	20	30	30
Liberty Mutual	20	30	30
Nationwide	25	40	10
Prudential	30	30	20
State Farm	20	30	10
Travelers	15	30	30
USAA	60	60	30

One insurer, United Services Automobile Association (USAA), not only gives air bag owners a 60 percent discount on premiums for medical protection but also gives a $300 direct payment to customers who buy an air bag-equipped car. USAA insures military officers and their dependents.

If you want a passenger-side air bag in an American car, you must buy a Lincoln Continental—hardly a money-saving choice. In an import, you may choose some Mercedes models.

If you like a car that buckles up for you, some automakers offer passive systems with belts that hug you as the doors close. These add far less to the cost of the car than air bags do. In some models, they are standard. And with some insurance firms, they earn a bigger discount than a driver's-side-only air bag. (See "Air Bags Mean Lower Premiums "on the opposite page.)

The simplest, cheapest way to protect yourself in a crash remains buckling the standard seat belt in your car. If you don't like reaching for your wallet, reach instead for your seat belt.

Money-Saving Maintenance and Repair

Should You Join an Auto Club?

Auto clubs can be little more than an extra insurance policy against towing or battery costs, or they can be a purveyor of convenience services at discount or no extra fee. The biggest club in the country—and the oldest—is the American Automobile Association (AAA), with about 29 million members. For a fee of about $18 to $100 a year, depending on where you live and how many drivers are in your family, you get free towing (up to a limited number of miles) and trip planning services, including maps. The towing is supplied by a nationwide network of participating dealers. Theoretically, this eliminates the need to find a station in the middle of the night, because AAA will find one for you.

Other services supplied by auto clubs may save you money. With trip planning, for instance, you get maps at no extra cost. If you travel a lot, the maps may be worth the fee. (Those free maps that came with the name of your service station on them went the way of cheap gas. Maps may cost $1.50 to $3.00 these days for a single state or city.) Other services included with your dues: discount title and notary fees if you buy or sell a car, no-cost traveler's checks, hotel and car rental savings, bail if you are arrested and charged with a violation, up to $1,000 in lodging costs if you break down away from home, and in some cities, legal insurance. (The legal insurance alone often can be worth the membership fee if you use it merely to file a will.) In states with hard-to-get auto insurance, club membership can even help you get coverage.

Compare Auto Clubs and Their Services

Before you join an auto club, determine whether you really need the services. If you primarily want towing costs, see if your car insurance has that protection (this usually costs only $5 to $10 a year in states that allow it). Your insurance carrier also likely provides bail assistance. Compare details on service: Can you be towed anywhere or only to a member garage? Does towing cover only a limited number of miles? How far away from home must you be for lodging reimbursement?

You can get more information about these established auto clubs by calling their toll-free numbers:

AAA (check your local
   phone book listings)

Allstate Motor Club
   1-800-323-6282

Amoco Motor Club
   1-800-334-3300

Cross Country Motor Club
   1-800-225-1575

Montgomery Ward Motor
   Club
   1-800-621-5151

U.S. Auto Club
   1-800-348-5058.

Do-It-Yourself Maintenance

By doing your own simple car repairs, you'll save two ways: You'll cut labor costs, which often run far more than the cost of parts, and you'll pay less for parts when you buy them from discount houses than you would from garages doing the work for you.

For instance, a garage might charge you $39.95 to tune your four-cylinder car, plus as much as $3.25 for each spark plug. You can buy the same brand-name spark plugs at discount for $.75 to $.99 each. Your first two tune-ups would save you enough to pay for the tools you'll need: a spark plug socket wrench, a timing light, a meter to set engine speed, and a booklet to show you how to do it. You probably already have assorted screwdrivers and wrenches.

Tools of the Trade

A few well-chosen, properly cared-for, quality tools will help you perform multiple car repair duties, and they will last for decades. (See the table "The Right Tools for the Right Job.") Start with a good repair manual, but forget the official, high-priced factory repair manual. Look instead for do-it-yourself repair manuals at your local auto parts store. The Chilton Book Company of Radnor, Pennsylvania, produces service manuals for specific models, as well as professional manuals that cover all models made over several years.

Quality tools are as near as your local Sears store, which guarantees its hand tools for a lifetime. They're frequently on sale singly or in sets. Discount stores such as K-mart sell a variety of tools of varying quality; look for established names like Stanley. The U.S. General Supply Corporation, a mail-order house with several retail stores, offers quality tools at discount. You can write to them at 100 Commercial Street, Plainview, NY 11803. To save the most money, shop garage sales. Good hand tools don't wear out easily, and a quality screwdriver for 10 cents is hard to beat.

Be Choosy
about a Mechanic

The best way to choose a mechanic is through word of mouth. Use the one your family has used successfully, or one a neighbor recommends. Don't ask for a reference and leave it at that; ask why a mechanic is good.

- Does he charge reasonable rates?
- Does he perform satisfactory repairs?
- Is he prompt?
- Does he discount parts?
- Does he guarantee his work?
- Does he warn you when parts are beginning to show wear, rather than waiting until they fail?

If you hear horror stories about the corner garage or the nearest dealer, keep searching.

Shop for Repair Rates

Generally, the highest repair rates will be charged by dealers, with large chain retailers, such as those owned by tire stores, not

The Right Tools for the Right Job

TOOL	FUNCTION	COST ($)
To tool up for car repairs, start with these basics:		
Adjustable wrench	Oil change, misc.	10 or less
Battery cables	Jump starting (dead battery)	10 to 25
Grease gun	Lubrication	5 to 15
Jack stands or ramps	Oil change, lubrication	15 to 25
Oil drainage pan	Oil change	5 or less
Oil filter wrench	Remove oil filter	5 or less
Pliers	Hose clamp, filter replacement	3 to 10
Screwdrivers (Phillips)	Lamp replacement, hose clamps	1 to 5
Screwdrivers (slot)	Lamp replacement, hose clamps	1 to 5
Socket set	Tune-up, misc.	20 to 100
Add these more sophisticated tools later:		
Mechanics creeper	Exhaust, suspension work	15 to 30
Open-end, box wrenches	Miscellaneous tasks	10 to 50
Specialty tools	Spring compressor (suspension), brake work	5 to 50
Timing light	Tune-up	25 to 50
Torque wrench	Changing alloy wheels, engine work	10 to 50

far behind. Your corner garage will have the lowest hourly rates, but it may also have the mechanics with the least training and the least sophisticated equipment. Electronics and complicated emissions controls have made repairs on modern cars far more difficult than on older models. The wrong equipment will hinder proper repairs.

Insist on an Estimate

Always get a written estimate before you authorize any repairs on your car. (Once the work is done, your bill should not exceed the estimate.) Some shops will give you an estimate without charge. Dealers, however, almost always charge a diagnosis fee, even if it's simply to tell you what you already know—that your muffler has a hole in it, for instance.

If work is done on your car that you didn't authorize, don't pay for it. If you must pay for it to get your car, explain to the manager that you will take legal action. Pay by credit card if you can; doing so allows you to stop payment if the work is unsatisfactory. You can also cancel a check if you're not satisfied, but fees can be as high as $30, and you must act quickly to stop payment.

Be Wary
of Discount Repairs

Consider discount repairs, but be careful. If a sale is advertised, it should be a temporarily low price, not a price that's offered every day. Be careful of "special purchases"; such parts may be of lower quality than those normally sold. If you take your car in for one repair and are told of a long list of other things the mechanic was "lucky" to discover, get another opinion and another price estimate before having the work done.

Don't Buy
Full-Price Tires

Tires are almost always discounted—never pay list. Make sure when you compare prices that you're comparing the same services. Always price tires by having the store include the cost of mounting, spin balancing (better than static balancing), rotating (if you are buying only two tires), and installing new valve stems.

To figure your best buy, determine the cost per mile for each tire you consider. The government rates tires three ways to help you do this:

■ Traction ratings: These are A (best), B, and C. The ratings indicate how much better a tire will cling to a wet road. This is important in cornering and stopping, so any money you might save with a lower rating is offset by the safety concerns.

- Heat resistance ratings: These indicate how the tire will stand up to highway speed and long-distance driving. As with traction ratings, A is preferable to B and C despite any possible purchase savings.
- Tread-life ratings: These are number- rather than letter-based. Each tire is assigned a grade, as low as 50 and as high as 340. This number times 200 gives you the estimated tread life. For example, a 200 rating × 200 equals 40,000 miles estimated tread life.

To determine the tire's cost per mile, divide the cost of the tire by the estimated tread life. So, if your tire costs $40 and it has an estimated tread life of 40,000 miles, divide $40 by 40,000 to come up with $.001 a mile.

Avoid Road Hazard Warranties

A road hazard warranty is an insurance policy against tire damage from bad roads or debris on the road. It is a prorated, limited warranty: An amount equal to the unused life of the damaged tire is applied toward your next purchase. So if you've driven 20,000 miles on a 40,000-mile tire when it becomes damaged, the unused life of the tire is 20,000 miles (or 50 percent). That means you'll get 50 percent of the price you paid for your damaged tire to put toward a new, identical tire. (The warranty locks you into buying the same brand and model of tire.) If you bought the original tire on sale but have to buy the replacement tire at the list price, your savings will be all but eliminated. Unless you drive on really hazardous roads, don't pay the fee for this insurance (usually $5 a tire). Be aware that salespeople often won't mention the hazard warranty and will automatically add it on to the price of the tires. Make sure you don't end up paying for insurance you don't want and don't need.

Retreads Save, but Watch Those Ratings

Retreads are used but sound tire carcasses with new treads that have been applied in a heated curing process. They can save up to 50 percent on the price of a new tire, an especially attractive alternative for a second car.

Avoid poor-quality retreads, which can separate under high-temperature conditions. Ask for the National Tire Dealers and Retreaders Association rating of the plant where the tires were rebuilt. An A or B rating is acceptable, but tires rated C through F are best avoided.

Use Cheaper Gas

Gasoline is likely to be your biggest automobile operating expense. On a car that averages 30 miles per gallon, you'll spend about $565 a year on gasoline that costs $.85 a gallon. On a car averaging 20 miles per gallon, you'll spend $850. If you spend a seemingly inconsequential $.15 a gallon more on premium gasoline that you don't need, you'll boost your annual bill by $85 to $150. So learn which gasolines run best in your car, and use the cheapest ones. Only a few high-performance engines require premium gasoline (91 octane and above) to avoid pinging. The rest run on 87 octane, which is $.10 to $.25 a gallon cheaper. If one brand knocks, try others until you find one that works. If your car does require higher octane, try a middle-grade gasoline (89 octane). It's priced between the others and may work fine.

Psst . . . Save a Bundle!

Pump Your Own

The easiest ways to get discounts on gasoline are to pump your own (as much as 15 cents a gallon cheaper than using full service) and pay cash (usually 4 cents a gallon cheaper than when paying with a credit card).

When You Need a Detergent Gas

. . . you don't necessarily have to buy premium-grade gasoline. If your car has multiport fuel injection (with a fuel nozzle for each cylinder), you must use a gasoline with detergent additives. It will keep the nozzles clean and avoid costly repairs. That doesn't mean, however, that you must buy premium fuel. If your brand adds detergent to its premium grade only, look for a brand that adds detergents to all grades. If your car has a carburetor or single-point fuel injection, you don't need detergent gasoline. But twice a year, clean the carburetor or fuel injector by adding a carburetor cleaner, such as Gumout or STP Gas Treatment, to a tank of gas.

Cut Oil Expenses

Consult your owner's manual for the correct grade of oil for your car. Buy only a detergent grade that meets or exceeds manufacturer's specifications. Oil comes in varying weights. The lightest is 5-weight, or 5W, and the heaviest is 50W. Multiviscosity oils, such as 10W–30, work in all kinds of weather. For extra-cold temperatures, use 5W–30. (Some manufacturers are no longer recommending oil heavier than 10W–30. A very few high-performance engines may require unusual oils such as 5W–50.)

Learn to add your own oil (your owner's manual should explain how), and buy it on sale at discount stores. Oil at the service station can cost close to $2 a quart. Sale prices and mail-in rebates can lower your store-bought cost to less than $.50 a quart.

Avoid costly oil additives. They thicken oil and starve the engine of lubricant while it's warming up; in winter, they hinder starting. You're better off changing your oil and filter more frequently than the manufacturer suggests—about every 3,000 miles instead of the 7,500 that's usually recommended.

Wheeling and Dealing

Know Where and When to Buy

New-car dealers are called that for a reason: They deal. To pay the list price for a new car—any car—is entirely unnecessary. To pay more than list because of what dealers euphemistically call ADP—Additional Dealer Profit—is downright wasteful (ADPs are standard on Japanese cars).

Where you buy will make a difference. High-volume dealers will likely charge the least, and small dealers will likely charge the most. But high-volume dealers in high-rent districts may have to charge more to recoup high costs.

When you buy also matters. Shop when sales are slow to get a better deal. If you're likely to be the only sale that day—say, the day of a snowstorm—your chances of striking a good deal also increase, unless you're buying a four-wheel drive. Buy one of these in the summer. By the same token, purchase a convertible in the winter. And if you read in the newspaper that a certain model isn't selling—and that dealers have more than the typical 60 days' supply—it's a good time to shop for that model.

Do Your Homework

Before you shop for a new car, learn about the model you want and about models that compete with it. Read road tests of the cars in such magazines as *Consumer Reports, Motor Trend, Car & Driver,* and *Road & Track.* Also learn what a dealer pays for options and what the manufacturer's suggested retail price is. You can buy a list of such costs at $11 per model from Consumers Union, the publishers of *Consumer Reports.* (Lists for two models cost $20; lists for three models cost $27. Each additional list beyond three models costs $7.) Far cheaper—about $4 for every make and model available—but quite reliable is *Edmund's New Car Prices.* It is updated as prices change, with one book for domestic cars and another for imports. You can find it in bookstores and at newsstands.

Drive a Tough Bargain

The difference between the dealer cost and the manufacturer's suggested retail price is profit. (Some price services, such as those mentioned above, list a typical selling price for you to use as a guide.) Your goal is to get a better buy—which means reducing the dealer's profit—so you'll have to be tough. Bargain for every penny, but not option by option. Instead, add up the total cost, including freight (sometimes called destination charge), and use the total as your bargaining point. Note which options require other purchases. Does an automatic transmission require a bigger engine? Does air conditioning require tinted glass? Don't allow a salesperson to claim he or she didn't know about these "required options," and then try to charge you more at delivery time. Remember that heavily advertised, specially priced packages, sometimes advertised as "free," might have been bought at discount by the dealer; that means he or she may raise the price on the basic car to recoup some of the loss on the option package.

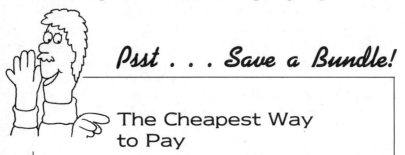

Psst . . . Save a Bundle!

The Cheapest Way to Pay

Avoid borrowing money to buy your new car, and you'll save money. Borrowing costs more because you'll pay interest. The more you borrow, the more interest it will cost you. Borrowing for a longer period costs you not only because you'll pay interest longer but because you'll pay it at a higher rate.

If you're concerned with total payments, here's how buying methods are likely to rank, from cheapest to most expensive:

cash
big down payment, short-term loan
smaller down payment, short-term loan
bigger down payment, longer-term loan, higher rate

Dealing with the Dealers

If you want a specific make and model of automobile with certain equipment, price at least three, and preferably five, car dealers. Try to get your offers in writing. (Some dealers won't do this.) If you'll consider a comparable model from a different manufacturer, get three prices for that one, too.

Before you get a price, make sure you're getting the same price from each dealer: what it will cost you, in cash, to drive the car home, equipped as you want it, including taxes and all fees, with tags on the bumper and the title in hand. Make it clear you want no additional charges added later—not even a notary fee. (Once you have a price, you can arrange for your lowest-cost financing. You can also, after getting the price, ask what you'll get in trade for your car, but you'll likely get hundreds more if you sell it yourself.)

The salesperson will give you a high price. Say that you're shopping around. If you're asked what you think is fair, use your knowledge from the price lists to pitch a price $100 or $200 over dealer cost. If the salesperson says no, insist on his or her best price, then compare it with others. Don't be surprised to find prices differing by as much as 20 percent. If you get two good prices, give each dealer a chance to come in lower.

Take a Look at the Interest

If you're considering borrowing money to finance a new car, be aware that you will end up paying a lot more than the selling price. See the table "The Cost of Borrowing $10,000" to understand how the interest adds up when you take out a loan.

Whatever the terms of your loan, make sure you can prepay the principal—the amount you borrowed—without penalty. Prepaying has the same effect as a bigger down payment: The more and sooner you pay, the more you'll save in interest and the sooner your payments will end. You can save hundreds by prepaying just $10, $20, or $25 a month toward the principal.

Understanding Incentives

When car sales are slow, manufacturers offer big incentives to lure you into buying. Incentives fall into three categories: reduced rates on option packages, cash rebates, and low-interest loans.

Option packages are good deals *only* if they contain options you really want. For example, don't buy a package with lots of bells and whistles you don't want just to get the air conditioner you do want. Even if these other items are listed as "free," the dealer paid for them, probably at discount. To get his or her money back, the dealer will offer less of a discount on the car. Were you to buy a car with the air conditioner alone, you'd get a better dealer discount.

You often have a choice between a cash rebate and a low-

The Cost of Borrowing $10,000

RATE (%)	TERM (YEARS)	MONTHLY PAYMENT ($)	TOTAL INTEREST ($)	TOTAL COST ($)
8.0	3	313.37	1,281.32	11,281.32
8.0	4	244.13	1,718.24	11,718.24
8.5	3	315.70	1,365.20	11,365.20
8.5	4	246.50	1,832.00	11,832.00
9.0	3	318.00	1,448.00	11,448.00
9.0	4	248.90	1,947.20	11,947.20
9.5	3	320.40	1,534.40	11,534.40
9.5	4	251.30	2,062.40	12,062.40
10.0	3	322.70	1,617.20	11,617.20
10.0	4	253.70	2,177.60	12,177.60
10.5	3	325.51	1,718.36	11,718.36
10.5	4	256.10	2,292.80	12,292.80
11.0	3	327.40	1,786.40	11,786.40
11.0	4	258.45	2,405.60	12,405.60
11.5	3	329.76	1,871.36	11,871.36
11.5	4	258.50	2,408.00	12,408.00

interest loan. The best deal is to take the rebate, then secure your own loan. You can apply the rebate toward your down payment, thus reducing the amount you borrow. And be aware that when automakers offer bargain loan rates, so do the banks, which compete for your business. Your bank's interest rate will probably be more than the automaker's, but you'll be borrowing less after you throw in the rebate. The difference that will make over the life of the loan could be hundreds or even more than a thousand dollars—that's money in your pocket.

Buying from the Lot

Dealers want to sell you from their stock first. That's because in-stock cars are typically ordered with many options, so they may cost you more, and the dealer is paying interest on loans to own those cars. Insist on deletion of or steep discounts on options you don't want. Beware, too, of dealer-installed "options" that you are required to take. Typical are unneeded items such as rustproofing (today's cars are guaranteed by manufacturers for years against rust-through) and an upholstery protector (tell the salesperson you'll buy a can of Scotchgard for $3). Remind the salesperson of the incentive to reach a deal: The sooner he or she sells the car, the sooner the dealer's costs are lowered.

Is It Better to Lease?

Leasing a car instead of buying one can considerably reduce the amount of money you pay up front and the amount of money you pay monthly, but it will cost you more in the long run. Why? Because when you're done paying monthly lease payments on a closed-end lease, you have nothing left but a need for another car, and the dealer owns the car you leased. When you're done buying the same car, you retain ownership of that car—and its residual value—when your payments end. The value of the car after four years should far exceed the difference between what you paid for it and what you would have paid had the car been leased.

Residual value—the estimate of what the car will be worth when the lease ends—determines the cost of your lease. For two different makes costing $15,000 to purchase, the one with the higher resale or residual value will likely cost less to lease. Cars that are trouble-prone or have poor safety reputations will have much lower residual values, making them less attractive leasing choices.

Don't take any lease except a closed-end, no-down-payment lease. Some companies advertise artificially low monthly payments but in the fine print indicate that a large down payment is required. This defeats the whole purpose of leasing, which is a low cash outlay and no down payment. Also avoid open-end leases, which require that the car be sold at the end of the lease (to you or someone else). If the leasing company doesn't receive a predetermined price when it sells the car, you must make up the difference.

Leasing makes sense only if you lack cash for a down payment and taxes but can afford a sizable monthly payment. On a $15,000 car, for instance, a minimal 10 percent down payment would require $1,500, and sales tax (say, 6 percent) would require another $900. That's $2,400 up front. To lease the same $15,000 car, there is no down payment, although you would probably have to pay the first month's payment and one more month as a security deposit. That's about $600 up front. You would pay about half as much in sales tax, and the tax would become part of your monthly lease payment, rather than be due up front.

Try Renting First

It's hard to know how much you'll like a car until you live with it. Try renting a model identical to one you might buy—with similar equipment, including engine and transmission.

Many dealers offer rental cars, sometimes at rates lower than those of the big car rental firms, especially for local use. Try to work out a deal in which your rental fee would apply toward a pre-arranged purchase price. Renting a car with a few thousand miles on it will give you a chance to see if the car remains sound after use. If you like the particular car you're renting, ask the dealer to give you a price on that one. Because it's technically a used car, it should sell for hundreds less than a brand-new one.

Big vs. Small Cars

Big cars have two advantages: They usually offer the most room and travel comfort, and they sustain less damage in a crash. They also have strong disadvantages: They're more expensive to buy, much more expensive to run, and sometimes impossible to park.

If you need a big car's luggage capacity and travel comfort for only one or two weeks of vacation travel each year, buy a smaller car for everyday use and rent a big car for vacations. If all you need is more luggage space, consider equipping a small or intermediate car with a rooftop luggage carrier. Get the type that's weatherproof and lockable, available for $50 to $75. A carrier will at least double the 13- to 15-cubic-foot capacity of trunks in most small cars. While a rooftop carrier will reduce fuel mileage somewhat when in use, it can be unbuckled and stored in a garage or basement when not needed.

The toughness of big cars in a crash translates to better safety for the occupants—something that's impossible to value. It also can mean a discount on insurance, saving $200 to $500 a year. But the discount on insurance won't be enough to make up for the higher costs of running a big car. For example, a big car that averages 20 miles per gallon on a trip might get only 12 to 14 mpg around town. Compared with a four-cylinder compact that gets 30 mpg on a trip and 22 mpg around town, that bigger car could cost $300 or more in gasoline per year. And tires for a big car will cost perhaps twice as much as those for a compact, and they're likely to wear out faster. Couple these costs with car payments that may run $1,000 to $2,000 a year higher, and small definitely looks more beautiful.

Used Car Know-How

Buy Smart

You'll save money if you buy a used car, because a car loses the biggest part of its value in the first year of ownership. It loses a smaller percentage of its value in succeeding years. For identical used cars, you'll pay the highest price to a new-car dealer of the same make, less to a new-car dealer of a different make, still less to a used-car dealer, and the least to a private owner. But remember, you save only if the car has sound mechanicals and body. Be sure to thoroughly inspect the car before you buy.

Once you find a used car that you've inspected (see the tips below) and would like to buy, ask for the name and telephone number of the previous owner. Call the person and ask what the mileage was when the car was traded in, how often the oil was changed, and whether the car had problems. If you can't get the name and number, don't buy. (It may mean that the car came from the auto auction, where dealers and rental firms typically send their problem autos, admittedly along with some good ones.) Insist on taking the car from the lot to your own mechanic for a safety inspection and diagnosis, including an engine compression check. If you can't take it with you, take the hint, but not the deal.

Check the Mechanicals

If you're in the market for a used car, don't dress up—you have work to do. You should thoroughly inspect a used car before you even consider making an offer. Start with the mechanicals:

■ Always insist on a test drive. Walk to the car; don't allow the salesperson to bring it to you. Look under the car where it has been parked. Are there spots under the engine? (Oil leak.) Transmission? (Transmission leak.) Wheels? (Brake leak.)

- Put your full body weight on each corner of the car and then let go. If the car bounces more than twice, it may need shock absorbers.
- While the car is cool, run your finger along the inside of the exhaust. An oily, black buildup could mean a valve or valve-seal problem. Have the salesperson start the car while you stand back and look at the exhaust. If it blows smoke, it may require expensive repairs.
- Drive the car in typical conditions: over side streets and highways, in stop-and-go traffic, and at high speeds.
- Apply the brakes hard from speed. Does the car pull to one side? It may need expensive brake rebuilding. Does it take much longer to stop on the second or third stop? The brakes may need new linings.
- Park the car and let it idle for at least 10 minutes with the air conditioner running to be sure the engine doesn't overheat. Try the heater, radio, and wipers. Don't be hurried.
- With the parking brake on and the car in drive, try to accelerate. The engine should stall or nearly stall. If the car moves easily, the brake may need repairs. In an automatic, failure to stall or stumble may indicate wear in the transmission.

Take a Close Look

Once you've checked out the mechanicals of a used car, give it a good visual once-over, following these guidelines:

- Look at the car in daylight only, and never in wet weather. (Rain makes even weathered paint look shiny.)
- Does the paint match on all the panels? A brighter color on one or two means accident or rust damage.
- Press your cheek to the side of the car and look down the length of the car. Wavy areas indicate body repairs. Place a small magnet against the wavy area; if it won't stick, the area is plastic body filler. Find out what the damage was.
- Look underneath the car. New undercoating is probably covering rust. Poke with a penknife. Also check for rust inside the trunk and under the hood, especially at the tops of shock absorbers.
- Look under the hood. Are there leaks? Greasy or oily spots? If the engine is spotless, it might have been steam cleaned to eliminate evidence of problems.
- If trim, weather stripping, or windows have an overspray of

paint, the car was painted. That could mean past rust or accidents.

■ Are tires evenly worn? Cupping or uneven wear could mean a need for alignment or expensive parts.

Research for Recalls

If you're thinking of buying a used car, find out if it was ever involved in a government-ordered recall for safety defects. It could save you hundreds of dollars in repair bills. If the car has a problem that was covered by a recall, but it was never taken care of, you can have the repairs made free of charge, no matter how long ago the recall took place. You'll need to know the year, model designation, and some details on equipment (power brakes or engine option, for instance). Then call the toll-free number of the National Highway Traffic Safety Administration (NHTSA): 1-800-424-9393, or 366-0123 in Washington, D.C., only. Call the manufacturer, as well, to find out if the car was subject to any voluntary recalls. This information may not be available from NHTSA.

Extending the Life of Your Car

Change the Oil—Frequently

There's only one time that you shouldn't follow the recommendations in your automobile's owner's manual: when you exceed them. The best place to overdo it is in changing the oil and filter. Taxi owners who want 200,000 miles out of their cars change both every 3,000 to 4,000 miles. (Your owner's manual may recommend an oil change every 7,500 miles, and a new filter every 15,000.)

You can do the work yourself with tools that cost less than $15: an oil filter wrench, an adjustable wrench, and a plastic drain pan. A garage will charge you $12 to $25 for a filter and oil change;

the do-it-yourself cost for oil and filter from a discount parts house will be $5 to $7, and an oil and filter change takes only about 15 minutes (although you may spend up to an hour the first time you do it). Doubling the frequency of oil changes over the first 100,000 miles may cost you $70, but your engine will last years more. The alternative is an engine rebuild, which may cost $1,200 or more, or a new car. If your chassis requires grease lubrication, do it with each oil change.

Keep Those Tires Turning

Buy a tire gauge (about $3) and an air pump (about $5 for a manual model; $10 to $20 for an electric one). Check your tire pressure monthly and add air when needed. Properly inflated tires can last twice as long as underinflated ones.

If you rotate tires, keep radials on the same side as you move from front to back. On cars with front-wheel drive, front tires will wear out much faster than back tires. Some tire stores will rotate tires free for their tire customers. That could save you $12 to $25 a year.

Do-It-Yourself
Preventive Maintenance

Some car parts just plain wear out. Learn which ones will, and when they are likely to, and you can replace the part before your car breaks down. (You'll save a $40 to $60 towing fee, you'll get to pick your own mechanic, and you'll be able to buy your own part at discount.) See the "Maintenance Timetable" for a general schedule for preventive maintenance. (Refer to your owner's manual for more specific maintenance information.)

Carry Spare Parts

If you're planning a vacation by car, perhaps on the road for thousands of miles, carry spare parts: a headlamp, fuses, accessory drive belt, tube patch (for hoses), antifreeze, and a spare tire. If your car comes only with a temporary spare, consider buying a used tire of the same size and type from a salvage yard, but be sure it will fit in your car's spare tire well. Also carry jumper cables, which could save you the need to call an expensive service truck.

Maintenance Timetable

ITEM	MILES	FREQUENCY	WHAT TO DO
Antifreeze/ coolant	1,000	Monthly	Add if low; replace alternate years
Brake fluid	1,000	Monthly	Check; add if low; correct leaks
Oil	1,000	Monthly	Add if low
Tires	1,000	Monthly	Inflate if low
Transmission fluid	1,000	Monthly	Add if low
Window fluid	1,000	Monthly	Add water in summer, antifreeze in winter
Battery	2,000	Bimonthly	Add water if low
Belts	2,000	Bimonthly	Tighten if loose; replace if cracked or frayed
Hoses	2,000	Bimonthly	Replace if cracked, soft, swollen
Shocks	2,000	Bimonthly	Replace if car bounces or sways
Wiper blades	2,000	Bimonthly	Replace rubber blade only, leave arm
Brakes	6,000	Twice a year	Replace if worn

Stay Out of Heated Garages

Protect your car from the weather, but don't put it in a heated garage. (It can cause condensation in cold weather and speed rust.)

Keep It Clean

Use clear water to wash off your car, or a mild soap when needed. Wax it twice a year, and apply silicone protectants to vinyl and rubber parts. (Silicone makes blackwall tires look great, too.) When metal is exposed by scratches, remove wax with a solvent, sand off the rust, and touch up, first using a primer and then the body-color paint. Cover again with wax.

Don't Ignore the Underside

If you live in a snowbelt, wash off salt after each storm. Don't ignore the underside: Those $.50 or $.75 car washes that let you direct high-pressure streams of water are great at cleaning around wheels and between underbody parts. When undercoating is chipped, touch it up with aerosol applicators available at auto and discount stores. A couple of times yearly, remove and clean out plastic grommets on the car's underside to prevent water collection. With today's antirust guarantees, save $200 or more by skipping after-market rustproofers, which are not likely to do more than standard treatments. If you live in the Sunbelt, covers made to fit your car will help prevent sun and heat damage. Get the kind that "breathe"; they let air filter through but keep out moisture.

Some Inside Tips

Caring for the interior of your car is just as important as caring for the exterior. Follow this advice:

■ Vacuum cloth seats and carpets monthly, and before washing. To keep stains out, apply aerosol water and stain repellents.
■ Clean the seats twice a year: with a mild detergent for cloth seats or vinyl cleaner and a soft-bristle brush for vinyl seats. Wipe with a sponge. Apply a silicone-containing protectant twice a year to vinyl seats after cleaning.
■ Don't use the same cleaners on real leather that you use on vinyl. Use saddle soap to get stains out, and a leather conditioner to keep them out.
■ Don't allow dirt and grease to set. On cloth seats, blot stains and wash with clear water as soon as possible. Don't rub stains in. If a stain remains, use a biodegradable cleaner that has grease-cutting agents to spot clean.
■ Use a cardboard windshield shade to protect against sun damage to the interior. These list for about $4 but often sell for less than half that. A shade can prevent fading of cloth and cracking of vinyl seats and dashboard padding.

Theft Deterrence

Lock Them Out

The cheapest deterrent to theft is to lock your car and take the keys. While it's true that thieves can steal even a locked car, there's no sense in inviting joyriders by leaving the keys inside.

Also avoid leaving keys in a conspicuous place, such as in the glove box or in a magnetic key holder under the instrument panel. A better choice is a plastic duplicate of your key set made into a credit card-size sheet of plastic that fits in your wallet. These keys come standard with Chevrolet Beretta and Corsica models, but are available from auto parts stores for other makes.

Sound the Alarm

There are many types of electronic burglar alarms or combination alarms/fuel starvation systems available for your car. Installed, the systems can cost $100 to $250. The systems work by disabling the car or sounding an alarm—or both—when the driver's door is opened and an override switch is not activated. The override is hidden from the thief's sight. They're effective, but only if you remember to set the alarm when you leave your car. (And you mustn't forget to throw the switch when you get back in, or you'll set off the ear-piercing alarm.) To get adequate protection, you'll need to put a sensor on each door, not just the driver's door. That will cost more money.

Alarm systems are discounted, so shop for the best price. To save the most, consider installing a system yourself, but only if you are at least a moderately experienced backyard mechanic. You can also buy at discount through mail-order advertisements in respected magazines such as *Road & Track, Car & Driver,* and *Motor Trend*. You can install your own for as little as $50 by purchasing from a discount store. At the least, get a system that trips your auto horn (or a very loud alarm) and flashes your headlights. Some alarms are barely audible above heavy traffic.

Cheaper alternatives to alarms are steel bars that lock onto your steering wheel and sometimes the brake pedal. The car won't move until the bar is unlocked or drilled free. These won't stop thieves, but they will slow them down.

Avoid Flashy Accessories

Sometimes components in a car, and not the car itself, are the targets of thieves. The high-line radio in Volkswagen models, for instance, is a favorite with thieves; so are the removable roof sections on T-roof cars. Fake radio fronts are available to mask a high-priced model. High-performance tires and aluminum-alloy wheels are also frequently stolen—keep them locked on with key-locking lug nuts, about $8 at auto parts stores. Don't buy a car with accessories such as these if you will be parking it unattended in a high-crime area.

3

DRESSING
ON A SHOESTRING

It's fun anticipating a shopping spree, or even the purchase of just one particular item of clothing. But once you get to the store, you're in for sticker shock. There you are likely to discover that the look you dreamed of costs a mint. But with our help, you can achieve the style you want, yet spend less. The buying and shopping hints in this chapter are designed to save you money while helping you look your best.

Clothes for Less

Plan Your Wardrobe

The key to buying clothing for less lies in planning—and wardrobe planning begins with your closets and drawers. First review what you've got, weed out and give away anything you haven't worn in several years, and mend anything that's in disrepair. You'll probably want to do this at the beginning of each fall-to-winter and spring-to-summer season.

Next, write down the purchases that will round out your wardrobe. Is it a new pair of navy slacks? A white dress shirt? Black shoes? A bone-colored handbag? A brown belt? With this basic planning done, you're ready to consider what's on the market and, of course, where you can get the best buy.

Go Versatile

Whenever you can, get one piece of clothing to serve two or more uses. That way, you can cut your clothing expenditures by 50 percent or better. For example, buy long-sleeved shirts to use year-round, and roll up the sleeves in the summer instead of buying long-sleeved shirts for cool weather and short-sleeved ones for summer. Another wardrobe extender is an all-purpose raincoat with a zip-out lining. You'll be able to get through three seasons with just one coat.

Mix and Match

If "mix and match" sounds more like the name of a new board game than a way to save money on clothing, it's probably because you haven't learned that mix-and-match separates can extend a wardrobe. Here's how. These seven pieces of clothing—a navy blue skirt, a navy blazer, a blue-gray tweed skirt, a white blouse, a light blue blouse, a pair of navy slacks, and a gray sweater vest— make 16 different outfits. Base your mix-and-match wardrobe on your favorite basic color, such as navy, brown, gray, black, or dark green. Then, as you add new purchases, be sure they complement existing pieces.

Accessories Work Magic

Use accessories—jewelry, belts, ties, scarves—to expand your wardrobe without spending a fortune. You can change the look of a suit with the change of a tie, or with the addition of suspenders. A simple dress can turn sophisticated with a silk scarf or a string of pearls.

To keep the cost of accessories low, choose simple, classic designs that can be worn with more than one garment. And look for sales. Then, buy quality merchandise that will look rich and last for years.

Fad or Fashion?

Fads in clothing come and go. One season balloon skirts are in; the next they're out. And once they're out, you'd look sadly out of date wearing them. But fashion classics survive season after season, year after year. Witness the tweed blazer, the oxford cloth shirt with button-down collar, the A-line skirt, the knitted vest, or the neutral-colored trenchcoat. While it's perfectly okay to have a few faddish clothes in your closet each season, your best bet is to base your wardrobe on the classics. You'll never be out of fashion, and you'll save a bundle by not following those here-today, gone-tomorrow fads.

When to Get the Best Buys

SALE! This is a welcome sign to most clothing buyers. When can you expect to see it? Traditionally, stores run their best sales right after Christmas, right before school starts (for children's clothing), and at the "end of the season." Other good sale times are presidents' birthdays (February), Easter, Memorial Day, and Labor Day. Generally speaking, the end-of-season sales have the lowest prices because stores are trying to clear their stocks to make room for the next season's clothing. These sales usually run in January, April, June, and November. Prices can be anywhere from 10 to 50 percent off.

Clothing Care and Repair

Reinforcement Helps

As soon as you get a new garment home, take steps to keep the garment in like-new condition. Reinforce seams and hems that are sewn with nylon thread, since its slippery nature often allows stitching to come out. Also, nylon thread, which is very strong, can cut the fibers of less strong fabrics.

On casual jackets and sweaters, consider adding good-looking suede patches to the elbows. Reinforcement of wear areas such as these will extend the life of the garment. Jeans, corduroys, and other slacks will benefit from reinforcement, too. Apply a sturdy denim or twill patch to the wrong side of the fabric at the knee.

Secure buttons by sewing with a double strand of matching thread. Ready-made garments are notorious for sporting loosely attached buttons.

Resew seams that have been chain stitched. One break in the thread of a chain-stitched seam will cause the entire seam to unravel rapidly.

A Stitch in Time

The old adage "A stitch in time, saves nine" might also read "A stitch in time, saves a dime." The next time you pop a button, split a seam, or tear a hole in a garment, repair the damage right away. You'll save time because a small repair is quicker to fix than a large one. And you'll save money because a small repair is unnoticeable, so you needn't relegate the garment to the rag bag.

Join a Fabric Club

If you make your own clothing, consider joining a fabric club. You can often save at least 20 percent on the fabric you buy—special sales offer up to 50 percent off. Many of the clubs also guarantee 20 percent savings on such items as patterns, linings, and notions. With each mailing, you receive swatches of fabric with descriptions and ordering information.

Fabric Clubs

Save money on fabrics and notions by joining a fabric club. Here are some of the more popular ones:

Lineweaver
1515 W. Cornwallis Dr.
Suite 206
Greensboro, NC 27408

Fashion Fabrics Club
Dept. SN
10490 Baur Blvd.
St. Louis, MO 63132

Natural Fiber Club
521 Fifth Ave.
New York, NY 10175

Seventh Avenue Designer
Fabric Club
Dept. SE 6
701 Seventh Ave.
Suite 900
New York, NY 10036

Stretch and Sew Fabrics
Swatch Club
7100 Brookfield Plaza
Springfield, VA 22150

Shop Smart

Department Stores

Department stores, especially the larger ones, offer a wide range of quality and prices in ready-to-wear clothing. They also provide conveniences: credit, private fitting rooms, delivery, appealing displays of merchandise. Frequently the better department stores will surprise you with buys that are comparable to or lower than those offered in economy stores. If the store commissions major manufacturers to produce clothing, you can expect good quality and save up to 20 percent. End-of-season and clearance sales are usually top-notch.

Specialty Shops

Just as you might expect from the name, specialty shops specialize in only one type of merchandise—shoes, handbags, women's clothing, tall and large men's clothes, uniforms, children's clothing, and so on. Alteration services are often available. Generally speaking, the quality is high and so are the prices. During sales, however, you can pick up some excellent buys.

Discount and Chain Stores

Some discount and chain stores offer a variety of products ranging from greeting cards and clothing to sports equipment, garden supplies, and automotive parts. Others stick with one item. Although dressing rooms exist, privacy and mirrors are minimal. Prices are usually a cut below those of department and specialty stores, but quality is generally lower, too. Your best bets in these stores are jeans, underwear, socks, pajamas, sweatshirts, and work clothes. Be wary of special purchase sales. These are not regular items with prices reduced, but are often bulk quantities of inferior merchandise bought and advertised specially to attract customers.

Factory Outlets

At one time, the term outlet most often referred to merchandise sold directly to the public by the manufacturer. The items included manufacturing overruns, display goods, samples, overstocks, and seconds, or irregulars. Today, these outlets still exist, but the term also can apply to independently owned outlets that carry discontinued lines and surplus stocks as well as the seconds from a variety of factories. Some outlets have dressing rooms, but you can't expect the privacy of an individual booth. Other amenities are minimal.

You can get some terrific buys at outlets, but you must be a cautious shopper. Much of the merchandise is seconds—clothing items that don't meet the manufacturer's quality-control standards. So they are sold "as is" and cannot be returned. Check them carefully for size, flaws in the fabric, tears, and broken zippers. Also look for sleeves that are put in backward and pants legs with mismatched lengths. Some outlets mark the product flaw with a piece of tape; others aren't so helpful. Returns are sometimes possible, but refunds are rare. Many outlets will accept only cash or checks with identification.

Army-Navy Stores

Known for their surplus military supplies, Army-Navy stores also stock lots of camping, backpacking, and athletic supplies. As with other outlets, you must check quality versus price. Sales can be very worthwhile.

Catalog or Mail Order

Some stores have both retail and catalog divisions. In most cases, you'll find lower price tags on catalog orders even when you figure in the shipping and handling charges. If the operation is strictly mail order, you can anticipate savings because the distributor doesn't have the high cost of operating a retail outlet.

The advantages to shopping by mail are that you can review the catalog at your leisure, then order day or night by mail or phone. Big establishments even offer toll-free numbers. Payment is by check or credit card and sometimes COD. The disadvantages? You have no opportunity to try garments on and may need to return them because you ordered the wrong size. You also have the inconvenience of having to wait anywhere from 10 days to a month for your order to arrive.

Thrift Stores

Thrift stores specialize in used clothing. They're sponsored by the likes of Goodwill and the Salvation Army and obtain their merchandise through donations. The best buys here are in worn-once and cast-off evening wear. Children's clothes are also bargains since kids outgrow clothing faster than they wear it out. Prices are a steal, and you can find clothing that looks like new.

Consignment Shops

There's a growing number of consignment shops, and they usually feature women's or children's clothing. Consignment shops carry barely worn, still up-to-date fashions. The garments accepted for resale must be immaculate. For the shopper, that means good-looking clothes at bargain prices.

Consignment shops also offer you the chance to make money on the clothing you no longer want. You bring in your old clothing for the shopkeeper to evaluate and price. If an item is sold, the shop will split the sale with you fifty-fifty.

Look for Signs of Quality

Well-made clothing retains its shape and good appearance through many wearings. It's more expensive to buy than cheaper clothing, but if you can use an article for several years, it's the most economical alternative. Here's what to look for when you buy:

armhole and crotch cross seams that match up
even, close stitching, about 10 to 12 stitches per inch
even gathers
evenly woven fabric with no flaws
flat, smooth pockets with reinforced corners
inconspicuous, smooth facings and interfacings
neatly secured zippers, snaps, buckles, and other trim
pinked or overcast seams

plaids and stripes that match at seams
reinforced buttonholes, as well as ones that are sewn through
    both sides of the fabric
smooth seams with no puckering
symmetrical darts, lapels, and points on collars
uniform-width hem with stitches invisible on the outside
woven lining in skirts and jackets

Sweater Smarts

When buying sweaters, you'll get longer life from your purchase
if you give special attention to these areas:

- Construction. Is it full-fashion or seamed together? Full-fashion
sweaters keep their shape better.
- Grosgrain backing to the buttons and buttonholes. Is it well
placed and secure?
- Ribbing at the neck, sleeves, and waistband. Is it well finished?
Does it hold its shape? Does it have enough stretch, or does it
bind?

The Inside Story
on Underwear

Articles of underwear seem so simple, you probably wouldn't
think to check for quality construction, but you should. To really
get your money's worth, you not only want underwear that's comfortable but also durable. When buying men's underwear, check
for:

- Adequate fullness in length and width of T-shirts and briefs
- Fabric protection from shrinkage
- Rows of stitching in the elastic waistband of briefs (to prevent
rolling)

    Women's underwear requires a look at:

- Elastic. Is it of high quality?
- Seams. Are they double stitched, edge stitched, or overcast?
- Straps. Are they securely fastened? Are they adjustable?
- Trim. Is it as durable as the rest of the garment? Does it take
the same care?

Read the Label

Be on the lookout for dry-clean-only labels on clothes. Even if they're priced right, in the long run these clothes will cost a bundle. Dry cleaning is expensive—it can cost $2.75 just to have a single pair of slacks cleaned. Clothes that can be hand or machine washed cost just pennies to clean. *Do* read the labels carefully. Many people send clothing that can be washed at home (such as silk items) to the dry cleaners because they never bothered to check the laundering instructions on the label!

Mirror, Mirror on the Wall

When buying a new outfit, a good mirror can be your best friend, telling you truthfully if the style, fit, and color are right for you. That bargain dress may look great on the rack, but if you don't like what the mirror reveals, save your money for a better purchase.

Try It On

Don't waste your money on clothes that don't fit. There is little standardization of sizes in the clothing industry, so you're taking your chances if you buy clothes without trying them on first—particularly when the item is on sale and not returnable. The few extra minutes you spend in the dressing room can save you the time and aggravation of having to return the item later on, and will definitely save you money if you're buying nonreturnable items.

Get Your Money Back

You buy a pair of corduroys that look great on you in the store and are just the right color. You bring them home, and hang them in the closet. A few days later, you put them on and the zipper breaks. May you bring them back? You bet, but don't procrastinate. Most stores have a clothing return policy that's good only for 7 to 10 days. Take the clothing back and ask for a refund or for a replacement that's not defective. (Some stores will not refund your money, but will give you a store credit if you can't find a suitable replacement.)

Not all clothing is returnable, especially if it was bought on sale or in an outlet. In all cases, make sure you know what you're getting by trying on and carefully examining the item, and ask what the store's return policy is before buying.

Quality to Match the Occasion

When should you be willing to spend more money for higher quality clothes: when you need a gown for a special dinner or dance, or when you need a coat you'll wear every day from early fall to late spring? Even though it's tempting to go all out for the quality gown, it's most economical to put more money into the coat. After all, if you buy a cheap coat and it falls apart after a month or so, you'll have to buy another. But since you'll probably only wear the gown once, you can take a chance on buying a less expensive one.

Psst . . . Save a Bundle!

Free Clothes for Kids and Moms-to-Be

Don't overlook your family and friends as sources of kids' clothes and maternity clothes. Because kids grow so fast, a lot of hand-me-downs have hardly been worn. Baby clothes, especially, may be brand new because they were the wrong size from the start. And maternity clothes usually end up in the back of a closet after the baby's born. If you're pregnant, ask your friends for their maternity hand-me-downs.

Take the Children Along

When children need clothing, take them shopping with you. If you think it's too much of a hassle, keep this in mind: It's far better (and cheaper) to put up with an aggravating hour or two of shopping with your picky 12-year-old than go alone and buy clothes he or she hates and refuses to wear.

If you're buying for a young child, be sure to buy items such as shirts a little big. Buying a shirt one size bigger means it can be worn for a longer period of time before it's outgrown.

Save on Pantyhose

It's no secret that the pantyhose brands sold in supermarkets and drugstores cost less than the brands sold in department stores. But did you know you can undercut the price of many of these brands, including the higher-priced department store pantyhose? You can save up to 50 percent by purchasing slightly imperfect pantyhose through the mail. You can order a full range of colors, styles, and sizes. The imperfections range from something like a slightly uneven waistband to imperfections that are only notice- able to the manufacturer's quality-control experts. Two sources of these practically perfect pantyhose:

L'eggs Showcase of Savings   Rolane Direct Marketing
   (L'eggs and Hanes brands)   (No-Nonsense brand)
L'eggs Brands, Inc.   P.O. Box 23368
P.O. Box 1010   Chattanooga, TN
Rural Hall, NC 27098-1010   37422-9988

These catalogs also offer good savings on brand-name socks, lingerie, and men's underwear.

Spare Legs

Next time you need pantyhose, buy two or three pairs in the same style and color. That way you'll have spares to match up when you get a runner in one leg. Here's how: If one leg has a runner, cut it off right below the panty. When another pair gets a run or snag, cut that leg off. Then, you can wear the two panty tops—with a good leg each—at one time.

Make Sure the Shoe Fits

Since shoes are expensive, one way to save is to buy fewer pairs, then wear those shoes for a long time. This means buying shoes that fit well and will last. Here's how:

- Take your time in the store and always try both shoes on. Walk around. If either shoe is uncomfortable, don't buy. You shouldn't have to break in new shoes for them to feel right.
- If one foot is slightly larger than the other, fit your larger foot. Then, if you need to, put a half-sole in the front of the shoe for your smaller foot.
- Stand still and check the length and width of each shoe. The shoe should be $\frac{1}{4}$ to $\frac{1}{2}$ inch longer than your longest toe. The shoe should be wide enough for you to wiggle your toes. The toe box should not press down on the top of your toes. Don't forget the heel. The back of the shoe should grip your heel and not slip when you walk.
- In sandals or sling-backs, check to see that neither your toe nor your heel extends beyond the sole.
- The most comfortable heel height is between $\frac{1}{2}$ and 2 inches.
- Don't insist on always buying the same size. Sizing varies from one manufacturer to another, so spend a bit of time trying on different sizes.
- Try on shoes late in the day when your feet are swollen. Be sure to wear the type of hosiery that you'll be wearing with the shoes; hosiery thickness affects fit.
- Look for classic styles: docksiders, loafers, plain pumps, wing tips. These never go out of style.

Clothing Care for Longer Wear

Be Kind to Your Clothes

To get the most from your wardrobe, it pays to treat your clothes with care. Here's how:

- Dab perfume on your skin instead of on your clothing. The chemicals in perfume may weaken the fabric or stain it.
- Apply lipstick or other cosmetics after dressing. Lipstick or blush stains can be impossible to remove from fabrics.

- Alternate clothes to give them a chance to return to their natural shapes. Ideally, clothing should hang for at least 24 hours between wearings.
- Hang up or fold what you take off. That way, you'll spend less time pressing garments, and they'll last longer.
- Fold sweaters and other knits instead of hanging them. Hangers can distort knits at the shoulders.

Clean Garments Regularly

Fibers release fresh soil and stains readily and quickly. But dirt that has been set by exposure to air, light, and heat can be difficult, if not impossible, to remove.

Sort Your Wash

Your clothes are subjected to tumbling, crumpling, and spinning every time you wash them in a washing machine. One item can pick up dyes and lint from another. You can help extend the life of your clothes by sorting them before they're washed. Separate white, dark, light colored, and heavily soiled clothing. You'll avoid bleeding dark colors onto whites, and you won't share the dirt from heavily soiled clothing. If you have several different kinds of fabrics, you can separate towels and other lint producers, permanent press fabrics, delicate fabrics, and woolens.

Load It Lightly

Don't load your washing machine to the brim. If you pack in as much as you can, permanent press articles will become very wrinkled. Other garments may be damaged by the agitator action in a tightly packed washer.

Close Zippers

. . . and snaps, hooks, and Velcro closures before laundering. Garments retain their shapes better, and fabrics get fewer snags and pulls from the rough edges of the fasteners.

Empty Pockets

. . . then brush lint from pocket seams before laundering. A stray piece of gum or crayon, or a forgotten carbon receipt can make an incredible mess once the item is in the washer or dryer. The resulting stains can be impossible to remove.

Use Chlorine Bleach with Care

A small amount of chlorine bleach helps keep clothes white; too much weakens the fibers. The result is tiny holes in the fabric where weak fibers have torn.

Off-Season Storage

To get more wear from your clothes you not only need to clean them carefully but also store them properly. Before storing any garment, launder or dry clean it, but don't starch. Cellulose-based starches attract silverfish and carpet beetles. Allow plenty of time for items to dry before packing them away. Dampness encourages mildew—and mildew stains can be permanent. To prevent moth damage to woolens, store these clothes in sturdy cedar chests. Potpourris may also discourage attacks by moths.

The Everlasting Shoe

Frequent Care for Longer Wear

Good routine care will keep your shoes in tip-toe shape. Here are some pointers:

■ Before wearing new leather or imitation leather shoes, give them a protective coat of polish. Protect canvas shoes by spraying them with silicone.
■ After each wearing, dust or brush your shoes to remove any dirt.
■ Once or twice a week, polish with a neutral paste or cream—or one that matches the shoes' color. Apply the polish and let it dry. Then rub well with a soft cloth and buff with a soft brush.
■ For shoes with wooden heels, apply lemon oil to the wood.

- Apply a light coating of castor oil or petroleum jelly to patent leather shoes.
- Remove water and salt stains from leather shoes by rubbing with a cloth dipped in a dilute vinegar and water solution. Polish as usual when the shoes are dry.

Save Your Sole

If the soles of your new shoes are leather, take them to a shoe repair shop and have thin rubber sole guards put on them. This is expensive ($12 for ladies' shoes and $16 for men's), but it will make your shoes last longer and look better as they age.

Slip into a Driving Shoe

You can always tell a long-distance driver by the back of his or her right shoe. The heel and the back are scuffed from rubbing against the floor of the car. Avoid this premature aging by wearing a driving shoe. Keep an old shoe in the car and get into the habit of slipping it on before you buckle up.

Stormy Weather

Water, mud, snow, salt—they're tough on your car and your shoes. If you know you're in for soggy weather, wear an old pair of shoes you keep just for that purpose. You can change into your regular shoes once you get inside. Your other option: Treat your leather shoes with Original Mink Oil to help make them water repellent.

If your shoes do get wet and muddy or salty, rinse them in cold water. Then, stuff them with newspaper or insert wooden shoe trees. Dry away from heat, which can make leather dry and stiff. When dry, give the shoes a good rubbing with saddle soap, then polish.

Give 'Em a Breather

You don't have to walk through an ankle-deep puddle to get your shoes wet—just wear them. Research shows that your feet produce about half a pint of water every day. To make your shoes last longer, give them a drying out: Let them air at least 24 hours between wearings.

New Life for Old Shoes

The heels are worn down, the soles are thin, but the shoe tops still look great. Time to throw out the shoes, right? Wrong. If the shoes are good-quality leather, take them in for repair. Repairs cost only a fraction of the price of a new pair.

Children's Shoes for Less

Don't waste money on those tiny shoes for infants. Nonwalking children don't *need* shoes; in fact, their feet may not develop properly if they're put into shoes at too early an age. Most pediatricians recommend that children not wear shoes until they are walking on their own, and then, they should be worn only when the children are outside. Socks or soft-soled slippers are fine for indoor wear.

What to select when you do buy those first shoes? Look for firm but supple uppers, semifirm soles of rubber or synthetic material (leather is too slippery), and laces for a snug fit and to keep feet from sliding about inside the shoe. Don't buy off-the-rack shoes and guess at the correct size. Have your child fitted by a knowledgeable shoe salesperson for that important first pair.

Another way to save is to buy sneakers. They're fine for young feet of all ages if they are well made. Although many sneakers have Velcro closures, stick to shoelaces because they enable you to adjust for a snug fit. As with shoes, have the sneakers fitted by a professional.

Save on Grooming Costs

Cut Your Own

You can save at least 50 percent by doing your own cutting between professional haircuts. Your best bet is to take small amounts from the front and sides, which you can see and, therefore, handle most easily yourself.

Ask your barber or stylist for cutting hints. You'll learn tricks for maintaining your good cut and for stretching the time between visits. Many stylists will even give you advice on cutting your children's hair, and you'll save the entire cost of a child's cut.

Psst . . . Save a Bundle!

Need a Haircut? Go to School

If you've ever calculated a year's worth of haircuts, permanents, and manicures, you've no doubt discovered the total to be well over $200. So how can you save money but still get terrific styling services? The well-kept secret is a cosmetology school. There you'll find savings of up to 60 percent. Cosmetology schools are convenient to use because most don't require appointments. And you can feel comfortable about the services you'll receive (cosmetology students go through hundreds of hours of practice on mannequins and each other before working on customers).

Simple Substitutes Save

By substituting a few everyday products for expensive cosmetics, you'll save in grooming dollars. Take a look at the table "Cosmetics Substitutes" for some ideas.

Luscious Lips for Less

Ever wonder what you're getting for your money when you buy those high-priced lipsticks at department store cosmetic counters? Not much more than what's available in the inexpensive brands at the drugstore. According to *Consumer Reports* magazine, all lipsticks are created equal—or almost so. The basic ingredients—oil, wax, dye, and perfume—are the same whether you spend $2 for a tube or $15.

The high-priced versions offer you a heavier, nicer case, retractable lipsticks, stronger fragrances, and, of course, an upscale image. Otherwise, performance is about the same. So before you spend $10 or more on one tube of lipstick, take a look at what the local drugstore has to offer. For the same price, you can buy several different brands and/or colors.

Cosmetics Substitutes

COSMETICS	SUBSTITUTES
Bath oil	Baby oil or vegetable oil
Cold cream	Vegetable shortening
Deodorant	Baking soda
Perfume	Cologne
Talcum powder	Cornstarch or baby powder
Toothpaste	Baking soda

4

GREAT FURNITURE
YOU CAN AFFORD

Americans are rediscovering the joys of relaxing at home. Where else could you find comfort with the people and things you love? Unfortunately, even staying home can be expensive. If the furnishings and appliances you buy are of inferior quality, if they are energy wasters, or if they're just plain impractical for your lifestyle—no matter what they cost—they're bad buys.

So how do you furnish your home the way you want, but without spending a fortune? You have to be an educated consumer, asking yourself questions such as: Will it fit (physically and tastefully)? Is it versatile enough for future use elsewhere? Is it priced right compared with similar items? Will it last as long as I want it to? To find out more on how to shop smart, save money, and get the most from your furniture and appliances, read on.

Furniture Shopping Savvy

When to Buy

Unlike appliances, home furnishings still follow the traditional December-to-February and June-to-September "white sales" seasons. During these months, you'll find linens, mattresses, furniture, lamps, and floor coverings on special promotions at furniture and department stores. Of course, the careful shopper can find discontinued, marked-down, or "seconds" merchandise year-round at no-frills clearance centers, which are operated by major furniture and department stores. At most of these, you pay cash and take the furniture home yourself (delivery usually can be arranged for a fee).

Don't Shop
by Price Alone

Never judge a piece of furniture by its price alone. Read labels and ask questions about features you can't see. Don't necessarily shun quality veneered construction (a layer of one wood bonded to a lesser-quality base). It should be labeled as a veneered piece, but that doesn't mean it's inferior. The layered construction is actually stronger than solid wood, which can warp or split.

Buy for the Future

Your mother was right: If you can only afford one piece, choose one that's versatile enough to be used for years. Put your money in quality furniture for the rooms where you'll spend most of your time. For example, buy the best sofa you can afford, even if that means using bricks and boards for your bookshelves. Put function and comfort first, and you'll find that pleasing lines and proportions need not be top-of-the-line. However, as in building a classic wardrobe, the shrewd shopper buys a few good pieces that will last rather than choosing cheaper but poorly made and poorly designed items.

Be Prepared When You Shop

Once you've decided on the furniture you want and need, take measurements of the space you intend to fill. Take your tape measure to the store, too—size can be misleading there, as can color. If you want something to match, take along a paint chip, a remnant of carpet or wallpaper, or a swatch of fabric.

The Sour Side
of Furniture Suites

For decades, some stores have catered to insecure furniture shoppers by selling medium-quality preassembled suites for the living room, dining room, and bedroom. While these matched groupings take the guesswork out of buying a roomful of furniture at once, the store benefits most: It sells five or six pieces rather than one or two. Even when the whole bunch is offered at a bargain price, these suites aren't the way to go, unless you like being led to buy more than you really need. What's more, rigidly coordinated suites save you time and trouble at the expense of style and imagination.

If you're inexperienced at furniture shopping, but don't want a roomful that matches piece for piece in shape, upholstery, and scale, don't buy them. Take a deep breath and confidently choose related furniture from one manufacturer, which is designed each season to work together. You'll save money because you'll be buying only the pieces you want, and you'll create a room that looks like home—not a store display.

Case Out the Case Goods

When buying "case goods" (chests, desks, tables, and so forth) there are very specific things that you should look for that are sure signs of quality. The back panel should be inset and screwed into the frame, not tacked on flush with it. Cabinet doors should hang true on their hinges and fit flush when closed. Hardware should be heavy and securely attached. Drawers should have center or side guides and automatic stops and shift only a quarter inch to either side. Normally hidden wood surfaces (on the back and underside) should be sanded and stained to match the rest of the piece.

Discount Furniture by Phone

North Carolina, where much of America's furniture is made, is also home to a new breed of retailers. Using toll-free telephone lines, they quote prices up to 50 percent below retail on top-quality, name-brand furniture. Callers need only specify manufacturer's name and stock number for each piece ordered. On top of these savings, orders shipped out of state rarely collect sales tax, although freight charges may cancel out much of that benefit.

To determine your savings, visit retail stores to price pieces you like. Copy all the information and numbers from its hang tag (if the floor sample has none, ask a salesperson). If you see an item you like in a magazine, consult the magazine's buying guide section for the manufacturer's name and address. Write them for the stock number, including the fabric number and grade on upholstered pieces.

Call or write each telephone retailer for a list of the manufacturers it represents. If you have questions about an item's style or suitability, don't hesitate to ask. Many firms have designers on staff to help. Once you decide to order, follow up a telephone quote with a written one, and ask for written confirmation of your order in case someone gets a number wrong. Since these are special orders, mistakes are not returnable. Be sure you understand the discounter's responsibility in case a piece arrives damaged. If you doubt a firm's reliability, check with its local chamber of commerce or the Dun and Bradstreet directory at your public library.

Now the bad news: When you order, you'll likely be asked for a deposit (up to 50 percent, but some accept credit cards). And delivery can take months, depending on the manufacturer's production and the shipping method to your town. Freight charges are computed by weight and distance (more expensive the farther you live from North Carolina). The remaining charges may be due upon shipping or delivery, often by a certified check or cash. If you can live with these restrictions, though, the savings can be sizable.

Many telephone retailers advertise in the classified sections of decorating magazines. You can also write to the following for lists of firms:

Chamber of Commerce   Chamber of Commerce
P.O. Box 5025   P.O. Box 1828
High Point, NC 27262   Hickory, NC 28601

There's No Such Thing as a Free Lamp

Don't be misled by stores that boast free accessories when you buy a roomful of furniture. Price each piece so you'll know just how much you're paying for each. Ask if the package price drops if you don't take the freebie; if it does, that lamp was a hidden charge and the store is deceptive.

Take a Look at Lighting Stores

Lighting supply stores often have good sales, their selection is almost always far more extensive than that of local department and furniture stores, and their salespeople are usually more knowledgeable than their department and furniture store counterparts. If you're renovating or building and will be purchasing a quantity of lighting supplies, many of these stores will give you a renovator's discount. Be sure to ask about it. And be on the lookout for "lighting labs"—a new concept in retail stores. The consultants in these labs will show you all types of lighting schemes in different room settings. You can bring in floor plans or photos of your rooms to get their advice on lighting needs. Lighting labs also offer renovator discounts.

Carpet Smarts

The Fifth Wall

Carpet, the fifth wall of a room, is an investment you'll live with for years to come. Aside from its decorative use, it can provide sound and heat insulation and increase the resale value of your home. Learn all about the carpet style you're considering. Ask about construction, appearance retention, durability, twist, and density. Artificial light tends to gray some colors, so take samples home and place them in the room to see how they look in both daylight and lamplight.

How Is Carpet Priced?

Carpet is priced by the square yard, and the more expensive carpets should be denser, better made, and available in more colors and weaves. The texture and type of fiber you select determines how your investment wears. The more resilient the fiber, the better the carpet will look over time. Look for tightly twisted yarns and a pile dense enough to make it tough to expose the backing. Here's how carpeting is likely to rank, from most expensive to cheapest:

wool	polypropylenes
wool/nylon blends	other synthetics
nylon	

Nylon Carpeting

Nylon is the strongest man-made fiber as well as the most popular for carpeting. It has excellent color retention, bulk, and softness. Most nylon blends are easy to clean; some newer lines are treated to be especially soil and stain resistant.

Polyester Carpeting

This type of carpeting has good "hand," or feel. It dyes well, is nonallergenic, and is reasonably durable. It's inferior to nylon in stain resistance and matting.

Acrylic Carpeting

Resembling wool, acrylic carpeting is crush resistant and soft, but some blends pill with wear.

Olefins/Polypropylene Carpeting

This type of carpeting is strong, colorfast, and durable. Most indoor-outdoor carpeting is made from olefins/polypropylene.

Wool Carpeting

Wool has a warm, natural look and feel. It's also very durable and flame resistant. But its colors are often not as bright as the man-mades, and this classic still commands the highest price.

How Much Should You Spend?

Determine your carpet budget, then buy the best quality you can afford. Don't economize for high-traffic areas; quick wear out can make that a false economy. Be sure the price quoted for wall-to-wall carpeting includes installation and padding. Also find out who will do the work and how it is guaranteed. Installation fees vary little; it should be the carpeting itself you invest in.

Wall-to-Wall for Less

For the wall-to-wall look without the same expense, have carpeting cut just shy of your room's exact dimensions, then bound on the edges. It will be easy to turn this carpet for even wear, and you can take it along when you move. To save on expensive padding, check wholesale foam rubber outlets for thin sheets you can use instead.

Look for Discontinued Deals

Dealers sometimes offer good buys on discontinued lines, or on remnants from a special order or dye job. Just be sure to buy all you need at one time.

Width-Wise Buys

If your room is large, look for carpet in the new 15-foot width (instead of the usual 12). You'll reduce or eliminate seams, which can be unattractive and can wear quicker. You'll also save on installation costs because sections won't have to be pieced together.

A Bargain May Not Be One

Be wary of this rip-off scheme that persists in the wall-to-wall carpeting business: A price that seems too good to be true may be quoted per square *foot*, while the standard is the square yard. There are nine square feet in a square yard, so multiply your bargain per-square-foot price by nine and see what you come up with. Most likely, it will be a sum that surpasses legitimate sales offers elsewhere.

Steer Clear of This Offer

Those "three rooms for . . ." deals are suspect. Find out the actual total square footage you'd get, and inspect samples first.

Upholstered Furniture

Judging
Upholstered Furniture

Upholstered furniture that looks good in the store may not last long in your home. No matter what the price, a good buy is a piece that is made strong where it will take the most wear. A smart shopper will look at specific parts of an upholstered chair before shelling out the cash for it.

Test the piece by pushing on the arms and back. Then sit down and move from side to side. There should be no creaks or wobbles. The frame should be well padded so you can't feel it.

Look for quality tailoring. Cushions should have concealed zippers, straight stitching, smooth seams, matched patterns, and secure buttons. Reversible cushions are a plus because by switching them you can reduce the show of wear. Lump-free cushions of polyurethane foam wrapped in down or solid polyester fiberfill (with a density of at least 1.8 pounds per cubic foot) are best.

If the frame is wood, it should be seasoned hardwood (check for the Hardware Manufacturers' Association hang tag). If the frame is metal, the joints should be welded, riveted, or bolted together. Look for craftsmanlike joinery such as mortise-and-tenon or tongue-and-groove details. Legs should be an extension of the frame or joined to it with interlocking pieces, not metal plates. The back legs should match those on the front in size and finish.

Eight-way, hand-tied steel coil springs are best. These coil springs should be wrapped with a thick layer of foam or down.

Which Fabric Is Best?

Tightly woven fabrics wear better than loosely woven ones. (Hold the fabric sample up to the light; you should not see light through it.) Lightweight fabrics should be quilted so the fabric can stretch under stress.

Fabric with the design woven in is of higher quality than one that is printed on. If the fabric pills up when a sample is rubbed against itself, it won't take heavy wear and will need to be replaced sooner.

In general, man-made fabrics (acrylic, nylon, rayon, and olefin) are more durable, resist soiling, and fade less than natural materials. But for better absorbency and feel, go with cotton, linen, silk, or wool. A blended fabric is the best compromise. Look for a low synthetic to high natural fiber ratio.

Chintz vs. Chintzy

"You get what you pay for" isn't always the case when it comes to upholstered furniture. Often a sofa or chair gets its high price mainly from its fabric. Check the hang tag or ask if it can be ordered with a lower-grade (and more inexpensive) upholstery. Lower grade doesn't necessarily mean poorer quality. It may mean a line of fabrics that aren't in this season's trendy colors, or ones with more simple weaves.

A growing number of furniture stores take the Chinese menu approach: You choose the chair or sofa you want, then pick the fabric from swatches displayed around the showroom and arranged by color group. Salespeople are happy to suggest companion prints or advise whether or not a fabric is suitable to the item's shape or style.

Furniture Tips from the Pros

Gallery Shopping

Take advantage of furniture galleries—a marketing phenomenon of the '80s. Major furniture manufacturers (Thomasville, Baker, and Pennsylvania House among them) use room settings as showrooms. Everything is for sale in one place, from major pieces to accessories, and all is chosen and updated by professional designers. You can browse through and get some great decorator ideas without having to hire a decorator. Knowledgeable consultants are on hand to answer your decorating questions. Some stores even hold seminars or lend videos to introduce the public to new styles or decorating ideas.

Get Free Advice

Not everyone can afford a professional interior decorator. If you're totally in the dark about decorating, or if you have ideas but lack the confidence to carry them out, ask about free advice or buying suggestions from the professionals in furniture or department stores. Many stores provide free in-home consulting services. Even if there is a slight charge, professionals can save you money by finding bargains, making the most of inexpensive pieces, and helping you avoid costly decorating errors.

Also study a store's model rooms, or vignettes, that show furnishings arranged creatively. Sometimes these feature design collections—fabrics, wallcoverings, rugs, linens, and accessories with patterns and colors that coordinate to make it easy for you to shop. Top-name design collections that are available in retail stores include Gear, Marimekko, Laura Ashley, Ralph Lauren, and Diane Von Furstenburg.

Buy Where the Decorators Do

In major cities, design centers or showrooms are *the* wholesale source for top-quality furniture, but most are open only to the trade. To even see what's there, you have to go with a design professional—an architect, designer, or decorator who acts as middleman—or at least carry the person's business card or letter of introduction. Rules on who can get in and who can buy vary from center to center. One solution is to get a resale license from your state tax department. This often gives you access to a design center. Once admitted, you may save up to 40 percent off the list or retail price. But before you place an order, compare prices with those at retail stores.

How to Read a Showroom Price Tag

Once you get inside a designer showroom you will probably be confounded by the price tags, mysteriously coded so the client can't tell what the pro pays. Most likely it's the "5-10" code: You subtract 5 from the figure on the left and 10 from the one on the right, then add the totals. So if, for example, the tag says 85-15, subtract 5 from 85 to get 80 and subtract 10 from 15 to get 5. Then add 80 and 5 to get $85.

Select Your Decorator with Care

Using the services of an interior decorator needn't be expensive. Look for a decorator who charges only a small markup over wholesale or one who works on a flat fee for time or the job. His or her access to a design center may well be worth the fee.

Frugal Furnishings

Double-Duty Furniture

Conquer a space squeeze, and buy two pieces for the price of one with multifunction furniture. Look for tables that change from low (at the sofa) to high (for dining) by flipping the base, or a hutch or china closet with a fold-out dining surface. Trunks or cedar chests can act as tables, with room inside to store linens, games, crafts projects, and so on. Futon furniture folds to serve as a chair or sofa, or unfolds to a bed. These pieces are especially handy if you move often because they adapt to many spaces.

Bidding for Bargains

Unfortunately, it's rare that you'll find a "steal" at a country or estate auction. Antiques dealers spot the best things, too, and sometimes they bid high with a particular collector in mind. However, you can save about half of what a store would charge on practical, everyday furniture—perhaps a piece that needs refinishing or slipcovering. But be careful. Never bid on a piece you haven't examined first during the preview (usually held just before the auction). Assess its value (including repairs or reupholstering) and decide how much you'll pay. An honest auctioneer sells damaged items "as is" or points out their flaws.

Also beware of bidding fever. Once the dealers have left for the day, impatient buyers may try to make up for lost time by buying something they don't really want or by paying more than it's worth. Don't act emotionally. And don't appear too eager about something you're desperate to have. When bidding gets close to your predetermined limit, pretend to lose interest to discourage competing bidders. Then, as others drop out, and if it's still within your limit, make your final offer.

Thrift-Shop Savings

Don't be too proud to visit Goodwill, the Salvation Army, or charity-run thrift shops. Sometimes you can find furniture here in good repair at a fraction of its original cost, and you can feel good knowing your money is going to a good cause.

Score Big
with Secondhand Goods

Country barns full of secondhand stuff are often cold and dirty, but they are bursting with a bit of everything. Shopping here is like a treasure hunt; the proprietor may not know what he has. Even if he does, feel free to haggle. And be ready to pay in cash. Most owners of secondhand shops won't deal with the hassles of credit cards and are leery of checks. You can drive a better bargain when you pay in cash.

Garage Sales Spell Savings

Garage-sale mania continues to be America's favorite way to recycle. The furniture you find here should be priced one-third to one-half of the retail price or even lower, depending on wear. Again, these are cash-only deals—and be prepared to haggle. Tip: If the garage sale is set up every weekend, you're dealing with pros—they're in business, they're not just cleaning house—so don't expect to find real deals.

Get Paid for Your
Old Furniture

Consignment stores benefit both buyer and seller, and you can be both. These locally managed outlets take furniture on consignment, turning part of the selling price over to the former owner, and keeping the rest as commission. When an item is slow to sell, many consignment shops mark the price down automatically—20 percent off after the first month, for example, so you can find some real bargains here.

Try a Kit

Kit furniture is a Shaker concept that brought quality furnishings to isolated settlers. Today kit furniture brings that same quality to our homes. Many of the kits available are reproductions or adaptations of museum pieces, or pieces in traditional styles. When you buy kit furniture, you get the satisfaction of playing a role in the craftsmanship, you choose the wood's color and finish, and you pay a lot less than you would for comparable pieces in furniture stores.

Look for kit furniture in department stores, home centers, or by mail order. Some kit prices include the finishing materials, so keep this in mind when comparison shopping. Much of the kit furniture is made from solid wood, commonly maple, which is nicely grained and takes a finish well. You can find cherry and oak in expensive pieces, and pine with fiberboard in budget pieces. If you're new to working with wood, check first about an item's level of difficulty. Many involve simple sanding, gluing, and clamping; for more complex projects, ask your supplier for help.

Psst . . . Save a Bundle!

Knock-Downs and Other Bargains

If your budget is limited and you need well-designed, casual furniture—and you don't mind doing some time with a screwdriver—visit the "lifestyle" furniture section of your favorite department store or retailer such as Ikea, Conran's, Crate & Barrel, Storehouse, and Workbench. Here you'll find a range of pieces, mainly contemporary in design, that are labeled "knock-down" or "ready-to-assemble" (RTA to the trade). Prices are low because pieces are often imported, and flat cartons cost less to ship from overseas. Parts, hardware, and instructions are included. Just attach shelf A to frame B and celebrate your handiwork. These stores sell assembled, higher-end furniture, too, plus rugs, lighting, housewares, and accessories.

The Joys of Catalog Shopping

The Benefits of Buying by Mail

Whether you live in a city or in the country, shopping by mail-order catalog makes sense. The selection is wide, no salesperson will pressure you, and you avoid crowds, parking, and bad weather. It's easy to furnish an entire home—from sofa to silverware—without leaving it.

The "Big Three" and More

Sears, J. C. Penney, and Spiegel—the "big three" catalog firms—offer the widest variety, but specialty catalogs are growing by the thousands each year. From Laura Ashley's English country-look pieces to Conran's Euro design, there's a style for every home. Items on sale are infrequent (and then quantities may be limited), but catalog goods are often of the type and quality that are hard to find across much of the country. Just be sure you're dealing with a reputable mail-order firm that has a no-charge, hassle-free return policy.

If You Need Help

If a dispute occurs when you order from a catalog, you can complain about this by writing to the Direct Mail Marketing Association, 6 East 43d Street, New York, NY 10017.

This is also where to write if you want to receive catalogs from member companies. You'll probably find that once you order from one, your mailbox will seldom be empty again.

Antique Reproductions by Mail

Can't afford antiques? You can get the look for much less with reproduction furniture, available in both kit and finished form through established mail-order sources. Some pieces copy important designs from the Museum of American Folk Art or settlements like Sturbridge Village and Colonial Williamsburg, offering an affordable way to live with history. Prices vary according to how true the piece is to the original. The most expensive, a replica, must be made with the same materials and methods as the museum piece. A reproduction might fudge on the type of wood or joinery used. An adaptation, generally least expensive, may alter the classic's scale, finish, or detail. Write the following for catalogs:

Cohasset Colonials
  by Hagerty
Cohasset, MA 02025

The Bartley
  Collection Ltd.
3 Airpark Dr.
Easton, MD 21601

Shaker Workshops
P.O. Box 1028
Concord, MA 01742

Sturbridge Yankee
  Workshops
Blueberry Rd.
Westbrook, ME 04092

Yield House
Dept. 6850
North Conway, NH 03860

Unexpected Sources for Furniture

Buy after Others Have Rented

What the clever consumer lacks in funds, he or she makes up for in creativity. Why limit your shopping to furniture stores when you can find hard-working, good-looking bargains where no one else would think of going? Take furniture rental agencies, for instance: They have fair-quality, if generally unimaginative, pieces they let go for one-third to one-half of their retail price after a certain length of time. Evaluate these furnishings carefully, though.

Like rental cars, they often receive rough treatment. As long as the frame is sound, professional cleaning can usually make a slightly dingy upholstered piece look like new.

Bedrooms for Less

If you want basic bedroom furniture (not mattresses) for a vacation house or guest room, try a hotel or motel that is undergoing refurbishing or going out of business.

Move the Outdoors In

End-of-season sales at outdoor living, pool, and spa retailers often yield patio furniture that would work just as well inside as out. Import shops are excellent sources for bamboo or wicker furniture that works equally well on a porch or deck or inside in a casual family room.

The Office Look for Less

Your home office will look and feel more professional—whether it hosts clients or not—when you use school or commercial desks, chairs, storage units, and lighting. Office supply stores often have floor samples or leftovers from an office order; don't be afraid to ask if you don't see any on display. And keep an eye out for school closings or renovations; call the administrative office and ask if any furniture will be available. .

Don't Buy at All

If you move frequently or need to furnish a home on an extremely limited budget, rental showrooms are one alternative. Without long-term commitment, you can try out pieces and styles before you're ready to buy. Shop around for selection, which will also affect fees. If what you're renting is not new, it should have been thoroughly cleaned before being delivered to you. Furniture groupings may rent for as little as $50 or as much as $500 a month, depending on quality. The Furniture Rental Association estimates sofas will run $10 to $45, chairs $10 to $30, and end tables $5 to $15 per month. Expect to pay a security deposit of one month's rent and to give a 30-day notice to terminate the contract.

5

PUTTING A CEILING
ON HOME EXPENSES

It doesn't fit in a safe deposit box, and you can't trade it on the New York Stock Exchange. But buying a home remains the most important—and largest—investment most of us will ever make. This chapter can help you make a wiser choice when it's time to buy a house. More importantly, the tips that follow will help to guarantee that your house won't cost you money in the long run.

Here are tips on how to get the best financing when you buy, and how to find a home that is sure to appreciate in value. Here are also ideas about how to improve the value of your property without spending a bundle. You'll also learn ways to spend less on ongoing maintenance, and how to assess when you can do a job yourself and when you should turn it over to an expert. We've even included guidelines for hiring the right professional for a job, since hiring the wrong one can cost you more money. Read on, and learn how to keep Home Sweet Home from becoming Home Sweet Headache.

A Top Priority When Buying

North, South, East, West

As every real estate agent will tell you, the three most important considerations when looking for a new home are: location, location, location. Whether you're looking in a city or intent on country living, these factors are always worth considering:

- Look for well-kept neighborhoods that are convenient to shopping, churches, schools, recreational facilities, and other amenities. Heavily trafficked streets are usually less desirable. At the same time, being close to public transportation can be a plus.
- Check out the zoning for surrounding properties. What looks like a nice open field across the road could become a factory or large shopping mall in just a few years—and your property value will suffer. Make sure your neighborhood is zoned for residential use only.

Buy Low, Sell High

The home buyer's dream is to buy a bargain home and cash in later when values soar. One way to accomplish this is to choose an area where homes will significantly appreciate in value, and buy before the increases occur. Although it's difficult to predict exactly where housing prices will skyrocket, an older, working-class neighborhood just outside the city is a likely place for a renaissance. Contact a local historic preservation organization. These groups often know which areas are historically significant and likely to be up-and-coming.

The Handyman Special

Purchasing the handyman special or fixer-upper—the home that needs a lot of work—is a good way to stretch your dollars. Such homes usually sell for significantly lower prices than other homes in the neighborhood. If you can do some or all of the work yourself, you'll reap bigger profits at resale time. (See "How Much Can You Save?" on page 126.)

If you're considering a handyman special, here's what to look for and what to avoid:

- If the work that needs to be done is mostly cosmetic (painting, wallpapering, and the like), this is a good investment. If the rest of the house is structurally sound (good roof, solid foundation, and so on), just making the property look better will mean a big return when you sell.
- If the house needs major work—new wiring, for example, or extensive shoring up of the foundation—the return on what you invest may be relatively low. If you can't make such judgments yourself, hire someone to evaluate that charming white elephant before you close the deal.
- No matter how minor or how extensive your fixing up must be, weigh which jobs you can do yourself versus which you would have to hire someone to do. If you have to pay someone to do most of the costly work, the house may not be a bargain in the long run.

Follow the Yellow Brick Road

Is a major highway being built that will make commuting to a metropolitan area a breeze? Is a major company moving into town? Anything that might make an area more attractive can signal that this would be a good place to buy—before everyone else catches on and housing prices rise to meet the demand.

Grade the Schools Before You Buy

Evaluate the Local Schools

When you're in the market to buy a house, you'll want to know how the schools near your prospective new home measure up. Even if you don't have youngsters, you still should be looking at the caliber of the local schools. Why? Because the person who buys your home five or ten years later may have children, and the quality of local education could make or break the sale. You're protecting your investment when you consider the future buyer's needs as well as your own. Schools are usually very high on every house hunter's list of priorities.

Don't Pay for Information

How can you assess your future school district? By doing some research. Beware of computer services that provide information about school districts for a fee. While they may have valuable information, ask for examples of the kinds of things they report. If you're willing to make some phone calls yourself, you can bypass a bill of $50 to $100 per report.

Visit the Schools

By visiting the schools in your prospective new town, you'll be able to see the condition and quality of the facilities. Many districts will give prospective students and their parents a tour by appointment.

When you call or write for your tour, contact an official in the school district and ask about specifics such as average class size, district-wide results on standardized achievement tests, what special classes are available, and the number of students who go on to pursue college degrees.

Do Your Homework

Don't take the official word at face value when it comes to judging school quality—administrators often paint a rosier picture of their schools than is known to be true in the community. But how can an out-of-towner learn the inside scoop? Start by going to the library in your prospective new town and looking up newspaper articles about local schools. These can give you some real insights into what's happening and can alert you to potential problems.

Next seek out parents whose children attend the schools and ask for their candid opinions. Try asking parents of older children, as well as those whose children are the same age as yours. Parents whose children have already completed elementary school may have a better perspective about the primary grades. Similarly, those with college-age youngsters may have a better handle on what was good—or bad—about the local high school.

In the Market

The Best of Times

Try to buy a home when it's not peak selling season. You will pay top prices in March, April, and May when the housing market traditionally is booming. But if you wait until mid-July, you just might get a bargain. A disheartened seller who has had his house on the market for three or four months may be ready to negotiate. Using the same strategy, keep track of that dream house you saw in June. If it's still available in August or September, you may be able to negotiate a better price.

Don't Let the Snow
Slow You Down

If you don't mind house hunting in the winter, it's possible to find excellent bargains during December. Although there are fewer properties to choose from, sellers are more anxious during what is traditionally the slow season.

End-of-Summer Sales

Shopping for a summer vacation home? Try looking at the end of the season. You'll get the lowest price then, although you will have to maintain the property before you can use it the following spring and summer.

Be Smart
in a Seller's Market

If you shop for a home in a seller's market (one where demand exceeds the supply of housing), beware of paying more than the fair market price for a house. Don't get locked into a bidding war with another buyer. Instead, always keep in mind what you can afford to spend and what the house is worth.

Psst . . . Save a Bundle!

For Sale by Owner

One of the easiest ways to save money when buying a home is to buy directly from the owner. At the very least, you'll save the real estate agent's commission. That's 6 percent on the average these days. That's $4,800 on an $80,000 home. Many homeowners who choose to sell their homes themselves adjust their price to reflect the fact that no one is paying the real estate agent's commission. However, if you choose to buy this way, hire a lawyer to go over the paperwork. She or he will help ensure that you get what you pay for.

The Mortgage Maze

Which Way to Pay?

Now that you've found your dream home, how are you going to pay for it? Today's mortgage options are mind boggling: Some mortgages save you money up front by cutting your closing costs; others cost more up front but less each month in payments. How do you determine which mortgage option is best for you? Start by estimating how long you think you will be in your house and how long you will pay on that mortgage. The average American family moves about every seven years—some move much more often, some not at all. Figure out where you are likely to fall, then take a look at your mortgage options.

No Points

Some banks will charge you no points at closing (a point is 1 percent of the principal) on a standard interest rate. The standard rate may not be the lowest rate available, so you'll pay more each month due to the higher rate, but you won't be paying any cash upon signing because there are no points due. You will, however, almost always pay a 1 percent loan processing fee up front.

Some "no points" loans require the points up front, but provide you with the money to pay the points if you're short of cash. This loan can still be attractive if you don't plan to stay in your house more than a few years, but it would cost you more over the total life of the loan, as shown in the third entry in the table "No Points vs. Points."

Adjustable Rate

Adjustable rate mortgages, or ARMs, have lower payments the first two or three years. Usually, by the third year, the rate is equal to or higher than a fixed-rate loan. The rate is generally a bit more than 2 percent lower than the conventional fixed rate. The rate is set at an agreed-upon percentage over a specified index—treasury bond rates or money funds. It will be adjusted—up or down—annually.

Adjustables help a lot of first-time buyers because more peo-

No Points vs. Points ($100,000 loan)

POINTS ($ DUE)	RATE (%)	MONTHLY PAYMENTS ($)	PAYMENTS AFTER 3 YEARS ($)	COST AFTER 3 YEARS ($)
0 (0)	11.0	953.0	34,308	34,308
3 (3,000)	10.25	897.0	32,292	35,292
3 (0)	10.25	923.91	33,260	33,260

ple can afford these initially low-payment adjustables in the first and second year. But to make sure you can afford the mortgage past those first inexpensive years, insist on a cap—2 percent per year and 6 percent over the life of the loan is typical.

Adjustable Convertible

These mortgages have built-in refinancing. They start with a low rate, because they're adjustable, and they change annually with the rise or fall of the mortgage's index. But for a fee, usually about 1 percent of the principal, you can switch to the current fixed rate. This is thousands cheaper than refinancing.

Some of these loans limit conversion to certain times—often between the 13th and 60th month of the life of the loan. Be sure you completely understand the terms of this loan before you sign, then read your newspaper's financial pages to anticipate the best time to convert.

Conventional

As mortgages go, conventional is the standard, although it's far less popular than years ago. The advantage to you is that the monthly payment never changes. The advantage to the bank is that it can charge you a higher rate than with adjustables because it takes the risk that the cost of money will go up before you pay

PAYMENTS AFTER 7 YEARS ($)	COST AFTER 7 YEARS ($)	PAYMENTS AFTER 10 YEARS ($)	COST AFTER 10 YEARS ($)
80,052	80,052	114,360	114,360
75,348	78,348	107,640	110,640
77,608	77,608	110,869	110,869

off the loan. It also earns much more in interest in the loan's early years.

Conventional loans are available in almost any term or repayment period. The shorter the term, the higher the monthly payment, but the greater the savings over the life of the loan. A 15-year $100,000 mortgage will likely cost less than 60 percent of what a 30-year $100,000 mortgage will. (See the table "Comparing Conventional Loans.")

Comparing Conventional Loans
($100,000 loan)

PRINCIPAL ($)	TERM (YEARS)	RATE (%)	MONTHLY PAYMENT ($)	TOTAL PAYMENTS ($)
100,000	30	11.0	953	343,080
100,000	15	10.75	1,121	201,780
			Savings:	141,300

Bimonthly

Mortgages that require you to pay every two weeks instead of once a month cut interest, reduce the term of the loan, and build up equity more quickly. Each payment is about half of what a monthly payment would be on a 30-year loan. A bimonthly loan can reduce payback to about 18 years. For families with two paychecks, this may be a comfortable repayment plan.

You can, however, achieve the same—or even better—results by prepaying principal voluntarily. (See "Prepay Your Mortgage" below.)

Sweat Equity

If you're a do-it-yourselfer buying a handyman special, some savings and loans will lump your fix-up costs with your mortgage at the outset. You'll have to pay for a special appraisal—one that compares the value of the house in its current condition with the value after the planned work is done.

To qualify for this type of loan, be prepared to show that you have the know-how and the time to do the work. Present detailed plans and schedules, and make them as exact as possible if you're not using a contractor or architect.

Prepay Your Mortgage

Prepaying your mortgage can save you a fortune—perhaps even more than the price of the home itself on a 30-year loan. Make sure the terms of your mortgage allow prepayment (most do). What you are prepaying is principal—the amount you originally borrowed. If you borrowed $100,000, you will pay back $100,000 in principal whether you do it over 30 years or 15. But every dollar of principal paid early cuts the interest you will pay, because on a mortgage, you pay interest only on the part of the principal that's outstanding. So, the earlier you prepay, the more you save.

Prepay any amount, monthly or sporadically, but keep a record. Make principal prepayments by separate check and clearly mark them as such. Remember that even if you prepay principal one month, you'll still owe your regular monthly payments on the dates in your coupon book. But once the principal has been paid, your payments will end entirely—years early. For instance, on $75,000 borrowed over 30 years, $25 monthly prepayments will save $34,000 in interest and will end all payments more than 5 years early. Monthly prepayments of $100 would save $78,000 in interest and end payments more than 12 years early. Prepayment creates similar savings on second mortgages and home-equity loans, too.

Smart Moves

Should You Hire a Mover?

When it comes time to move, should you do it yourself or hire professionals to lift and carry all your worldly possessions? There's no question that you'll save money if you handle the move with a little help from friends and relatives. It will probably cost less than $200 if you hire a truck and do it yourself. Contrast that with typical fees for professionals: A local move involving a few miles costs about $200 to $300. A long-distance move—from New York City to Pittsburgh, for example—could cost $500 and up. Factors such as the amount and type of furniture, how many stairways the movers must negotiate at your new residence, and other considerations can affect costs.

Go Local
for the Short Haul

For moving short distances, consider a smaller, local firm. Joe's Moving and Storage may charge lower rates than the bigger companies with nationally recognized names.

Pack It Yourself

Even if you decide to hire a professional mover, you can still save money by doing the packing and unpacking yourself. Just be sure to check with the moving company first. Some companies have do-it-yourself packing guidelines, which may specify the type of packing materials to be used. A few may stipulate certain rules for packing that must be adhered to before the company will assume liability for damages.

Check the Insurance

Before you hire a mover, get a written explanation of the insurance coverage offered by the company. Also verify how much time you have to file a claim. On a busy moving day, some damage might escape your attention. Ninety days is the standard amount of time for filing a claim.

Check to see if your homeowner's insurance will cover the move. If you have anything especially valuable—such as a priceless antique or a one-of-a-kind piece of art—you should ask about special coverage.

The movers will provide you with an itemized bill of lading after they have loaded the truck. It's a good idea to make your own list, detailing the number of cartons from each room and every item not packed in a carton. Then you can check your list against theirs. Your personal list is a good way to safeguard your property.

Guaranteed Delivery
Is Worth the Price

If you must get your possessions picked up and delivered on specific dates, pay for a guaranteed delivery. This really does not guarantee your delivery, but it does require the mover to pay a fine—an average of $125 per day—plus costs for you to stay in a motel if the date specified in the contract is not met.

The Plan's the Thing

Bargain Blueprints

You can obtain house blueprints by writing to your state land grant university. Address your request to the agricultural engineering office. These house plans may have to be modified to meet local code requirements, and you will probably need an architect to do this. But it will require a fraction of the time—and money—that is required to draw up a blueprint from scratch.

Psst . . . Save a Bundle!

Save on Architect's Fees

If you want a home that is designed to your specifications, you may need the help of a licensed architect to translate your dreams into a set of plans that builders and contractors can follow. If you do hire one, look for someone who is affiliated with the American Institute of Architects (AIA), which sets many standards in the profession. An architect's standard fee is usually 10 percent or more of the total cost of the house. So if you're building a $100,000 home, the architect's fee would be $10,000.

A cheaper alternative to a custom design is to buy plans from various companies. Often for under $200 (and, in some cases, for much less), you can order a house plan from a plans book that contains descriptions of dozens of tested plans and designs. Your local library can help you locate these plans books. Two companies that provide such plans are:

The Garlinghouse Company
34 Industrial Park Place
P.O. Box 1717
Middletown, CT 06457

Home Planners, Inc.
23761 Research Dr.
Farmington Hills, MI 48024

House plans are also available by writing to the Government Printing Office, Washington, DC 20401.

Go with a Standard Plan

If you do hire an architect, you can save money by choosing what is referred to as a standard plan instead of a custom design. Such a plan incorporates a design that has been previously used. A classic example would be the center-hall colonial. It is cheaper to have an architect modify an existing plan than draw a new one.

Be Your Own Contractor

You're in Charge

When it comes to building a home, being your own contractor puts you in charge of all the details. But instead of doing all the work yourself, you hire others—subcontractors—to do parts of the work you can't handle. Assuming this responsibility ensures that you'll get exactly what you want, and it also saves you money. If you hire a general contractor, he could charge 10 to 25 percent of the total cost of your project. On an $85,000 house, that can mean a savings of anywhere from $8,500 to $21,250; on a $100,000 house, it means savings of as much as $25,000.

Know What
You're Getting Into

The savings are attractive, but being your own contractor can cost you money if you can't handle all the details yourself. It's imperative that you understand construction and/or remodeling procedures. If you don't already have a working knowledge of most procedures, you can attend an owner/builder school, an institution that teaches people how to build their own homes and also offers courses in owner-contracting. But such schools are expensive, and a cheaper alternative would be to do some reading. Better yet, apprentice yourself to an expert who is willing to share some knowledge.

Time Is Money

If you're going to save money in the long run, the time you spend planning, soliciting bids, calling suppliers, and tracking down subcontrators will be worth it. During construction, you should plan to visit the site once a day. You'll be in charge of scheduling the subcontractors, making sure all supplies are on hand, and making sure all phases of a project are running smoothly. If details aren't your strong suit, or if you lack people skills, you could find that being your own contractor is the toughest job you ever assume.

And Money Is Everything

Everyone who builds a home is involved in the financing process, but those who opt to be their own contractors have more responsibility. You'll have to prove to the lender that you know what you're doing. The lender will want to see detailed plans and specifications, accurate estimates for materials, and a realistic time frame for completion. As the project moves along, you'll have to work out payment schedules and budgets for all phases of the project and keep track of who and what has been paid. By keeping careful financial records, you'll get the most from your lender and the most from the money you have to pay out.

Sign on the Dotted Line

Being your own contractor demands a knowledge of contracts and liabilities. Contact your lawyer, insurance agent, and local zoning officials to make sure you're meeting all obligations. Be sure you're covered in case of damage or mistakes. Hire subcontractors who are licensed and bonded—they will have insurance coverage for any mistakes made or injuries incurred. You should also make your subcontractors sign a no-lien agreement. This protects you in case your subcontractors don't pay their workers. Without the agreement, you will be liable for paying them if your subcontractors default.

The Owner/Worker

Do the Finish Work and Save

Even if you don't want to assume the responsibility for being your own contractor, there are still ways to save when you're building a home. If you have some do-it-yourself experience, you can cut thousands off your final bill by doing some of the finish work on your new abode. Exactly what you complete depends on your skill level and how much time you're willing to invest. The savings can be well worth it: You can cut the cost of some jobs in half if you do them instead of hiring a professional contractor. How much can you save by doing the finish work yourself? Take a look at the examples in the table "Do-It-Yourself Savings." They illustrate the tremendous savings that can be yours.

Negotiate with Your Contractor

Most contractors are willing to negotiate to leave some or most of the finishing to be done by the owner. Regardless of how much you decide to finish yourself, it's good to remember one rule when you're negotiating with a contractor: Don't try to nickel-

Do-It-Yourself Savings

JOB	CONTRACTED COST ($)	DIY FINISH COST ($)
Baseboard and trim	1,303	690
Cabinetry	7,865	5,900
Electrical fixtures	4,242	2,720
Insulation (fiberglass)	2,150	1,035
Interior wall finish	2,139	600
Shelving	617	200

and-dime him by offering to do parts of the job—such as cleanup—that will not yield significant savings. It's probably a good idea to allow the contractor and his crew to finish their work before you take over. That way, there's no danger that you'll hold them up.

Try Your Hand at Drywall

You can save a fair amount of money if you do your own drywall work. You'll need help hanging the drywall, but that takes more strength than skill. Then you can hire a pro to do the more exacting finish work or opt to do it yourself if you have some experience.

Hiring a Contractor

If you've decided to hire a contractor, follow these suggestions *before* you sign on the dotted line:

■ Use a contractor who is licensed in your area. Affiliation with a professional association such as the National Association of the Remodeling Industry, the Remodelers Council of the National Association of Home Builders, or the National Kitchen and Bath Association is a good sign.
■ Inspect other work that the contractor has done. Is it of good quality? Does it meet your standards?
■ Make sure the contractor secures all necessary permits. In general, a building permit is required whenever structural work is involved. You can't take care of this yourself because the person who obtains the permit is liable if the work does not comply with various building codes and regulations.
■ Make sure your prospective contractor is agreeable to your finishing all or part of the work yourself, if that's what you have in mind. Some contractors make a practice of refusing all jobs that involve subcontracting all or part of the work to the owner.

Do-It-Yourself
Doors and Cabinets

Prehung doors are simple to install, and cheaper than custom-size ones. Fitting and hanging doors in your own jambs is a little more difficult. You have to know how to use a level and have experience in finish nailing. But doing it yourself will save you dollars.

Prefabricated cabinets, vanities, and countertops take a lot of the headaches and the expense out of installing kitchen cabinets, bathroom vanities, countertops, and other built-in pieces.

Save on Shelving

Closet and pantry shelving is an inexpensive item, so don't run up its cost by having it professionally installed. This is an excellent job for beginners because the techniques aren't difficult to master and, if you do make a mistake or two, they are usually hidden behind closed doors.

Fasten Your Fixtures

Installing toilets, basins, bathtubs, showers, and sinks isn't that hard if you have the pipes installed beforehand. Bath accessories like shower doors, toothbrush holders, mirrors, and the like can be installed by just about anyone. Spas, whirlpools, and hot tubs, however, are major investments and are best left to the professionals unless you have considerable plumbing experience.

Appliance Acumen

If the electrical and plumbing connections have been done properly by your contractor, hooking up your appliances—such as washer, dryer, oven/range, and refrigerator—should be relatively easy. You may need some help situating the large, heavy pieces.

Installing an electric water heater is also a fairly easy do-it-yourself project. Be wary of installing gas units, which are complicated because of the gas connections.

Up on the Roof

If you can handle working in high places, you can handle installing gutters and downspouts, but a second pair of hands is definitely required.

Don't Do the Plumbing

. . . or the electrical work, either. Experts say that you should rely on professionals for all plumbing, heating, and electrical work. This is best because most local codes and ordinances require professionals to complete certain work. You'll waste a lot of time and money if you do it yourself and then find out it has to be redone by a pro, so don't balk at spending the money up front. And always hire a pro when you're not confident in your ability to do the work. A sloppy job done now spells trouble (and expensive repairs) down the road.

Go Fishing and Save on Electrician's Fees

While you should save the hard-core electrical work for the pros, there is one way you can do some electrical work and save: "Fish" the wires for electrical connections yourself, and let a professional complete the work. This is well within the limits of most laws and also is a safe procedure for a nonelectrician. Fishing involves running the wires up from the basement and pulling them through the wall via the outlet or light switch to which they lead.

The Whole Kit and Caboodle

Ever since Sears, Roebuck and Company sold homes from their catalog, Americans have been fascinated with manufactured houses. Also known as kit homes, these structures are no longer thought of as second-class alternatives to stick-built houses. Instead, they are a recognized way for homeowners to get more for their money. However, it's important to remember that, as the quality of kit homes has risen, so has the cost. Don't expect to get a home for 50 percent of its current market value.

The savings on kit homes average 25 to 35 percent below the cost of a similar structure built from scratch. Savings can be more dramatic, depending on how much of the work you finish yourself. If you act as your own contractor, you can realize an additional 15 to 20 percent savings. (See "Be Your Own Contractor" on page 120.)

Remodeling Revenues

Do It Yourself, but Do It Well

Remodeling some part of your home is usually more economical than moving to a new house that has the feature you desire. But it's easy to spend too much, or to spend foolishly, when you make home improvements. You can make every dollar count by tackling the job yourself instead of hiring a professional. But do so only if you are confident that you can handle it—it will cost you more money if a professional has to correct all your mistakes later. Similarly, a poor job could cost you money at resale time if a buyer thinks it looks cheap or poorly executed. So keep in mind that doing it yourself only saves you money if you can do it well.

How Much Can You Save?

You can expect to save 50 percent or more if you do a remodeling job yourself. Exactly how much depends on the job, the materials used, the age and type of home, and some other factors. The table "Do-It-Yourself Remodeling" compares the cost of eight jobs when undertaken by a professional versus the costs when they are do-it-yourself projects.

Let Your House Pay for Its Own Improvements

In the past, homeowners who wanted to build additions or replace their kitchens usually paid for the projects with home-improvement or personal loans. Today a home-equity loan is probably your best bet for lowest monthly payments and saving money at tax time. The Tax Reform Act of 1986 called for phasing out the deductibility of all consumer interest, except for mortgages on first and second homes. In 1989, only 20 percent of consumer interest from such debts as car loans, home-improvement loans, and credit cards can be deducted. That amount drops to 10

Do-It-Yourself Remodeling

PROJECT*	PROFESSIONAL JOB ($ COST/ % RECOUPED)†	DIY JOB ($ COST/ % RECOUPED)†
Exterior paint	3,500/18	190/1,301
Basement conversion (converting to living space)	6,720/84	2,360/232
Bathroom	3,590/98	1,290/228
Deck	3,500/66	1,010/219
Interior facelift (painting, wallpapering, new carpeting, and so forth)	3,900/105	2,020/202
Fireplace	3,010/85	1,280/200
Kitchen	6,930/85	3,150/184
Garage (adding one)	9,475/85	4,230/182
Central air-conditioning‡	2,100/110	N/A
Furnace replacement‡	2,100/82	N/A

SOURCE: The 1988 Home Improvement Survey conducted by *Practical Homeowner* magazine; based on assessments made by 20 realtors and real estate appraisers in ten cities across the United States.
*Costs are for improvements to a 25-year-old ranch.
†The percentage of the cost you can expect to recoup when it's time to sell your house (roughly how much value this improvement will add to your home).
‡Not recommended as a DIY project. Hire a professional.

percent in 1990. By 1991, consumer interest will no longer be deductible, but the interest paid on a home-equity loan will be.

Equity is the difference between your home's current market value and any outstanding mortgages on the property. Fixed- and variable-rate home-equity loans tap into this equity. You may deduct the interest on your federal income tax if the equity loan does not total more than the original purchase price of your home plus the actual cost of improvements. Interest is also deductible if the loan is used directly for new improvements to your home, for financing educational costs, or for uninsured medical costs.

Home-equity loans offer lower interest rates and a longer repayment period than do home-improvement or personal loans. The equity loans are usually for a fixed rate with a set payback period of 10 to 15 years. Interest rates are comparable to those for first mortgages. The interest rates for home-improvement and personal loans tend to be higher, and the repayment period is short (often as little as two or three years). However, unlike home-improvement or personal loans, if you default on an equity loan, you risk losing your home.

Be Sure It Fits In

If you want your improvements to add value to your home, consider other houses in the neighborhood. If your improvement makes your house the fanciest one on the block—significantly larger, or with superdeluxe kitchen or baths—chances are that you'll never get your investment back if you sell. A luxury improvement such as a swimming pool or hot tub may also be out of place in a moderately priced neighborhood.

Stick Around

Think about how long you're planning to live in your house after you remodel. In general, the longer you remain after a project is completed, the more money you'll recoup from the cost of the renovation. And many improvements yield actual savings—such as energy-saving windows or better insulation—but these take time to accrue.

Is It What You Want?

The most basic consideration on any remodeling job should be whether it's something that will enhance your lifestyle. If you'd love a swimming pool, put one in but be aware that it may add little to your home's resale value. If you're planning to stick around and enjoy it, it may be worth the investment. And always remember that a remodeling job should be done in good taste so that it won't detract from your home's value. If you've got your heart set on painting the interior black, you may suffer the consequences when it comes time to sell.

Taxing Considerations

Remodeling can put more money in your pocketbook by helping to lower your taxes. When you sell, you can deduct the cost of all improvements and the original purchase price of the house from the selling price. The amount that's left is the capital gain that is subject to taxes. It doesn't take a mathematical wizard to see that a substantial number of improvements can mean substantial tax savings.

To guarantee that the improvements will lower your tax bill, you must understand the difference between improvements and repairs. Repairs keep your house in operating condition. Improvements extend its life, increase its value, or adapt it to another use. Patching a leaking roof is a repair, but replacing it is an improvement. Refinishing a floor is a repair; replacing it is an improvement. Improvements can include everything from an alarm system to central air-conditioning. Other improvements include adding insulation and installing storm windows and doors.

Be sure to keep good records of all improvements so you can claim your deductions. Hold on to invoices showing the name of the supplier, the date, the cost, and the description, and save all your canceled checks.

Hiring Help

Shop Around

Whether you need the help of a plumber, electrician, carpenter, or cleaning service, you'll save money in the long run by shopping around. Ask people you know and trust for their opinions and recommendations. If you can, take a look at the work that was done for them so you can compare quality.

Choose at least three workers and solicit estimates before awarding a contract for a job. When you ask for estimates, offer as many specifics about the work as you can, or the bids may be inaccurate. If there are significant differences between bids, ask why. The lowest bid isn't necessarily the cheapest in the long run. It may be low because the worker plans on using poor-quality materials that will soon have to be replaced, which means you'll be paying twice for the same job within just a few years.

It's All in the Contract

Your best protection when hiring outside help is a clear, well-thought-out contract. Make sure you have a hand in writing it. More informal agreements—such as simple letters of agreement—will suffice for jobs costing $1,000 or less. In addition to specifying starting and ending dates, the contract should include:

- Total cost and an outline of payment. Don't pay too much up front. It's better to save your largest payment for last.
- A description of the work area, with clearly described boundaries and a description of the work itself.
- A description of materials. This is also called drawing up specifications, or specs. Quality, weight, dimensions, color, and style are some of the information you should insist upon. Request guarantees of product life and performance, as well.
- The contractor's guarantee of his liability for personal injury and property damage on the job.
- A waiver of mechanics' lien rights. This states that subcontractors cannot try to collect from you if the contractor defaults on payments to them.

Retain the Right to Refuse

When drawing up a contract for outside help, ask for a right-of-refusal clause. This guarantees your right to reject a subcontractor whose qualifications don't meet your standards.

Architects for Less

If you'll be hiring an architect to help you design a house or addition, try some of these ideas (architects will perform most of these services for an hourly fee):

- Do all the work yourself and pay to have the architect critique your work at various stages. Or contract with the architect to help you work through the initial conceptual explorations, and then take it from there.
- Work through a design program, and ask the architect to prepare a conceptual sketch. You can prepare construction drawings from that sketch.
- Use an architectural drafting service to draw up the construction documents from the design drawings.
- Contact a nearby college or university with an architectural program and find the best student there. Contract with him or her to do the design work.

Employing Electricians

Of all the jobs you do on your home, electrical work is the one most likely to require a professional. Many people are wary of working with electricity—and rightfully so. You can be killed by less electricity than it takes to light a 10-watt light bulb. By the same token, amateur electrical work can be dangerous in another way: Fires can result if wiring is done poorly or incorrectly. So be sure to hire a professional. Follow these suggestions:

- Hire someone affiliated with the International Brotherhood of Electrical Workers (IBEW). This trade union has one of the longest apprenticeships in any of the trades.
- Hire a licensed electrician if licenses are required in your area. Try to find out if licensing requirements include real proof of expertise or if they are granted to almost anyone paying a fee.
- Make sure that the person you hire follows all electrical codes. Contracts should stipulate that all materials are listed with Underwriter's Laboratories, the Chicago-based testing lab that sets product standards in the electrical industry.

In Search of a Plumber

You may not have a choice about whether or not you should hire a professional plumber. Some state and local ordinances require a licensed professional to complete such work. Be sure to check the laws in your area.

Do you want to be sure that the plumber you've hired is the crème de la crème? Contact the National Association of Plumbing, Heating, and Cooling Contractors, 180 South Washington Street, Falls Church, VA 22046.

Or you can contact one of the more than 400 locals affiliated with this organization. A NAPHCC member is a Master Plumber who has completed a minimum of four years as a licensed indentured plumber and an additional five as a journeyman plumber. He or she must pass a stringent written examination, as well. Even if you don't hire a Master Plumber, you can find out whether your plumber-to-be participates in a recognized training and apprenticeship program by contacting the Department of Labor, Bureau of Apprenticeships and Training, 601 D Street NW, Suite 5000, Washington, DC 20213.

Is It up to Code?

When hiring electricians or plumbers, insist that all work and materials conform to code. You can obtain copies of the National Electric Code and the National Standard Plumbing Code, respectively, by writing for a copy from:

International Association of
   Electrical Inspectors
930 Busse Highway
Park Ridge, IL 60068
(National Electric Code,
   $16.50 a copy)

National Association of
   Plumbing, Heating, and
   Cooling Contractors
180 S. Washington St.
Falls Church, VA 22046
(National Standard Plumbing
   Code, $40 a copy)

Try Personalized Cleaning

If you're in the market for a cleaning service, you have your choice of two types: companies that are individually owned businesses or licensed franchises, and individuals operating independently. Companies offer the advantages of insured and bonded workers, some guarantees on their work, and their own cleaning supplies and equipment. The individual cleaning person, on the other hand, can offer more personalized service, greater scheduling flexibility, and, sometimes, lower fees because he or she doesn't have the expense of maintaining an office, advertising, and providing his or her own supplies.

Get the Most
from a Cleaning Service

To get the most for your money from a cleaning service, look for a company that offers seasonal cleaning if you don't need regular weekly or biweekly cleaning. Perhaps you need occasional help with big jobs, such as washing windows or cleaning carpets. There are companies that offer these services, and you can pay for them seasonally.

Also, look for a company that allows some flexibility in what work is done in each cleaning session. You may be getting more for your money if you can dictate what jobs you need done each time the cleaning service comes to your home. Be wary of the company that has a set routine and then charges separate fees for additional jobs. It can run into quite a bit of money if the basic package doesn't include the chores you need.

Free Housecleaning

Before you go to the expense of hiring outside help to clean your house, explore the possibility of trading household chores with a friend or relative. Maybe a relative will dust and vacuum your house in exchange for your doing their grocery shopping. Or perhaps you have a friend who honestly likes cleaning windows, but wouldn't be caught dead ironing a shirt. By making a few trade-offs, you may be able to make your house cleaner without spending any money.

Lower Your Property Taxes

You Can Appeal

You *can* fight city hall when it comes to your property taxes. According to the International Association of Assessing Officers, more than half of all homeowners who appeal their assessments get them reduced.

If you think you're being unfairly assessed, start by doing

some research, as outlined in the tips below. When you're done, you can file a formal appeal. Most towns have a specific process you should follow. If you can substantiate your claim that you've received an unfair assessment, you can win a reduction in your taxes.

Check the Math

Check the mathematics used to calculate your home's assessed value. (Assessed value is the basis for calculating all property taxes.) One of two methods is used. Using the full-value method, the tax rate is applied to 100 percent of the home's assessed value. For example, if your home is assessed at $50,000 with a tax rate of $2.50 per $100 of assessed value, you would pay $1,250 in taxes. Using the fractional-value method, the tax rate is applied to a specific percentage of assessed value. A home assessed at $50,000, with a local tax ratio of 65 percent of the assessment and a rate of $2.50 per $100, would have an $812.50 tax bill.

Set the Record Straight

Check the assessment record for your property. (You may be able to request a copy through the mail, or you may have to go to the assessment office.) This record shows everything the taxing body believes contributes to your home's value. Verify that details such as square footage, number of rooms, and type of construction are correct. Make sure that all information is up to date and correct. If, for example, the record shows that your house is twice its actual size, you'll be paying taxes on a bigger home until you set the record straight.

Compare and Save

Compare your assessment to your neighbor's. You may win an appeal if you have a higher assessment for no apparent reason. You can save the money you'd spend on a professional appraiser by doing some research yourself. Find three houses in your immediate neighborhood exactly like yours and ask the owners for their assessments. If they won't tell you, visit the assessment office, where it's a matter of public record. If you have recently added a room or made some other improvements that makes your home different from other comparably priced houses in the neighborhood, ask a real estate agent or appraiser to give you an adjustment factor to calculate the difference in market value.

Home, Safe Home

All Locked Up

When people think of burglar-proofing their home, they often think of fancy security and alarm systems. But there are more inexpensive ways to keep intruders out. Start by purchasing locks—

While the Cat's Away:
9 Free Ways to Protect Your Home

When you're away from home, the best protection against thieves is a house-sitter, and exchanging the service with a friend is the most inexpensive way to get that protection. If you can't get a sitter, follow these precautions:

- Alert local police and a trusted neighbor and ask them to keep an eye on things.
- Never publicize vacation plans.
- Cancel all deliveries, such as mail, newspapers, and so on.
- Have someone cut your grass. In fall, have someone rake leaves, and in winter, have someone shovel the snow.
- Put valuables such as jewelry in a safe deposit box.
- Don't leave lights on continuously. Use timers instead, setting them to turn lights on and off as you would normally use them. Vary times from one day to the next, if you can, and don't forget to use one on the radio or television.
- Turn down the bell on your telephone so a burglar can't hear it ringing unanswered.
- Close and lock the door on an empty garage.
- Store empty trash cans out of sight in a basement or garage.

don't try to be thrifty here. Most home security experts agree that the one place you can't cut corners is in buying locks. Inexpensive key-in-knob locks can be opened with a credit card or a screwdriver. Night latches and chain locks mounted on the surface of the door aren't much help either: They can easily be broken. Invest in good deadbolt locks, which come in several varieties, and you'll save in the long run because you won't lose valuables. Deadbolts should be one inch thick and have a one-inch throw.

On the Outside Looking In

If you're concerned about break-ins, think like a burglar when you assess the outside of your home. Landscaping may make your home look more attractive, but it can also help a thief gain entry. Large trees near the house could help a burglar climb in a second-floor window. Prune lower limbs to make this impossible. While you're at it, trim trees and bushes near doors and windows so that they won't provide a hiding place while a thief tries to break in. That rose trellis may be lovely to look at, but make sure it's placed so it can't be used as a ladder to windows.

Do you have a high wooden fence around your property? What you gain in privacy you may lose in a break-in: Criminals can work unobserved behind it. Make sure all porches, yards, and entrances are well lit. Although spotlights work well, a few less-expensive lights, strategically placed, can also be effective. And if you've been working outside, always be sure to put ladders and tools away. If you don't, a thief may use them against you to get into your home.

Close the Door on Break-Ins

Good crime prevention starts at your front door. Before you start investing in expensive locks, make sure the door itself is a good one. If it's a hollow-core door, it can be easily broken down. Entry doors should be metal or have a solid wood core at least $1\frac{3}{4}$ inches thick.

Reinforce Door Glass

Decorative windows or glass panels on doors can be easily broken. Then all a thief has to do is reach in and unlock the door. Instead of going to the expense of replacing a door, install a break-resistant plastic panel or a decorative grille over the glass. These should be attached with nonremovable screws.

If the Door Fits

A door should fit its frame tightly, with no more than a $\frac{1}{8}$-inch clearance between it and the frame. If the gap is too big, the door should be replaced. Since this can be an expensive proposition, a cheaper—and equally effective—alternative is to bolt a sturdy metal strip to the door edge. It boosts your security and adds energy savings, too. The strips are available at hardware stores.

Psst . . . Save a Bundle!

Free Protection

One of the best ways to prevent burglaries doesn't cost anything except a little time. Organize a Neighborhood Watch or Block Watch program to encourage people to keep a watchful eye on the houses nearest them. The idea is to get people to call police the minute they notice anything suspicious. Although a watch program can't replace good locks and other home security measures, it's added insurance against break-ins.

To get a Neighborhood Watch program going in your area, invite everyone to an organizational meeting. Ask the police to send an officer or sheriff to offer tips on home security, self-protection, and what kinds of behavior to report. Neighbors who are home during the day can watch the homes of others who are at work. There should also be a formal procedure for notifying participants when someone is going away on vacation or business so they can keep a closer eye on that home. And when any burglary or other crime occurs, a phone network among neighbors can put everyone on the alert.

Slip Sliding Away

You could find your prized possessions slipping through your fingers when a burglar breaks in through a sliding glass door. This popular home feature is easy to open. You can buy a special lock in addition to the one already on the door. An inexpensive alternative is to place a wooden dowel or broomstick in the track of the closed door. This blocks the door if a thief tries to slide it open after a lock is jimmied.

A sliding glass door can also be lifted off its tracks. Three inexpensive remedies can prevent it:

■ Adjust rollers so the door can't be pushed up and lifted off the track.

Keep Windows Secure

A good, inexpensive way to secure double-hung windows is to drill an angled hole through the frame of the lower window and partially into the frame of the upper window. Make a second set of holes with windows partly open so you can have ventilation. Secure with an eyebolt or nail (an eyebolt is best because it resists jimmying).

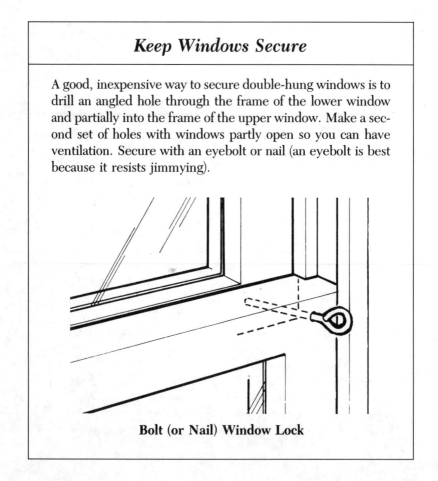

Bolt (or Nail) Window Lock

- Insert screws along the upper track. Screw them in far enough to allow the door to slide, but don't make them flush with the track. Leave enough protruding to keep the door from being lifted off its tracks.
- Drill a hole and insert a nail through the inside frame and partway through the top of the metal door frame. The nail can be removed when you want to open the door, but a burglar can't reach it.

Do-It-Yourself Tests: Radon

Beware of Swindlers

You won't know if your home has radon until you have it tested, and you don't have to spend a lot of money doing so. Beware of hucksters who try to scare you into purchasing expensive devices. Some may be worthless. Others may be the inexpensive home tests described below sold at a premium price. The legitimate ones that require a professional to administer start at $2,500 and soar to $10,000. With an at-home test that costs $50 or less, you can determine whether radon is contaminating your home.

Activated Charcoal Monitors

This do-it-yourself radon test consists of small metal cans that cost $10 to $25. You leave the cans in place for three to seven days, then return them to the manufacturer for evaluation. The charcoal detector works by absorbing gas from the surrounding air. The major disadvantage to this type of test is that it doesn't give a good picture of radiation levels over longer periods.

Alpha-Track Detectors

These radon-detecting devices, which aren't much bigger than a twist-off bottle cap, cost $20 to $50 and can be left in place from one month to a year. Unlike the charcoal monitors, they can track radon levels over a longer period. Like the charcoal device, they, too, are sent back to the manufacturer for analysis. Alpha particles emitted by decaying radon gas leave tracks on the plastic inside the cup. The more tracks, the higher the radon level. It is important to buy alpha-track detectors only from companies endorsed by the Environmental Protection Agency (EPA) and to use more than one detector in the house.

A reading of 4 picocuries or higher should be confirmed by a follow-up test by a professional firm using more sophisticated equipment.

Where to Find Radon Tests

For a list of companies offering EPA-approved home testing kits, write to the EPA Office of Radiation Programs, 401 M Street SW, Washington, DC 20460.

You can also contact your state EPA office. Many are making kits available at little or no cost. Your state EPA office is also a good source for lists of reputable professionals who do the more accurate follow-up tests.

Do-It-Yourself Tests: Water

What's in Your Water?

When it comes to drinking water, it's what you don't see that can hurt you. Although water that smells or tastes foul is a sure sign that something's not right, contamination is often undetectable to the naked eye, nose, and mouth. You need to have it tested to make sure it's safe. If you are hooked into a municipal water supply, you can request test results. If you still suspect that your water is contaminated, or if you have well water, you'll have to pay to have your water tested by a laboratory specializing in such procedures (there are really no do-it-yourself tests for water).

Contact your state department of environmental protection for a list of certified labs that can perform the service. Many labs will allow you to mail in water samples for testing. Their fees include prepaid overnight delivery, prepaid postal service, or UPS.

The fees for labs average $30 for basic potability tests; $40 to $55 for a basic test for about a half-dozen toxic or cancer-causing chemicals; $70 to $110 for more comprehensive tests for as many as two dozen chemicals; and $175 to $200 for "super tests" for just about all toxic chemicals, bacteria, and solvents.

Know What You're Paying For

Before you settle on a laboratory to test your water, make sure you get a complete breakdown of what its fee covers. One company, for example, may charge $10 more, but may test for another half-dozen chemicals. You may want the most comprehensive test you can find, or you may not need a super test, so it pays to understand your needs and then shop around.

Free Advice

Some water-testing labs offer suggestions for clearing up water problems. Be sure to ask about this before having any tests done—and before you rush out and spend money on a filtering or other cleanup device.

Home Remedy

If your water has a serious pollution problem, it may take a lawsuit or the action of a governmental agency to clear it up. But a water-filtering system can help keep things clean if your supply is relatively pure. When you are shopping for one of these devices, choose an under-the-sink type. Tests have shown that devices attached to the faucet don't work as well.

The under-the-sink filtering devices can screen out a variety of harmful substances, including excess chlorine, fluorides, organic halides, sodium, nitrates, and trihalomethanes. Don't expect them to remedy major problems, however. Most use some kind of carbon filter. In a product test conducted by Rodale's Practical Homeowner Institute, the most effective type was found to be a carbon-block filter. Granulated carbon filters were found to be less effective.

6

SAVE ENERGY, SAVE MONEY

If you're an average American homeowner, you'll spend more than $1,000 this year to heat your water, operate your appliances, and run heating and cooling equipment. The energy-saving measures in this chapter can help you cut that sum in half by focusing your time and money on those areas that provide the quickest return.

Since electric appliances will likely account for an increasing proportion of your total energy budget in the years ahead, the moment of purchase represents a golden investment opportunity; in other words, your goal should be to purchase the most energy-efficient appliances you can afford. To complement the information in this chapter, we recommend that shoppers obtain a copy of "The Most Energy-Efficient Appliances," a booklet ranking the most efficient appliances, air conditioners, and furnaces on the market. To obtain your copy, send $2 to the American Council for an Energy-Efficient Economy, 1001 Connecticut Avenue NW, Suite 535, Washington, DC 20036.

Save Energy with the Right Appliances

Big, Bright, Black and Yellow Labels

Since 1980, the United States government has required manufacturers of refrigerators, freezers, clothes washers, water heaters, dishwashers, room air conditioners, and furnaces to affix Energy Guide labels to their products. These big, bright, black and yellow labels are a real boon to shoppers. They'll tell you the estimated annual cost of operating the appliance in question and show you how it stacks up against the most- and least-efficient models in the same class. Of course, the most efficient model isn't always the best buy. That's why it's important to understand life-cycle costs. (See "Finding the *Real* Cost of Appliances" on page 145.)

With the passage of the National Appliance Energy Conser-

How Much Can You Save with Energy-Efficient Appliances?

	ANNUAL OPERATING COST ($)	
APPLIANCE	AVERAGE EXISTING APPLIANCE	NEW ENERGY-EFFICIENT APPLIANCE
Air conditioner (central)	300	150
Air conditioner (one room)	60	40
Clothes dryer (electric)	70	55
Clothes dryer (gas)	30	25
Clothes washer	90	45
Dishwasher	70	45
Freezer (frost-free)	135	75
Freezer (manual defrost)	75	40
Lights (household total)	75	25–50
Portable space heater	5–65	—
Refrigerator (manual defrost)	45	30
Refrigerator/freezer (frost-free	120	70
Range (electric)	60	50
Range (gas)	45	35
Television (color)	25	10
Water heater (electric)	300	150
Water heater (gas)	160	130

SOURCE: American Council for an Energy-Efficient Economy.
NOTE: Table assumes an electricity price of 7.5 cents per kilowatt hour and a gas price of 60 cents a therm. Operating costs for clothes washers and dishwashers include the cost of water heating.

vation Act of 1986, Energy Guide labels have become more important than ever. As a result of that law, a new generation of high-efficiency appliances will be entering the market between now and 1992. These new models will be 10 to 32 percent more efficient than their predecessors and will generate net energy savings worth $28 billion—nearly $300 per American household—through the year 2000. One of the best ways to keep track of these money-saving newcomers is to pay strict attention to Energy Guide labels when you go shopping.

Finding the *Real* Cost
of Appliances

One of the truest measures of appliance value is found by comparing life-cycle costs, which reflect both the purchase price *and* the lifetime operating cost of the units being compared. You can calculate life-cycle costs yourself by following these simple steps:

1. Determine the annual energy cost for the models you're considering. To do this, first find out how much you're paying for electricity (in cents per kilowatt hour) or gas (in cents per therm). The information is included on your bill or is available from your utility. Then check the yellow energy labels attached to appliance models on display. (The appliance dealer can give you ratings for models not on display.) Use this figure for A in the equation below.

2. Use the table "Average Lifetime and Discount Factor" to find the average lifetime of the appliance. Use this figure for B in the equation below.

3. Use the table below to find the discount factor. Use this figure for C in the equation below.

APPLIANCE	AVERAGE LIFETIME (YEARS)	DISCOUNT FACTOR
Clothes washers	18	0.78
Dishwashers	12	0.84
Refrigerators and freezers	20	0.76
Room air conditioners	15	0.81
Water heater (gas or electric)	13	0.83

SOURCE: American Council for an Energy-Efficient Economy.

NOTE: The discount factor is based on a 5% discount rate and a 2% annual increase in the price of energy above inflation. This method isn't valid for central air conditioners and furnaces.

4. Use the purchase price of the model in place of D in the equation below.

5. Do the required arithmetic. The model with the lowest lifetime cost is the most cost-effective choice over the long term.

$$[A \times B \times C] + D = \text{Life-cycle cost}$$

The example below compares two refrigerators—one selling for $800 with a yearly energy cost of $95, the other selling for $725 with a yearly energy cost of $115.

[95 × 20 × 0.76] + 800 = $2,244 Life-cycle cost

[115 × 20 × 0.76] + 725 = $2,473 Lifetime cost

The results show that over the 20-year life of the units, the more energy-efficient model would save the owner $229, although it costs $75 more to purchase.

Refrigerators and Freezers: Start Small

According to the Association of Home Appliance Manufacturers, today's refrigerators are more than 75 percent more energy efficient than those sold in 1972. But that doesn't mean you can't save even more. Because it's in use day and night, operating costs can add up to almost three times a refrigerator's cost over its typical 15-year lifespan.

To start saving, buy the smallest, simplest model that fits your needs. As a rule of thumb, a family of two needs 8 to 10 cubic feet of fresh-food space and 3 cubic feet of freezer space; add another cubic foot to both for each extra person. Don't forget to look ahead: Since a good refrigerator will last more than a decade, plan for your future family needs when sizing one.

Buying a Better Box

Buying a new energy-efficient refrigerator/freezer can be a super investment, yielding double-digit, tax-free rates of return. A power-stingy fridge will save you money on your electric bills year after year, sooner or later paying for itself in saved energy.

This is not to say that purchasing the most efficient refrigerator/freezer on the market is necessarily your smartest move—the price of the unit and various other factors need to be considered. To make a truly educated purchase, take the time to understand the concept of life-cycle cost. (See "Finding the *Real* Cost of Appliances" earlier in this chapter.) It's a nifty tool for appraising real value, not just for refrigerators, but for many other household purchases as well. Also, pay attention to the energy labels affixed to refrigerators and other appliances. They're a valuable source of objective, comparative information. When you're ready to buy, here are a few tips to help you choose the right box:

- It's much less expensive to buy and operate one big refrigerator than two small ones.
- The "energy saver" option is worth every penny.
- Manual defrost models typically use about half as much electricity as automatic defrost models, but if you don't keep up with the defrosting, the refrigerator's efficiency will drop.
- Side-by-side refrigerator/freezers typically use about 35 percent more energy than models with the freezer on top.
- In-the-door water and ice dispensers use more energy.

Should You Buy a Separate Freezer?

Think twice about buying a separate home freezer. It can be a convenience, but, unless you have a large family, it takes a lot of bulk buying, quantity cooking, and garden surplus to save you money. If a freezer makes economic sense for you, though, a chest style costs less to run than an upright because cold air doesn't "fall out" when it's opened.

In Search of the Frugal Dryer

In most instances, gas dryers cost less to operate than electric ones. Depending on the efficiency of the machines being compared and local energy prices, a gas dryer will typically cost one-half to one-third the amount it takes to run an electric model. The message is clear: Go with gas if you can, but make sure to get a model with electric ignition.

A moisture sensor control (to shut the machine off automatically when the clothes are dry) and a cool-down cycle (which uses cool air to complete the drying cycle) are nifty, money-saving features that will pay for themselves in short order.

It's unfortunate that new clothes dryers don't have Energy Guide labels to help shoppers compare. Nonetheless, you can make a smart choice by shopping around and asking some savvy questions about energy.

Smart Appliance Buying

Don't Buy More than You Need

Appliance dealers often stock loss leaders: no-frills, dependable items that offer real savings to buyers because they are sold at or near manufacturer's cost. Dealers advertise these bargains to bring you into the store, hoping that once you're there they can talk you into another—more expensive—model. They'll try to find fault with the no-frills model's styling or performance and/or they'll hype the more expensive model's high-tech features. This game of "selling up" is behind some displays that place low- and high-end items side by side. Wise shoppers will see past these tricks and buy the appliance whose features really suit their needs.

Seasonal Buys

If you're willing to shop around, you'll find the appliance you want on sale somewhere at any time of year. However, department stores still hold appliance clearance sales after Easter, after July 4, and after Christmas, and many continue to follow the traditional merchandise sale periods noted in the table "Calendar of Appliance Sales."

Take a Tip from the Pros

Take advantage of free (or nominal-cost) educational materials before you begin shopping for appliances. Maytag is just one manufacturer that provides free brochures to help consumers buy appliances wisely. These brochures contain information on dependability, energy efficiency, performance, and convenience. Their guidelines are applicable to any brand. To obtain these how-to-buy brochures on washers, dryers, dishwashers, electric ranges, gas ranges, and microwave ovens, write to the Consumer Education Department, The Maytag Company, One Dependability Square, Newton, IA 50208.

Calendar of Appliance Sales

JANUARY	JUNE
Freezers Ranges Refrigerators	Freezers Refrigerators
	AUGUST
FEBRUARY	Air conditioners
Air conditioners Ranges	SEPTEMBER
	Air conditioners
MARCH	NOVEMBER
Air conditioners Ranges	Ranges

Get the Scoop
on Gas and Electric Appliances

The American Gas Association's series "The Right Choice" explains the sometimes perplexing options found on the latest models of gas ranges, dryers, heating systems, and water heaters. For these and a guide to energy-efficient furnaces and appliances, write to the Consumer Information Committee, American Gas Association, 1515 Wilson Boulevard, Arlington, VA 22209.

Your local utility company can supply information on saving energy with your current electrical appliances or selecting the best of what's new on the market. Call or write and ask for the Energy Advisor program.

Compare Brands
the Easy Way

Consumers Union publishes *Consumer Reports* magazine and offers "Feature Finder" printouts that compare major appliances. The first printout costs $8, with reports on additional appliances costing $6 each. If you consider that you will spend several hundreds of dollars for an appliance, the few dollars you spend for these printouts to help make the best decision is money well spent. Write to Feature Finders, Box 17003, Hauppauge, NY 17003.

The Association of Home Appliance Manufacturers publishes three consumer selection guides—for room air conditioners, refrigerators and freezers, and humidifiers and dehumidifiers. Each is $1.50, postpaid. Write to the Association of Home Appliance Manufacturers, 20 North Wacker Drive, Chicago, IL 60606.

Check Out the Discounts

Appliance and electronics discount stores, catalog showrooms, and warehouse outlets have virtually eliminated the need to pay list price for these appliances. You can find some honest deals in these types of stores, but service often suffers, and the warning of "buyer beware" still holds. For example, check that the price tag reflects your total charges—including delivery and installation. Many times, these are add-on costs. Look at "sale" prices with a wary eye. Tags can compare the store's price with "manufacturer's list," "reference," or "suggested retail" prices, which may exist only on tags to make retailers look like good guys. (With the discounts and competition that abound, you'd be hard pressed to actually find a store selling these items at list or retail price, but you can use these prices for rough comparisons.) See what the identical appliance actually sells for elsewhere to determine if you're really getting a bargain.

Read the Warranty

When an appliance breaks down, it can be an inconvenience, or it can be a disaster. And the price of appliance repairs can be astronomical (starting with the fee that's charged just for sending a serviceperson to your house). Before you buy, read the warranty. If it's "limited" instead of "full," be sure you understand what the limitations are. You may want to check out a similar appliance that has a full warranty. Also find out where you need to go for service under the warranty. A local repair shop or the dealer from whom you bought the appliance is far preferable to a factory service center miles away.

Before you call for service, whether your appliance is under warranty or not, check the owner's manual. You may be able to save the cost of a repair—or at least pin down the problem—before you call for service.

Are Service Contracts Worth the Cost?

Once you've spent hundreds of dollars for an appliance, it makes sense to pay $60 more to cover it after the manufacturer's warranty runs out—at least, that's the salesperson's line. Do you fall for it?

Think twice about appliance service contracts (also called extended warranties). Like an insurance policy, your investment pays off only when the worst happens. Most appliances come with a one-year manufacturer's warranty—five years for big parts like motors—and you should have few problems during that time. If something does break, you can often fix it yourself with the manual and the manufacturer's toll-free help line.

A service contract is worth buying if you get a "lemon," if your family wears appliances out, or if repairs are expensive where you live. But premiums favor the seller. Why spend $60 for two or three years' worth of peace of mind when most refrigerators, for example, cost just $50 to fix during their 15-year lifespan? If you're sure yours will die the day *after* its warranty expires, bank that $50 instead of purchasing a service contract. If you need it, it's there; if you don't, it's earned you interest.

Understanding a Service Contract

If you're still interested in purchasing a service contract after reading the preceding tip, first read the actual contract, not just a brochure about it. Then ask these questions:

- What does the contract cover and what does it exclude? Are there extra costs or deductibles?
- Is there at-home service or must I bring the appliance in? Will I get a loaner while my appliance is being repaired?
- What regular maintenance must I perform to validate the contract?
- Can I transfer the contract if I sell the appliance?

If the contract is with the dealer and not the manufacturer, make sure the dealer will be around throughout the contract period. If the dealer goes out of business, your contract probably won't be honored.

Don't give in to a high-pressure salesperson. Be aware that if he or she has a quota to meet, a salesperson may sell the contract for less than the original price. Some stores even give you some time after the sale to decide whether or not you want to purchase the service contract.

Appliance Options

Store-Brand Clones

Major department and catalog stores sell lines of appliances under their own house name or private label, but they rarely actually make these products. Instead, they contract with national-brand manufacturers. For example, Montgomery Ward carries ranges made for them by Tappan; Sears' Kenmore line includes products from Whirlpool. A sharp-eyed shopper can often spot the similarities in styling and controls. These store-brand appliances are often priced lower than the name-brand versions, but don't assume this without first checking seasonal sales and warehouse or discount outlets. Also be sure to compare the name brand and store brand warranties and local service facilities.

Last Year's Models

Consider buying one of last year's models on special sale when new appliances are introduced. In many cases, the latest improvements in styling and gadgetry make an appliance more appealing, but not more efficient or practical. If a particular appliance line is being discontinued, be sure the guarantee or warranty will still apply and that you'll still be able to get parts.

Used/Rebuilt/Reconditioned Appliances

Buying a used, rebuilt, or reconditioned appliance is a bit of a gamble, but there are ways to lower your risks of getting a lemon.

Buying from a private party (check your newspaper's classified ad section) can be a good source. People sometimes sell appliances that are in good condition when they move because it's smarter to sell them than to pay to transport them. It's easy enough to spray paint these appliances if you don't like the original enamel (use heat-resistant paint on ranges).

When buying appliances secondhand from a reputable dealer, be sure you get a warranty in writing. Used-appliance terms can be confusing: "Reconditioned" means the appliance has been cleaned, adjusted, or had minor repairs, but not rebuilt. "Reconstructed" or "rebuilt" appliances have been taken apart, repaired (with new parts), put back together, and refinished. Such an appliance should work almost like new and come with a comparable warranty. In one way, these are better than new because hidden defects have already been found and fixed. As with new appliances, compare prices, warranties, and dealer service facilities. If you're in doubt, check with past customers and the Better Business Bureau.

Cut Your Electric Bills

Shop for Bargain Power

Taking advantage of time-of-day electric rates can save you up to $500 a year on your electric bills. This is accomplished by shifting some of your power consumption to off-peak periods when your local utility has an abundant supply of electricity offered at relatively low prices. Not all utilities offer these innovative new rate schedules. But a recent study by the Electric Power Research Institute found that 74 out of the 158 electric utilities surveyed now offer some type of time-of-day program for residential customers. Some utilities will even help pay for new meters, thermostats, and appliance timers that enable you to automatically shift your usage into off-peak periods.

Of course you don't need a lot of fancy new hardware to get started. Just being aware of when that bargain power is available and rescheduling certain household chores can save you a pretty penny. The differential, or spread, between on-peak and off-peak prices can be as much as 14 cents a kilowatt-hour, so it really pays to educate yourself and take advantage if you can.

Off-Peak Savings

You can install thermostats and appliance timers that give you real flexibility, with built-in energy savings. For example, shifting part of your water heating load to off-peak hours can deliver hefty savings, and by using a clock thermostat, air-conditioning can be cycled off and on to accommodate daily schedules, saving energy in the process. Swimming pool pumps and dishwashers can be timed to work at night when power is cheapest. The table "Saving with Off-Peak Rates" shows the potential savings available through a time-of-day rate schedule currently offered by a Northern utility. Keep in mind that time-of-day rate programs vary greatly from one utility to the next. Some companies offer very attractive rates that are worthwhile for almost any homeowner. Other programs are too restrictive or don't offer enough savings to be of interest. Investigate your local options. You might end up with an electrifying bargain.

Freezer Facts

The money-saving tips listed for refrigerators (see "Refrigerators: 9 Cool Tips to Cut Electric Bills" on page 156) also apply to the operation of stand-alone freezers. When buying new, bear in mind that chest freezers tend to be more efficient than upright models, and that manual defrost models use less power than units with automatic defrost.

Don't Let Your Dishwasher Do the Drying

"Air power" and/or "overnight dry" settings can cut your dishwashing costs 10 percent by automatically turning the machine off after the rinse cycle. If you don't have an automatic air-dry feature, turn the machine off after the final rinse and prop open the door.

Saving with Off-Peak Rates

APPLIANCE OR USE	POTENTIAL SAVINGS WITH OFF-PEAK RATES*
Electric water heating	Substantial savings†
Clothes washer	Substantial savings†
Electric baseboard heat	Cut heating bills by 20%
Heat pump	Cut heating and cooling bills by 20%‡
Central air conditioner	Save $17 a month
Dehumidifier	Save $15 a month§
Swimming pool filters	Save $14 a month§
Water bed heater	Save $8 a month‖
Clothes dryer	Save $6 a month
Dishwasher	Save $2 to $3 a month
Baking and cooking	Impractical
Hair dryer	Impractical

*Estimated for an average family based on a price differential of 7.7 cents per kilowatt-hour between peak and off-peak rates.
†Varies with household use.
‡Would require new microprocessor setback thermostat.
§Shifting entire load to off-peak.
‖ With new insulating liner.

Operate Your Dishwasher Wisely

You can cut the electric consumption of your dishwasher just by following some easy and sensible tips. First, don't run your dishwasher until you have a full load. Your dishwasher uses three to seven gallons of hot water each time you use it, so choose the shortest cycle that will clean your dishes and be sure the machine is full. If you have a few heavily soiled dishes, scrub them before you put them in the dishwasher to avoid using the rinse/hold cycle. Run the machine at night in hot weather. This reduces your air-conditioning load and takes advantage of off-peak electric rates. (See "Shop for Bargain Power" on page 153.) If your dishwasher is next to the refrigerator, put a layer of insulation between them.

Refrigerators:
9 Cool Tips to Cut Electric Bills

Unlike most appliances, refrigerators run 24 hours a day, 365 days a year. With that in mind, it's easy to see why they're one of the biggest energy guzzlers in the home. Typical households spend $50 to $180 a year running their refrigerators, depending on the size and efficiency of the unit and the local price of electricity. But if you've got a real Edsel on your hands and live in a utility district where electricity is pricey, you may be paying as much as $300 a year!

Buying an efficient new refrigerator to replace a tired old clunker can be one of the shrewdest investments a homeowner can make. But if your current unit is relatively efficient and has a few more good years on it, you can still save yourself some bucks by being a smart operator. Here's how:

■ Set your refrigerator at 38° to 40°F and the freezer at 0° to 5°F. Settings just 10 degrees lower can raise your operating costs a whopping 25 percent!

■ Clean the coils with a vacuum or brush two or three times a year. (They're behind or underneath the unit.)

■ Clean dried food off the door seals to make sure they work properly. Cracked gaskets need to be replaced.

■ Both refrigerators and freezers work better when they're full. If you don't store enough food packages to keep the freezer full, use bags of ice.

■ If your refrigerator is located next to your stove or other heat-producing appliances, and it's not feasible to relocate them, insulate the space in between. Sunlight also has an effect. Window treatments that shield the refrigerator from direct sun will help it work more efficiently.

■ If your refrigerator has an "energy saver" mode, use it whenever possible (see unit instructions for details).

■ Manual defrost models should be defrosted regularly. Allowing ice to build up over $\frac{1}{4}$ inch hurts their efficiency.

■ Avoid leaving the refrigerator door open for long periods of time.

■ To keep humidity under control, liquids stored in the refrigerator should always be covered.

Psst . . . Save a Bundle!

Bullish on Booster Heaters

Would you like to invest in something that can give you an 1,100 percent payback over the next 12 years? No, there's nothing illegal about it. All you have to do is get a booster heater on that new dishwasher you're buying. It'll cost you about $30 extra—that's the up-front investment. But over the 12-year life of the dishwasher you'll save about $360 on water heating bills. Without the booster, you'd have to keep your water heater set at 140°F to satisfy the dishwasher's specifications. With the built-in booster, you can reduce your tank setting to 110° to 120°F, saving yourself a bundle in standby losses.

How to Pool Big Savings

If you own a swimming pool, you can pocket big savings by cutting the number of hours you use your filter pump. Suppose you have a one-horsepower motor and are able to reduce your pumping time from eight hours to four hours a day (without sacrificing water quality). Your annual savings, assuming electricity costs $.07 a kilowatt-hour, would be $148.19 a year. With a two-horsepower motor and electricity at $.09 a kilowatt-hour, you'd bank $302.22! Any way you look at it, that's a lot of suntan lotion. Some utilities will even install the "trippers," or timers, on your pool system for free. You can also save money by using a pool cover (to retain heat) and by maintaining a clean filter (to reduce the load on the pump). If you're going to buy a new motor, opt for high efficiency.

Avoid Water Bed Nightmares

You may love the luxurious, undulating feel of a water bed. But did you know that it costs $100 to $200 a year to keep it heated? Water beds are like huge, uninsulated water heaters, drawing a continuous stream of electricity. They are never going to be cheap to operate compared to conventional bedding.

But if you have a water bed, there are some tips you can follow to help you sleep easier knowing that you are keeping electricity costs down. Set the water bed heater thermostat as low as comfort allows. Tests show that every degree above 85°F uses an additional 10 to 15 kilowatt-hours a month. Insulate under the mattress and along the sides with one inch of rigid insulation. Make your bed when you get up. This helps insulate it. Keep heavy covers on the bed, even in summer. Find out if it's worthwhile to use a timer to shift heating to off-peak hours. (See "Shop for Bargain Power" on page 153.)

Psst . . . Save a Bundle!

Get a Handle on Laundry Costs

You may be able to save $200 a year just by altering the way you use your washing machine. Conserving hot water is the key, since up to 90 percent of the cost of washing clothes is attributable to water heating expense. By using the water level and water temperature controls on your machine, you can score big savings day in and day out. Be sure to match the water level to the size of the load. Remember that the temperature of the rinse cycle *does not* affect cleaning, so always use a cold water rinse. As the table on the opposite page illustrates, simply changing your rinse cycle from warm to cold can save about $70 a year. Hot-water washes should be reserved for heavily soiled clothes that have been presoaked to ensure good results. Some brands of detergent are specially formulated for cold-wash, cold-rinse performance.

It's More Than Dirty Laundry

WASHING MODE	COST PER LOAD (¢)	ANNUAL OPERATING COST ($)
Hot wash/Warm rinse	58	211.70
Hot wash/Cold rinse	40	146.00
Warm wash/Warm rinse	40	146.00
Warm wash/Cold rinse	21	76.65
Cold wash/Cold rinse	3	10.95

NOTE: Estimates are based on electric water heating at 7.63 cents per kilowatt-hour and 365 loads a year. Typical costs and savings would be substantially less with gas water heating.

Washday Tips

To make the most of your washing machine's capabilities, follow these tips. Don't overload your machine, and don't use too much detergent—oversudsing makes your machine work harder. By boosting the efficiency of your water heater and pipes, you score indirect savings in the cost of running your washing machine. (See "Water Heating within Means" on page 167.) When buying a new washing machine, remember that efficiency pays over the long haul. That so-called inexpensive model may use up to three times more energy than the most efficient models on the market. Use Energy Guide labels and life-cycle costs to make a smart choice. Remember, front loaders typically use less energy than top-loading machines.

Put a Damper on Dryer Expenses

Any steps you can take to shorten the time your clothes dryer runs will save you money. The biggest saver of all, of course, is to forget the machine and dry your clothes outdoors. But solar drying isn't always possible or convenient.

A state-of-the-art dryer comes equipped with a built-in moisture sensor control, which automatically shuts the machine off when the clothes are dry, and a cool-down cycle, which tumbles the clothes in cool air during the final 10 to 15 minutes of the cycle. These features can save you bundles of money over the life of the machine. Use them! If your machine doesn't have these money-saving controls, make a mental note to buy a model with these features when it comes time to replace your current dryer.

Operate Your Dryer Wisely

You can cut the operating expense of a dryer by following these simple suggestions. Don't overload your dryer—it wastes time and energy. If you've only got a few items to dry, wait till you have enough for a full load or make use of a small indoor drying rack. Clean out the lint screen after each load. Overdrying wastes energy, sets wrinkles, shortens fabric life, and generates static electricity. If your dryer has a moisture sensor, temperature sensor, or timer that permits automatic shutoff, use it to full advantage. Separate loads by weight. Quick-drying synthetic and permanent press fabrics take less drying time than heavy fabrics. Dry one load right after the other to take advantage of residual heat. Check the flappers on your exhaust vent from time to time. A clogged exhaust impedes drying and increases energy use.

Tapping Free Heat with Two "Ifs"

Perhaps you've walked outside your house on a cold winter day, seen billows of steam pouring out the dryer vent, and wondered if there wasn't some way to put all that wasted heat to use. Well, you can, with two very important "ifs."

If your home is dry inside during the winter and if you have an electric dryer (never do this with a gas dryer!), you can detach the vent pipe from the outside vent, cover it with a piece of cheesecloth or nylon stocking to serve as a lint filter, and redirect that wasted heat back into your house. Come summer, you return the vent to its normal position.

If you want a more formal device, you can buy a heat diverter attachment ($7 to $8) at your local hardware or appliance store and install it yourself. It makes winter-summer conversion a snap.

Bear in mind that there is a lot of moisture contained in that diverted heat, so you need to keep an eye out for condensation, mildew, and other problems related to excess moisture. This technique is *not* advisable in areas with humid winter climates or for homes with humid indoor air.

Psst . . . Save a Bundle!

Free Lunches? You Bet!

The word "free" has been so often misused and abused that we tend to view free offers as marketing gimmicks or outright fraud. But the fact remains, many utilities are giving away things for free. Valuable things. Things like water heater wraps, home energy audits, low-flow shower heads, portable electric heaters, and fluorescent lights. What's more, half of all the utility customers in America are eligible for cut-rate weatherization loans or rebates for purchasing energy-efficient appliances and heat pumps. Utilities aren't doing this out of the goodness of their hearts. They've discovered that it's a lot cheaper for them to conserve electricity than it is to build new power plants. Smart homeowners will embrace a similar philosophy. Call your local utility. Find out if they've got a free lunch or two waiting for you.

How Savvy Chefs Cut Electric Costs

Don't Peek!

Opening the oven door and lifting pot lids lets heat escape. Cracking the oven door just once lets 20 percent of the heat out. Use the timer and oven window instead.

If the Pot Fits

Use pots and pans with tight-fitting lids and flat bottoms that match the size of the burner.

Free Heat

Get in the habit of turning off the oven and rangetop burners a few minutes early. The residual heat will finish cooking the food for free.

Which Is Best?

Whenever possible, use the rangetop instead of the oven. Pressure cookers, Crockpots, and steamers are generally more efficient than rangetop pans or the oven and also tend to preserve the nutritional value of foods better. For heating small meals, a toaster oven takes just half as much electricity as a full-size oven.

Frozen vs. Thawed

Unless instructions indicate otherwise, thaw frozen foods before cooking in the oven. Frozen meat takes up to 20 minutes longer per pound to cook than thawed meat.

When to Preheat

Avoid preheating the oven or broiler, except for baked goods that require precise starting temperatures.

The More the Merrier

To take full advantage of the heat in an oven, try to select foods that bake at the same time and temperature. If one dish calls for 325°F, another for 350°F, and a third for 375°F, set the oven for 350°F and adjust their respective baking times to compensate.

Unclog Those Ports

If you have a gas range, keep the burners clean and unclogged. The flame should be blue and cone shaped; a yellowish flame usually indicates an adjustment is needed. You can unclog burner ports with a piece of wire or pipe cleaner. If that doesn't help, call an appliance service representative.

Clean Reflectors Pay Off

Keep reflectors under burners clean. They save you money by reflecting heat where it's needed.

Smart Use of Self-Cleaning

Use the self-cleaning cycle on your oven sparingly. Start it immediately after baking when the oven is already hot.

Foil Can Foil Heat

Never place aluminum foil on the bottom of the oven. It can block vents and impair heat circulation, reducing oven temperatures by as much as 50 degrees.

Why Gas Is Better Than Electricity

Despite all the promotion that's gone into the all-electric home concept in recent years, we think there are sound reasons for choosing a gas range. First, gas provides more sensitive control over cooking, without warmup or cooling delays. Second, natural gas has a price advantage over electricity in most markets, and that advantage seems likely to grow more pronounced in the years to come. A gas range may cost more up front than a comparable electric, but it will return that money and more in lifetime energy savings.

So consider gas when you go shopping for a range, especially models with electronic ignitions. Pilot lights add about 30 percent to the cost of cooking and heat up the kitchen.

There are two other useful, money-saving features to look for in ranges, both gas and electric. You can reduce cooking times and temperatures by buying a convection oven, which uses a small fan to circulate heat inside the oven. Self-cleaning ovens offer a double plus. They eliminate the chore of manual cleaning and—thanks to their superior insulation—also save energy.

Induction Cooktops
Aren't a Good Buy

Induction cooktops, which cook food magnetically, are making their debut in American kitchens. They use less electricity than conventional electric ranges and allow more sensitive control over cooking. Since the elements are tucked away underneath a smooth, glass-ceramic surface that stays cool during cooking, induction cooktops are a breeze to clean.

As one might expect from a system that relies on magnetism, induction cooktops work exclusively with steel and iron cookware. You can't cook with glass, copper, aluminum, and other materials. Because they cost four to five times as much as conventional electric models, induction cooktops can't be justified on their energy-saving merits alone. Magnetic cooking may be the big wave of the future, but at today's prices, not many people will be induced to buy.

Microwaves—
Quick and Cheap

The popularity of microwave ovens is easily explained: They save both time *and* money. A study by Wisconsin Power and Light found that for 85 percent of your cooking tasks, a microwave oven can cut energy costs by 50 percent or more.

Microwaves are most efficient heating small to medium-size quantities of food that are low in moisture. For example, to bake four potatoes, a microwave uses 65 percent less energy than a standard oven. However, to bring four cups of water to a boil, a microwave uses 10 percent more energy than a rangetop.

Illuminating Advice

Try Compact Fluorescents

Most homeowners know by now that a fluorescent light is a big winner compared to an incandescent bulb. Not only does it last up to 15 times longer, it also uses 75 percent less electricity. But did you know that there are new kinds of *compact* fluorescent bulbs that fit most standard lighting fixtures and that are as warm and easy on the eyes as incandescent bulbs? The availability of these power-stingy compacts and new kinds of electronic ballasts could make incandescent bulbs obsolete in the years to come.

Now, lest you get sticker shock when you go shopping for these compact fluorescents—they cost $15 to $20 each—consider these facts. To match the 10,000-hour lifespan of the fluorescent, you'd have to buy and install eight to ten ordinary bulbs. Moreover, the compact fluorescent will save you $20 to $40 on your electric bill over its lifetime. So the compacts, by virtue of their longevity and efficiency, are a sound investment.

Nevertheless, we don't recommend that you install them in every fixture in your house. In fact, do not use any fluorescent bulb in a lighting fixture equipped with a dimmer or three-way switch, as the reduced voltage is likely to damage the bulb.

Until their price comes down, the best way to use compact fluorescents is in those fixtures that you use all the time—a reading light in the living room, for example, or a much-used light in the kitchen. That way you guarantee yourself a fast payback.

Gas Lamps: Pretty Pricey

Outdoor gas lamps may be pleasing to the eye, but as energy guzzlers they have no peers. In fact, it's hard to imagine a *less* efficient approach to outdoor lighting. Keeping just eight such lamps burning year-round uses enough natural gas to heat an average-size home for an entire winter season! If you're thinking of installing a gas lamp, think again. If you already have one, turning it off will save you $40 to $50 a year on your gas bill.

Sun-Powered Landscaping Lights

Illuminating walks, driveways, and flower beds with small, ground-level electric lights is a beautiful but extravagant use of electricity. If you can't resist the idea of providing night lights for your pansies, consider using solar-electric lamps to do the job. These stand-alone units need no utility hookup. They convert sunlight to electricity during the day and store it in a small, built-in battery to run the light at night. They're somewhat more ex-

Lighting:
16 Enlightening Ways
to Cut Electric Bills

Depending on your lifestyle and how much you pay for electricity, you're probably spending $50 to $150 a year on lights. You can save up to two-thirds on your lighting bill by heeding these commonsense tips:

- Replace incandescent bulbs with money-saving fluorescents wherever you can.
- Use "energy miser" and "supersaver" incandescent bulbs. While they cost a little more than regular bulbs, they save you money over the long haul by using 5 to 13 percent less electricity.
- Install solid-state dimmers and high-low switches; they will pay for themselves over time.
- Use one large bulb rather than several small ones—it saves electricity.
- Concentrate lighting in reading and working areas.
- Use long-life incandescent bulbs only in hard-to-reach places. They're less energy efficient than ordinary bulbs.
- Use natural daylight wherever you can.
- Buy new energy-efficient night lights—they use only $\frac{1}{3}$ watt versus the old 7-watt models.
- Remove one of the bulbs from a multibulb fixture to save energy. (Leave a dead bulb in the socket for safety's sake.)
- Keep bulbs and fixtures clean and free of dust.
- Don't overlight.
- Don't waste money on light buttons. While they do extend the life of the bulb, they also cut its efficiency.
- If you're shopping for a new lamp, consider buying one with a three-way switch to give you more lighting control.
- If you plan to redecorate, remember that light-colored draperies, upholstery, rugs, and walls will reflect light and reduce artificial lighting needs.
- Use reflector bulbs in pole lamps to get better lighting.
- Need we say it? Turn out the lights when you're not using them.

pensive than conventional fixtures, but by the time you add up the cost of trenching electric cables all over your yard and installing switches, and the higher electric bills you'd be paying with conventional landscaping lights, solar-electric lamps start to look like a bargain.

Stand-alone, solar-electric lighting can also make sense for other applications—especially those that require long stretches of new electric cable. For example, a security light that's distant from your house or other existing sources of utility power might be a good candidate for solar.

Lighting
the Great Outdoors

Using incandescent flood lights to illuminate your yard or provide nighttime security is a big waste of energy. There are lots of money-saving alternatives, including mercury vapor, metal halide, and low- and high-pressure sodium bulbs. These cost more up front, but when you stop to consider how many hours an all-night security light burns over the course of a year, you can readily understand how a power-stingy bulb will save you money. It's also worthwhile to put a timer or photocell switch on these installations so they automatically turn themselves off when they're not needed.

If you tend to use your porch lights a lot, you can save money by putting in compact fluorescents. But you may need to equip the fixtures with low-temperature ballasts to ensure they work properly, since ordinary ballasts are adversely affected by cold weather.

Water Heating
within Means

Why It Pays to Save

About 30 percent of the energy spent in the typical home is used for water heating. In fact, next to space heating, water heating is usually the biggest energy gobbler. With that in mind, a prudent homeowner will find ways to cut the water heating bills without sacrificing comfort.

A Measure That Pays for Itself

Install one-way valves on your tank's hot and cold water lines. These devices, also known as heat traps, save energy by preventing hot water from rising and cold water from falling in your pipes. Priced at about $30, one-way valves will pay for themselves in less than a year.

A Drop Is a Lot

Fix leaky faucets. A one-drop-per-second leak can mean the loss of 2,400 gallons of hot water a year. That's money down the drain.

Drain the Tank and Save

Over time, sediment builds up in the bottom of your water heater and reduces its efficiency. You'll save money by opening the tap at the bottom of the tank and draining a bucketful of water a couple times a year.

When You Are Away

Turn your water heater off when you go on vacation. Why pay for what you won't use?

Showers or Baths

Take showers instead of tub baths—showers use up to 40 percent less hot water.

When Cold Will Do

Do as much house cleaning as you can with cold water. Also, you can save *loads* of money by washing laundry in warm or cold water (instead of hot) with a cold rinse. (See "Get a Handle on Laundry Costs" on page 158.)

Psst . . . Save a Bundle!

Water-Saving Fixtures: Better Than CDs!

In a world competing for your investment dollar, you'll find that high-efficiency shower heads and faucet aerators give you a better return than money markets, CDs (certificates of deposit), or government bonds! And that's not even considering the added savings you'll enjoy on your water bill.

You can use water-saving fixtures without altering your lifestyle or sacrificing comfort. Water-saving shower heads (not to be confused with flow restrictors) produce a pleasurable shower while maintaining high pressure by mixing air and water. Most models have a stop button so you can turn off the water while you're soaping up or shampooing without having to readjust the hot-cold mix.

Homeowners with electric water heating will enjoy the biggest savings, since electric water heating typically costs more to begin with. But homeowners using natural gas will also realize big savings.

Low-flow shower heads ($8 to $15 each) and sink faucet aerators ($2) are inexpensive and easy to install. You'll recoup your investment in just a few months and keep on saving money year after year.

When You Are Asleep

A $30 timer on your water heater will pay for itself in saved energy in less than a year. The unit turns the water heater off while you sleep and then back on again in plenty of time to heat water for morning showers. Also, consider taking advantage of off-peak electric rates. (See "Shop for Bargain Power" on page 153.)

Why Superheat Your Water?

Why pay money to scald yourself with 140°F water when 110° to 120°F water is perfectly adequate? By resetting your tank thermostat you'll chop 3 to 5 percent off your water heating bills for every 10-degree reduction you make. And it's an easy job! Just follow these steps:

1. Disconnect the circuit breaker or fuse controlling the water heater.
2. Remove the top and bottom cover plates and push back the insulation to expose the thermostats. (Some small tanks have only one thermostat.)
3. Use a screwdriver to readjust the settings. Some models have numerical settings; others are marked *High–Medium–Low*. Reset both thermostats to 110°F or *Low*. If this proves to be uncomfortably low, you can always bump the settings back up a little.
4. Replace the insulation and plates. Turn the circuit breaker back on (or replace the fuse).

Lowering the tank temperature *isn't* recommended if you have a dishwasher without a booster heater, since the machine needs 140°F water to do its job properly. The advantage of having a booster heater on your dishwasher becomes obvious when you stop to think that without it, you're heating *all* your household water to 140°F just to accommodate the dishwasher. (See "Bullish on Booster Heaters" on page 157.)

Wrap Up Some Savings

Perhaps no energy conservation measure has been so widely promoted as insulation wraps for water heaters. And with good reason. It's a quick, simple, cost-effective step that will pay for itself in four to seven months.

There are ready-made wraps available for about $30 that are a cinch to install. You can get even better results by spending $20 on a roll of six-inch builder's insulation and wrapping the tank yourself. (On gas water heaters, take care not to restrict air flow around the combustion chamber at the bottom of the tank or around the vent stack on top. On electric models, the overflow valve and control panel should be left uncovered.) Many utilities provide free tank wraps. And some will even do the installation for you.

Insulate the Pipes

In addition to insulating the water heater, you'll want to insulate your hot water pipes, especially if they run through unheated space. Foam or compressed fiberglass tubing insulation costs 30 cents to 80 cents per foot and typically saves about 50 cents per foot a year. But before you start, give your local utility company a call. Many utilities provide free pipe wraps (along with free tank wraps). Some will even do the installation for you.

The Hot Water Saver

The Hot Water Saver is a small, insulated expansion chamber plumbed into the top of the water heater. It goes to work after a hot water faucet is turned off, drawing hot water back into the water heater instead of leaving it in the pipes to turn cold. The device sells for $200 and requires about an hour's worth of a plumber's time to install. Tests show that the unit can cut water heating costs 20 to 40 percent. The Hot Water Saver will typically pay for itself in one to two years in homes with electric water heating and in two to four years in homes with gas. It's especially cost-effective when installed during home construction. The Hot Water Saver is available from Metland Enterprises, P.O. Box 7880, Stockton, CA 95207.

Graywater Heat Recovery

For years, business and industry have been saving money by reclaiming heat from used hot water before it goes down the drain. And a few adventuresome do-it-yourselfers have rigged "tempering tanks" to accomplish the same thing in their homes. Now there's an off-the-shelf system available for homes called the Earthstar Graywater Heat Reclaimer.

The device, which won the Department of Energy's 1986 National Energy Innovation Award, can save you up to 40 percent on your water heating bills. Instead of letting hot water from the shower, dishwasher, and clothes washer go straight down the drain, the Heat Reclaimer diverts it into a 50-gallon storage tank. The tank contains a heat exchanger to preheat incoming cold water so the water heater won't have to work so hard.

The system costs $475 installed and will typically pay for itself in two to three years. Its main drawbacks are the space required for the tank (41 inches × 26 inches) and the need to install new drain pipes from the shower, dishwasher, and clothes washer. The Earthstar Graywater Heat Reclaimer is available from Earthstar Energy Systems, P.O. Box 626, Waldoboro, ME 04572.

Choosing a New Water Heater

Don't be fooled by appearances—there can be as much as $5,000 difference in life-cycle costs between two water heaters that outwardly look the same. For example, a family of four paying $.10 a kilowatt-hour for electricity will spend about $8,200 for hot water over the estimated 13-year life of an electric water heater. That same family, using a high-efficiency gas water heater and paying $.75 a therm for gas, would spend just $3,360—a savings of more than $4,800!

You can compare water heaters of the same class by checking their energy factors, a measure of overall efficiency. Whatever model you choose, be sure it's sized correctly for your home. New high-performance gas water heaters have better insulation, burners, and heat transfer properties than their predecessors, and are up to 85 percent efficient. In most cases, they're a real bargain compared to electric.

Water Heater Options

If you don't have natural gas, consider an electric heat pump water heater (see "Heat Pump Water Heaters" on the opposite page) or a high-efficiency electric storage unit. Sears, Lowe's, Vaughn, and Rheem offer electric storage models with energy factors of 0.95 or better. Don't settle for less.

If you're about to buy a new furnace and/or air-conditioning equipment, or build a new home, an integrated gas appliance or three-way electric heat pump could be a superior choice. Integrated gas appliances, such as those available from Amana and Mor-Flo, provide both space heating and water heating in a single, compact unit. And they get great marks for efficiency on both counts. Integrated heat pumps, such as the new unit from Carrier Corporation, provide space heating, air-conditioning, and hot water in one efficient package. For more information on these various water heater options, consult your local plumbing and heating supply center.

Heat Pump Water Heaters

Heat pump water heaters use a refrigeration cycle to remove heat from the air and pump it into the hot water tank. Since they cool and dehumidify indoor air as a function of their operation, heat pump water heaters are especially attractive in warm, humid climates. Conversely, they lose some of their appeal in colder climates, because they pull heated air out of the home, and that warm air has to be replenished.

While heat pump water heaters cost about three times as much as ordinary electric resistance water heaters, they use only one-third as much electricity. Thus, on a life-cycle basis, heat pumps are less expensive than conventional electric water heaters, although still not as economical as gas.

E-Tech, Rheem, and Ruud offer add-on heat pump water heaters that can be attached to an existing tank. Therma-Stor, Reliance, and State Industries make integrated models that are designed to replace the existing tank.

Tankless Coils:
Notorious Villains

Firing a boiler all summer long just to supply a home with hot water is a flagrant waste of energy. If this is how you currently heat your water, there are two options that can save you big money fast.

First, you can buy an efficient gas or electric water heater and shut the boiler down during the summer (and swing seasons) when you don't need it for space heating. The system can be plumbed so that during the winter when the boiler is going full tilt to heat your home, you simply turn off the gas or electric water heater and pull hot water from the coil.

A second and perhaps better strategy is to install an indirect-fired storage water heater. These systems, comprised of a heavily insulated steel tank with a heat exchanger inside, are designed to be retrofitted to your present boiler. Thanks to the insulated storage tank, the boiler will only have to fire two to three times a day to meet household hot water needs instead of 12 to 20 times. Indirect-fired storage water heaters save money by cutting boiler standby losses, particularly in the spring, summer, and fall when the boiler has no constant space heating load. Amtrol, Inc. and

Arrow Heating Equipment, Ltd., companies that make the units, claim they can also be cost-effective replacements for conventional electric, gas, and oil water heaters.

Should You Let the Sun Shine In?

If you can answer yes to these questions, you're a good candidate for solar water heating. Are there three or more people in your home? Do you heat water with electricity or oil? Does your house have a good southern exposure?

One final question: Are you building or buying a new house? If so, you can install solar water heating at the time of purchase and finance it as part of your new mortgage. (FHA, Veterans Administration, and other government-backed mortgage agencies approve solar.) In this manner, you can enjoy positive cash flow on the system—that is, the monthly cost of ownership will be less than the monthly energy saved—from day one.

Sunshine Is Free, but . . .

Prices for solar water heating systems range from $1,800 to $4,000, depending on the type. *Passive* solar water heaters, with few or no moving parts, are champions when it comes to maintenance-free operation, but be sure you get a system with adequate freeze protection.

A good-quality, properly sized solar water heater will meet 60 to 85 percent of your hot water needs and yield a 10 to 12 percent tax-free return on your investment. You'll get even better returns if your state or utility offers solar incentives.

When You Buy Solar

Remember that the solar water heating system is no better than the company that stands behind it. Check to see how long the firm has been in business. Call the Better Business Bureau. Get referrals, especially from customers who have had their systems a few years. A strong warranty—at least a year on parts and labor; 10 years on the collector—is a must.

For helpful information before you buy, contact:

Conservation
and Renewable Energy
Inquiry and Referral
Service
1-800-523-2929

Solar Energy Industries
Association
1730 N. Lynn St.
Suite 610
Arlington, VA 22209

Inexpensive Ways to "Comfortize" Your Home

Caulk and Insulate

Up to 40 percent of furnace and/or air conditioner output is lost from uninsulated ductwork running through unconditioned attics and basements. You can fix this yourself with a caulk gun and a roll of 2-inch, foil-backed insulation. Caulk the cracks between each section of ductwork. Cut the insulation to fit and seal the wrap (foil side out) with duct tape. This simple measure will pay for itself in less than six months.

Repair deteriorated seals on storm windows and doors with caulk or weather stripping to cut heating and cooling costs.

Behind a Closed Door

Set back the thermostat in an unused room and close the door.

Beneath the Door

Use door sweeps or draft guards (cloth tubes filled with sand) to plug cracks underneath doors.

Use Fans Only When Necessary

Use kitchen and bathroom ventilating fans sparingly. Along with the fumes and humidity, they exhaust heated or cooled air.

Use natural ventilation, augmented by window fans, to help

cut back on expensive air-conditioning without sacrificing comfort. You can also use your air conditioner's fan-only setting to bring in fresh air without turning on the compressor.

Give Your Air Conditioner a Break

Cut the load on your air conditioner by scheduling cooking, clothes drying, and other heat-producing activities for the cooler part of the day.

Cold Air Doesn't Rise

Keep hot air registers and basement doors closed during the cooling season. Cold air flows to the lowest part of the house.

Getting Air to Where It's Needed

Adjust the dampers and registers on your system so they direct the right amount of cool or warm air to the right place.

Keep the Units Clean

Baseboard electric units, baseboard hydronic units, radiators, and air registers need to be kept clean and unobstructed.

Cheap Reflectors

Easy-to-make radiator reflectors can direct heat where you need it most. Simply cover a piece of insulation board with aluminum foil or other shiny material and place it against the wall behind the radiator. Heat will be reflected into the room instead of seeping out through the wall.

Cut the AC Power in Winter

Turn the power off on a central air-conditioning system during the winter; otherwise, the heating elements in the unit will consume power all winter long. Cover window units with tough plastic covers indoors and out to reduce infiltration.

Nix the Pilot in Summer

Don't forget to give the pilot light on your gas furnace the summer off.

Dress Appropriately

Clothing is the best wintertime insulation of all. In summer, peel down and let your body breathe a little.

Ready for Some Really Radiant Ideas?

Few homeowners realize that the radiant temperature of the things around them—walls, windows, furniture, even the family parakeet—affects how comfortable they feel. Heat always radiates from warm surfaces to cold surfaces. Ever wonder why you feel chilly sitting beside a bare glass window in the winter, even though the room temperature is a toasty 80°F? It's because your body is losing radiant heat to the glass.

You can raise the mean radiant temperature of your home and feel warmer without increasing the air temperature. Insulating floors, walls, and ceilings to raise their surface temperature is one approach. Adding rugs and wall coverings is another. Windows are notorious sources of radiant heat loss. Even a simple window shade can help cut radiant heat loss to the glass. (See "The Best and Worst Window Treatments" on page 182.)

The materials and colors you choose also affect the radiant heat environment of your home. Dull, dark surfaces (a shaggy brown rug) radiate more heat than shiny, light surfaces (bare white vinyl flooring). Cushy stuffed chairs add more warmth to a body than vinyl or wire-backed chairs. Whites, blues, and greens leave us feeling cold, experts say, while oranges, browns, and maroons impart warmth.

It's All Relative

The humidity level in your home has a profound effect on how comfortable you feel. If your house is too dry in the winter (telltale signs include dry throats and nasal passages, static electricity problems, and cracked book bindings) we suggest adopting some houseplants or putting a pot of water on the wood stove or radiator. The added humidity will make you feel more comfortable without raising the thermostat a single degree. But take care not to introduce too much humidity or you'll create condensation problems and have mold sprouting in your slippers.

Conversely, high humidity makes houses feel uncomfortably warm in the summer. You can address this by kicking some of your houseplants outdoors for the season and limiting cooking, dishwashing, and showers—all add humidity to the air. Consider installing kitchen and bathroom vents to expel humid air.

Weatherize and Save

Of Audits and Doctors

Hiring a professional energy auditor is a good way to get an *objective* overview of your home's energy situation and receive sound advice on where best to invest your time and money. An auditor can help you prioritize what needs to be done. Bear in mind that many utilities provide free or low-cost audits to their customers. Take advantage!

If you own an especially leaky house, you may want to go a step further and hire an "energy doctor." The application of high-tech tools, including blower doors and infrared scanners, enables energy doctors to precisely measure the amount of heat escaping from a home, pinpoint and plug the leaks, and run follow-up checks to make sure the tightening has been effective. You can expect to pay $.45 to $1 per square foot of heated space for this kind of testing and weatherization program. And it can be money well spent, returning your investment in three to five years. But beware of unscrupulous firms that stray too far from basic energy conservation measures. Get a strong warranty on the work, with specific promises on payback or utility bill savings spelled out in writing.

Weatherization: Priority #1

Living in a poorly weatherized home is like trying to draw a hot bath with the drain plug open. No matter how much energy you pour into it, it will never fill up. That's why energy experts so often recommend insulation, caulking, and weather stripping as a first step—they want to make sure the "drain plug" is in before they tackle other household energy problems. (See "Caulking, Weather-Stripping, and Insulating: 8 Places Not to Forget" on page 180.)

How much insulation is enough? In the northern half of the United States, don't settle for insulation values under R-38 in the attic, R-11 in the walls, and R-19 in the floor over an unheated crawl space or basement. (R-value is a standard measure of insulating power. For example, you would need 10 inches of fiberglass batt to attain R-30.)

In the South, where insulation saves both heating *and* air-conditioning dollars, homeowners should aim for at least R-30 in the attic floor, R-11 in the walls, and R-13 in floors over unheated spaces.

In most instances, it's worthwhile to upgrade your home to meet these standards, especially if you're heating and cooling electrically. Adding attic insulation is an easy do-it-yourself job that requires no structural changes. But beefing up the R-values in walls and floors isn't as simple. In older homes that have little or no wall insulation, it's often cost-effective to have a contractor fill the wall cavities with blow-in cellulose, fiberglass, or foam.

Two Birds with One Stone

There's an old saw in the building trades: *Insulation is cheap; finish is expensive*. Refurbishing your basement? Take advantage of the opportunity to add new insulation *before* the finishing work is done. Similarly, if you're going to put new siding on your home, consider adding new exterior insulation at the same time.

Outlets Let Out Heat

Electrical outlets throughout the home should be sealed with inexpensive gaskets to prevent heat loss. These gaskets are available at any hardware store. (Turn off the power before you remove the plate.)

Caulking, Weather-Stripping, and Insulating:
8 Places Not to Forget

Like most Americans, you've probably done some caulking, weather-stripping, and insulating work on your home. Still, it would pay you to take a second look. Caulk can crack and peel away; weather stripping wears out; and there are probably some places you missed entirely the first time around. Research shows that the greatest infiltration reductions are usually achieved by sealing air passageways in the basement and attic, which are often overlooked in the weatherization process. Be sure to give attention to these places:

- Check openings where pipes, ducts, or exhaust fans are cut through the attic floor. If you find gaps too big to caulk, stuff them with insulation.
- Check the seam where the furnace stack or chimney meets the wood framing of the house. Close the gap with fireproof caulk or insulation.
- Don't forget to insulate and weather-strip the attic door.
- Don't lay insulation over eave vents, recessed lighting, or other heat-producing fixtures. Build a drywall box over such fixtures and insulate the box.
- Caulk places in the basement (or ground floor) where plumbing and telephone wires pass through the wall of your house.
- Check the dryer vent and around window air conditioners. Make sure the edges are tightly sealed to the wall with caulk or fiberglass sealed with caulk.
- Use caulk and weather stripping to button up your windows and doors.
- Don't forget to caulk along the baseboards where needed.

An Easy Test for Infiltration

Windows, doors, and baseboards should be caulked and weather stripped. There's an easy test to determine airtightness. Move a lighted candle or incense stick around the frame and sashes of your doors and windows, and along baseboards. A dancing flame or shifting plume indicates you need to caulk or weather-strip.

You Get What You Pay For

Don't use cheap caulk and weather-stripping materials—it's an exercise in false economy. For example, silicone and polyurethane caulks are relatively expensive, but they're champions when it comes to shrinkage, flexibility, and durability. Likewise, pick out the right weather-stripping material for the job, and spend enough to get materials that will last. Pinching pennies up front could mean that you'll have to redo the job next year.

In Praise of Storms

Windows and doors are the weak links in your home's weather shield. By adding storm windows and doors, you may be able to chop heating and cooling bills as much as 15 percent. But before you start shopping around for storm windows, make sure your primary windows are in good shape. Repair broken or cracked glass. Install new sash locks if they're needed. Make sure windows close snugly. If you find cracks around the casing where the window meets the wall, caulk them.

Do-It-Yourself Storms

Do-it-yourself storm windows can be fashioned for about $2 per window by mounting clear plastic sheeting (at least 8 mils thick) to the inside of the window frame, completely covering the sash. Tape, glue, tacks, nails, or wood strips can be used to attach the sheet, as long as you achieve a tight seal. The obvious disadvantages in this approach are that you can't operate the window, and the materials may have to be replaced every winter. For about $15 per window you can buy a commercial kit—heavy-duty sheet plastic that is mounted on a frame—that can be reused winter after winter.

Permanent Storms

Permanent, combination storm-and-screen windows (triple-track) mounted outside your primary windows represent the best marriage of energy efficiency, durability, and convenience. They run $45 to $70 per standard size window if you have a contractor install them; $35 to $55 if you do it yourself. It doesn't pay to scrimp here—spend enough to get good, durable frames, tight seals, and weep holes to drain off excess moisture.

The Best and Worst Window Treatments

The most effective window treatments save energy year-round. These treatments insulate the windows, which means they reduce radiant heat loss during the winter and prevent unwanted heat gain in the summer. (See "Ready for Some Really Radiant Ideas?" on page 177.)

As you weigh various options, remember that the insulating power of blinds, drapes, and shades (measured in R-value) depends more on the tightness of the fit and seal around the window than it does on the material. R-values on window insulation products range from R-2 to R-5. Above R-5, the law of diminishing returns usually sets in. Prices range from $.50 a square foot for a simple pull-down shade to $50 a square foot for custom-designed window quilts.

Window Treatments

Here's how ten different window treatments stack up against each other in insulating value. From best to worst:

closely woven window quilts with lining	lined draperies
lined woven woods	unlined draperies
aluminized pleated shades	vertical blinds
unlined woven woods	metal miniblinds
window shades	sheer curtains

Steps to Ensure
Cheap Heat

Tune-Ups Save Money

Just as your car needs periodic tune-ups to keep it running efficiently, so, too, do furnaces, boilers, and heat pumps. A professional tune-up (about $50) can save you as much as 10 percent on
your fuel bill. Having your heating system checked out by a professional every year or two doesn't mean you can afford to
overlook routine maintenance, though. Be sure to follow all of the
suggested do-it-yourself measures below.

Check the Thermostat

Faulty thermostats are a notorious source of problems. A sticky
thermostat will be slow to activate the heating system when it's
needed and slow to turn it off when it isn't. The end result can be
wild and uncomfortable swings in temperature—and wasted
money. You can check thermostats yourself with an accurate thermometer and a bit of patience, or ask your service technician to
do it.

A Very Easy Task

The filters on forced-air heating systems need to be cleaned or replaced once a month during the heating season. If you are unfa-
miliar with how to do this simple task, read the owner's manual.
Or ask the serviceperson to show you how to do it when he or she
tunes up the system.

Set the Fan at 110°F

If you have a warm-air furnace, check the fan thermostat. It
should shut off at no higher than 90°F and come on when the furnace reaches 110°F. If the thermostat has just one setting, place
it at 110°F. If you can't find the fan thermostat, ask your service
technician.

Ducts Can Leak Heat

Check ductwork for leaks once a year. If you haven't already insulated ducts running through unheated space, do so.

Clean the Chimney

Woodstove owners should clean their chimneys in anticipation of the heating season. If creosote tends to build up quickly, it's wise to give the chimney a midwinter cleaning as well.

Psst . . . Save a Bundle!

Set Back and Relax

Setting back your thermostat before bedtime or before you leave the house is one of the biggest money savers around. For example, you can save as much as 15 percent on your heating bill (and up to 10 percent on cooling) simply by making a 5-degree setback while your family sleeps.

You can reset your thermostat manually, but it takes a superior memory and lots of dedication. Are you really going to remember to set back the thermostat every night, then reset again in the morning or on weekends when you're home more (or less)? Clock thermostats, which cost $30 to $280 and are easily installed, can do the job for you automatically. The more sophisticated models allow you to program your home's temperature throughout the day and night, with separate settings for each day of the week. In this fashion, you can save lots of energy while you're sleeping or out for the day, knowing that the thermostat will turn the furnace or air conditioner back on in anticipation of your awakening or arrival. Even the most expensive setback thermostats will generally pay for themselves in saved energy in a year or two.

Unclog Air Vents

If you have a steam radiator system, make sure the air vents work. Clogged vents will usually show themselves by blowing steam. Try removing the vent (with the steam off!) and soaking it in vinegar or boiling it in water. If this doesn't unclog it, buy a new one.

Bleed Radiators

Bleed the air out of hot water radiators once or twice each heating season. Hold a cup or pan under the valve and open the valve with a key. (Radiator keys sell for 25 cents.) Shut the valve when all the air has escaped and only water comes out.

You Need Water to Make Steam

Check your steam boiler once a week to ensure that it contains enough water and that safety switches work properly. Drain sediment from the system from time to time. If you don't know how to do this, ask your service technician.

Economical Add-Ons

Before you spend an arm and a leg for a new heating system, consider the cost-effectiveness of upgrading your current equipment. Obviously, you don't want to pour money into a system that has truly outlived its usefulness, but neither do you want to scrap it if it can be modified to work efficiently for years to come.

We've listed seven modifications in the table "Modifications for Heating Systems" that might make good sense, depending on what kind of system you have and its condition. It's a good idea to consult an independent energy auditor or engineer about the trade-offs involved in modifying a system versus buying a new one. Note that the savings on these options are *not* cumulative.

Reset and Save

You can save 5 to 10 percent on your boiler's fuel consumption by resetting the aquastat. Except on the coldest winter days, 150°F boiler water is sufficient to warm your house. You'll save money by manually resetting the low-limit aquastat on the boiler to

Modifications for Heating Systems			
ITEM	COST ($)	PAYBACK	COMMENTS
Smaller fuel nozzle	20–40	Less than 6 months	Trickier with gas systems than with oil
Barometric damper and baffles	20–80	6–18 months	Oil systems only
Modulating aquastat	150–350	1–5 years	Hot water boilers only
Flame-retention burner	300–500	2–3 years	Oil systems only
Gas power burner	400–600	2–4 years	For old oil and coal systems converted to gas
Electric ignition	150–300	3–5 years	Gas systems only
Automatic flue damper	125–400	3–10 years	A new burner is usually a better buy for oil systems

SOURCE: Massachusetts Audubon Society.

140°F and the high-limit to 160°F. For $150 to $350, you can install a modulating aquastat that will make temperature adjustments automatically. Payback varies from one to five years.

Smart Fires

In many homes, fireplaces are *net energy losers*. However, by operating your fireplace wisely, you can enjoy a heartwarming blaze without paying a big energy penalty. Here are some tips:

■ Turn off your central heating system when you have a fire going.
■ Build small, steady fires instead of roaring infernos—less energy goes up the chimney.

- Equip the front of your fireplace with a glass door—it's a real energy saver.
- Close the damper when the fireplace isn't in use.
- Some dampers leave a gap of an inch or more when closed. By stuffing that gap with insulation or making a flue plug, you can save up to $45 a year in wasted heated and cooled air.

Conservation— Casablanca Style

A ceiling fan can be a flexible energy saver, distributing warm air in the winter and creating an enjoyable breeze in the summer. The key is to choose a model with variable speed control. In the winter, especially in rooms with high ceilings (10 feet or more), heat stratification can be a problem. A ceiling fan in slow rotation (you don't want chilling drafts) can help redistribute warm air back down into the room where it's needed, thereby reducing heating bills. Come summer, you can let the fan fly, enjoy the breeze, and let the air conditioner take a rest.

When It's Time to Buy

If your old furnace or boiler has a seasonal efficiency of less than 60 percent (your heating service representative can calculate this for you), and modifications to the system don't appear to be cost-effective, it may be time to get rid of that old junker. No one enjoys dishing out $1,000 to $4,000 for a new heating system, but there's consolation in knowing that lower fuel bills lie ahead.

As with any large purchase, it pays to shop around. This is particularly true of heating and air-conditioning equipment, since big strides in efficiency are being made each year.

AFUE Is the Key When Buying

Furnaces and boilers, both gas and oil, are rated by their Annual Fuel Utilization Efficiency, or AFUE. This is a key consideration, along with price, quality, and warranty. Opt for an AFUE of *at least* 80 percent for new gas furnaces and boilers. For oil furnaces and boilers, an AFUE rating of 85 or better signifies high efficiency. These systems cost a few hundred dollars more than their inefficient cousins, but they'll save you $50 or more a year in fuel. Models of this caliber—and there are many of them on the market—would feature the following:

automatic vent damper or
   induced draft fan
electronic ignition
power or pulse combustion

If you have a long heating season, a condensing furnace (with AFUEs ranging up to 97) could be a wise investment. Be sure to get a good warranty on furnaces that employ "condensing technology," because the heat exchangers must withstand a highly corrosive environment.

Bigger
Isn't Necessarily Better

Before you purchase a new heating or cooling system, make sure that you've properly weatherized your house. A smaller load necessitates a smaller, less expensive mechanical system, and ensures lower fuel bills for years to come.

When you are ready to buy, make sure the system is properly sized. Have your contractor do heat gain and/or heat loss calculations on your home to make sure. Also bear in mind that while it pays to purchase high-efficiency heating and cooling gear, it may not be cost-effective for you to buy the *most* efficient model. Consider the trade-off between purchase price and operating cost, and the length and severity of your heating and cooling seasons.

Heat Pump Pointers

It pays to choose a heat pump appropriate to your climate. If your primary need is cooling, emphasize the Seasonal Energy Efficiency Ratio (SEER) rating in your selection. Conversely, if you have more heating than cooling load, focus on the Heating Season Performance Factor (HSPF). See "Understanding Energy Ratings" on the opposite page for definitions of SEER and HSPF.

Heat pumps generally perform best in climates where there's more air-conditioning demand than heating. They aren't a smart choice in really cold climates, because their heating performance suffers as outdoor temperatures fall. At about 15°F, most models shut themselves off, kicking in expensive electric resistance heating as a backup.

While natural gas will probably be the best overall fuel value in the years ahead, electric heat pumps are the most economical choice—that is, better than electric furnaces or baseboard electric—for homeowners who have to heat their homes electrically. The Air Conditioning and Refrigeration Institute, 1501 Wilson Boulevard, Arlington, VA 22209 offers a free brochure on heat pumps, and a product directory for $10.

Try Integrating

If you're building a new house or replacing old heating and cooling equipment, an integrated appliance could save you both money and space. Integrated appliances supply both space heating and hot water in one compact, efficient system.

There are several different makes to choose from. The System 2000, an oil-fired boiler made by Energy Kinetics, has an AFUE of 87 percent, and this doesn't include the water-heating bonus. Amana and Mor-Flo industries make gas-fired integrated appliances that get high efficiency marks for both space and water heating.

Carrier Corporation has taken the concept a bold step further with its new integrated electric heat pump, which provides heating, air-conditioning, and hot water in a single system. Early reviews give the Carrier unit excellent scores for efficiency and suggest that it can compete head-on with gas, even in cold climates.

Keep Your Cool

Understanding
Energy Ratings

Room air conditioners, central air conditioners, and central heat pumps are each rated by different standards. Room air conditioners can be compared by their Energy Efficiency Ratio (EER). An EER rating of 6 to 8 would designate poor to fair energy efficiency; 8.5 to 9.5 is good; anything above 9.5 is excellent.

Central air conditioners are assigned a Seasonal Energy Efficiency Ratio (SEER). A SEER of 6 to 9 denotes poor to fair energy efficiency; 9.5 to 11 is considered efficient. Very efficient systems have SEERs of 11.5 or better.

Central heat pumps, which provide both air-conditioning and heating, are given a SEER rating for cooling performance and a Heating Season Performance Factor (HSPF) to grade their heating efficiency. The most energy-efficient heat pumps on the market have SEER ratings above 10 and HSPFs of 8 or better.

Air-Conditioning Systems:
6 Money-Saving Maintenance Tips

To keep your central air-conditioning system running at peak efficiency, follow these maintenance tips:

- Perform a system check. When the unit is on, you should be able to feel air flowing from the vents at a distance of several feet. Tape a glass bulb thermometer to the supply air vent, and then to the return air vent. There should be a 17- to 20-degree difference in the two readings.
- Inspect the air conditioner's filter once a month. Some types are washable; others need to be replaced when they get dirty.
- If you have a belt-driven blower, check the belt occasionally. If it's slack, tighten it. If it's badly worn, replace it. Keep an extra belt on hand.
- Check thermostats with an accurate thermometer. We recommend 78°F as the best balance between comfort and conservation.
- Periodically clean the coils and fins on the outside condensing unit. Make sure shrubs aren't interfering with air flow.
- Have a professional inspect, clean, and tune your system every other year to ensure its efficiency and long life.

Evaporative Coolers

If you live in a hot, *dry* climate, consider an evaporative cooler. Priced from $400 (window unit) to $1,800 (ducted central system), evaporative coolers use about one-quarter the energy that an air conditioner requires.

Attic Fans:
Tried and True Energy Savers

Attic fans, sometimes called whole-house fans, can put a big dent in your electric bill by reducing the need for expensive air-conditioning. Studies show that attic fans can shorten the air-conditioning season by 30 to 50 percent with no sacrifice in comfort. In the South, this will translate into a cool savings of $100 to $200 a year. In the North, it may make it unnecessary to even turn on the air-conditioning.

Attic fans are usually mounted horizontally in the ceiling below the attic. Controlled by a manual switch, timer, or thermostat, they pull large volumes of cool, ventilating air into the house and vent it through the attic. At moderate humidity levels, an attic fan can make your home comfortable even when it's 85°F outside.

How Attic Fans Save Money

Every hour the fan is on and the air conditioner is off saves money. If you're paying 8 cents a kilowatt-hour for electricity, you can run a 400-watt attic fan for just 3.2 cents an hour. Compare that to the 34 cents an hour it costs to run a typical three-ton capacity air conditioner.

Installing an attic fan, complete with louvers and a timer, will cost $275 to $550, depending on its size and quality. Price, warranty, multispeed operation, and ease of installation are major shopping points. Remember that the louvers, which are used to hide the fan when it's not in use, are not designed to stop infiltration. To effectively seal the hole, you'll need a tight-fitting insulated panel with gaskets or weather stripping. Otherwise, wintertime heat losses will chew up all the money you saved on cooling.

Radiant Heat Barriers

For homeowners in the Deep South, installing a radiant heat barrier in the attic is an easy and cost-effective do-it-yourself project. Reinforced reflective foil (10 to 40 cents per square foot) is stapled to the roof rafters. The foil blocks heat that would normally radiate into the attic and living space below, saving up to 10 percent on air-conditioning costs. Hiring a contractor will add about 15 cents per square foot to the job.

Cool Window Treatments

When it comes to windows, one of the best cooling strategies is to block out the sun before it ever reaches them. Structural overhangs, trellises, and trees accomplish this very nicely. So do awnings, which can lower interior room temperatures 8 to 15 degrees and save you up to 25 percent on air-conditioning bills. Exterior sun screens and roll-up shutters are also good sun interceptors, but they can block cooling breezes and cut off views.

Various types of adhesive, sun-blocking films can be affixed to the inside surfaces of windows and doors. They range from $1 to $5 per square foot and have different shading coefficients. Remember: Darker isn't always better—you want to admit *some* light into the room.

As shown in the table "Comparing Sun-Blocking Window Treatments," sun-screening window treatments can be compared by their shading coefficients (along with price, versatility, durability, and so on). The shading coefficient indicates how much shading to expect from the product once it's in place. The lower the number, the more shading you get.

A Word about Precoolers

Adding a precooler to your central air-conditioning system can be a shrewd move, especially if you live in a hot, dry climate. A precooler is a water-cooled device that attaches to the condenser on your existing system. Using pads saturated with water, it cools incoming air before it passes over the condenser coils, enabling the air conditioner to operate more efficiently and decreasing total energy consumption. Precoolers cost $40 to $50 per ton of air-conditioning and can pay for themselves in saved energy in less than three years.

Comparing Sun-Blocking Window Treatments (Shading Coefficients)

WINDOW TREATMENT	COMBINED WITH SINGLE GLASS	COMBINED WITH DOUBLE GLASS
No treatment	1.00	0.88
Changeable Treatments		
Open-weave dark draperies	0.82	0.71
Medium-colored venetian blinds	0.74	0.62
Opaque dark shades	0.81	0.71
Light-colored venetian blinds	0.67	0.58
Close-weave light-colored draperies	0.48	0.45
Translucent light-colored shades	0.44	0.40
Opaque white shades	0.39	0.35
Permanent Treatments*		
Heat mirror	—	0.34–0.71
Awnings	0.20–0.50	0.20–0.50
Tinted glass	0.51–0.87	0.42–0.78
Reflective window films	0.20–0.94	0.15–0.58
Sunscreens	0.10–0.59	0.10–0.59

SOURCE: Compiled from *ASHRAE Handbook 1989* and other sources.
*When considering permanent sun-screening window treatments, be sure to check on visible light transmittance.

7

PRUNE THE PRICE
OF GARDEN
AND LAWN CARE

It's almost too good to be true: An activity as pleasurable and relaxing as gardening can reap an economic bonus as well! The National Gardening Association, using figures for 1987–88, estimates that the average vegetable gardener spends $45 a year on seeds, tools, and other aids to tend a 300-square-foot plot. From that garden patch comes a harvest worth $250—not a bad return on a season's worth of gardening!

Landscaping and lawn care is another area where do-it-yourselfers can save a bundle. Call up any professional landscaping or lawn care service in your phone book and ask for an estimate. Once you've recovered from the shock, figure that with a little know-how you can do the same thing for yourself at half or even less their price. There's an added financial incentive to landscaping: A nicely planted yard can add 7 to 14 percent to the value of your property.

Vegetable gardening, landscaping, and lawn care are the most obvious examples of how it's possible to save money. But there are lots of other ways you can be resourceful and trim down the cost of everything from starting seeds to mulching—without whittling down the fun of gardening one bit. By the time you've finished reading this chapter, you'll know all the tricks you need to be a money-wise gardener.

Soil Care for Dirt Cheap

Cover Crops
Cost Only Pennies

Here's a riddle: What costs only pennies, yet can improve your soil's fertility and structure, control weeds and erosion, encourage helpful soil microbes, and boost garden yields all at the same time? And, as a bonus, may even add extra nitrogen to the soil? Answer: a garden cover crop.

For less than a penny per square foot, your garden can be enjoying all the glorious benefits of a cover crop. (The average cost per half-pound of cover crop seed is $2.50, enough to sow 1,000 square feet.) It doesn't take much effort on your part. Once the crop is planted in the fall (after harvest), you leave it alone until spring when you turn or rotary-till the growth into the soil. Wait two weeks, then plant as usual.

Of Legumes and Grasses

Cover crops come in two categories: legumes (the nitrogen fixers) and grasses. Some of the more well-known varieties are listed in the table below. Check with your local extension service agent to see which one works best in your area and when it should be planted.

LEGUMES (ALSO CALLED GREEN MANURES)	GRASSES
Austrian winter pea*	Annual ryegrass
Crimson clover*	Oats
Fava bean	Winter barley
Hairy vetch*	Winter rye
Large white lupine	Winter wheat
White clover	
Yellow lupine	

*These tested well at the Rodale Research Center and are easy to turn under with a shovel or rotary tiller.

Sources for Seeds

Two good sources of seeds for cover crops are:

Johnny's Selected Seeds
Foss Hill Rd.
Albion, ME 04910

The Necessary Trading Company
New Castle, VA 24127

For 95 cents you can order the booklet "Green Manures—A Mini-Manual," filled with information at a terrific value.

Psst . . . Save a Bundle!

Free Soil Conditioners

Every good gardener knows that soil needs regular infusions of organic matter to stay in good condition (meaning it has good texture and water holding ability). And organic matter is essential when you need to transform problem soil into prime soil. Some of the best soil conditioners around are ones that money *can't* buy, such as the ones listed in the table "Yours for the Taking."

Rationing Plan for the Garden

Have you priced bone meal, blood meal, phosphate rock, or any other soil-improving rock powder or mineral recently? They're not cheap, but they're often one of the most effective ways to improve garden soil's texture and fertility.

Make your soil improver and your money go farther by using the powder or mineral only where it's needed—around the plant's roots. Instead of blanketing the whole garden, save the more costly soil additives for planting holes or trenches.

Soil-Testing Savvy

If you don't test your soil, you could be throwing away money on fertilizers your garden doesn't need. The best buy in soil testing is the service offered by your land grant college or university soil testing laboratory. For a modest fee (usually about $5) you will receive a soil sampling kit, lab analysis, and a set of recommendations. Usually within two to six weeks after you send in the sample you'll receive the laboratory reading of pH and nutrient levels. This analysis is very accurate, and the recommendations can help you correct soil problems. To get a soil sampling kit, contact your local extension service office. Some garden centers may also carry these kits.

Yours for the Taking

CONDITIONER	FREE SOURCE	COMMENTS
Animal manures	Riding stables or dairy barns, poultry farms, friend's pet rabbit	Don't use cat or dog manure in the garden; apply fresh manure in fall only—composted manure anytime
Chopped leaves	Anywhere there are trees	Chop with shredder or run over pile with lawn mower; add nitrogen source to soil to assist decomposition
Compost	Make your own; check to see if your town operates municipal compost piles	The garden equivalent of Geritol; makes any garden come alive with vim and vigor
Grass clippings*	Ask neighbors to give you their bagged clippings; ask the same of lawn services operating in the neighborhood	Grass clippings sealed shut in plastic bags really reek; work clippings into soil right away or spread in thin layer to dry
Leaf mold (decomposed leaves)	Where leaves have sat for a year or more and have rotted to crumbly, brown humus; scoop from floor of woods; under trees or along fences; compost your own leaves	Excellent tonic for sandy and clayey soils
Sawdust	School shop classes; friend or neighbor's wood shop; mill or lumberyard	Works wonders on clayey or sandy soils; add nitrogen source to soil to assist decomposition

*Do not use grass clippings from lawns that have been treated with chemicals.

No-Cost Soil Testing

Here are two quick and easy methods to test your soil. The first will give you a general reading of your soil's pH, and the second will give an indication of its texture.

To see how much lime is in your soil (meaning how alkaline it is), put 1 tablespoon of dry soil in a teacup and add 1 tablespoon of white vinegar. Cover the cup with a saucer, shake, then hold the cup close to your ear. A loud fizzing means there's too much lime in your soil, and you should add acidic material like peat moss, sawdust, or leaf mold. If the fizzing is weak or missing, get a more accurate pH test done.

Make a "soil shake" to learn the soil texture. Fill a glass jar with ⅔ water and ⅓ soil. Shake, then set on a table or counter to let the particles settle. In three days you'll have your diagnosis. The heavier particles sink first, in this order: sand, silt, and clay. Organic matter floats. If more than 70 percent of the particles settle in the bottom layer, your soil is sandy. When 30 percent or more rise to form the top layer, the soil is clayey. Good garden soil is 45 percent sand, 35 percent silt, and 20 percent clay; use these proportions as a gauge to judge your own soil's status.

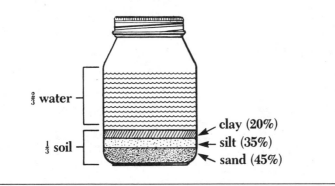

⅔ water

⅓ soil

clay (20%)
silt (35%)
sand (45%)

Make Your Own Potting Soil

Why spend money on bags of potting soil from the store when you can go out in your backyard and dig it up for free? The only thing you need to do before you use this garden soil is sterilize it to kill bacteria and weed seeds. Then it's ready to use for houseplants, window boxes, and even seed starting. Use one of these sterilization methods:

- Oven method: Place 2 to 3 inches of moist garden soil in an aluminum foil baking pan and cover tightly with foil. With the oven set at 200°F, monitor the soil heat with a meat thermometer. Once the temperature reaches 150°F, let the soil heat for 30 minutes, then remove. Be forewarned: Baking soil does *not* have a pleasant aroma!
- Microwave method: Place 2 pounds of moist garden soil in a plastic bag (polypropylene baking bags work best). Close by twisting loosely. (Don't seal tightly or you risk an explosion!) Heat on full power for 2½ minutes. Let the soil stand uncovered until cool. Clean the oven thoroughly when you're done, paying close attention to the door seal.
- Wheelbarrow method: Fill a wheelbarrow with a 2- to 3-inch layer of garden soil and cover with a sheet of clear plastic. Let the wheelbarrow bask in full sun for eight hours or more, turning the soil two to three times during that period.
- Backyard grill method: Start the coals, then fill an old roasting pan or aluminum foil pan with a layer of garden soil. Cover tightly with foil. In about 30 to 45 minutes the soil should heat to 300°F. Stir once or twice during that time.

Homemade Soil Mixes

You can make your own soil mixes for seed starting or houseplants that are better and cheaper than the kinds you see on garden center shelves. Try one or several of these recipes:

- Soilless Mix for Seedlings. Blend 3 parts peat moss and 1 part coarse sand, perlite, or vermiculite. To each bushel of mix add 6 ounces ground limestone.
- Seedling Mix with Soil. Mix 1 quart sterilized loamy garden soil, 1 quart peat moss, and 1 quart sharp sand.
- Houseplant Mix I. Add 2 parts garden soil, 1 part compost or leaf mold, and 1 part sand or perlite. Add 1 tablespoon bone meal per quart of mix. Sterilize in 150°F oven for 30 minutes.
- Houseplant Mix II. Mix 1 part garden loam, 1 part sand, and 1 part peat moss or leaf mold. Add 1 tablespoon bone meal per quart of mix. Sterilize as for mix I.

Fertilizers for Free . . . Or Next to Nothing

Garden Gold from the Compost Pile

The best fertilizer for your garden isn't for sale—it's *free* for the making. Compost has its humble beginnings in garden clippings, kitchen scraps, and other discards, but by the time they've all decomposed you have the nutrient-rich equivalent of garden gold.

For the complete word on composting and its many variations, see *The Rodale Guide to Composting* (Rodale Press, 1979).

Four Cheap and Easy Compost Bins

Page through garden supply catalogs, and you'll see commercial versions of compost bins that carry hefty price tags. One catalog listed a wooden bin for $100 and a simple wire bin for $50! Any resourceful gardener with the knack for recycling materials can make bins for a fraction of these prices. Here are four ideas for thrifty do-it-yourselfers:

■ Snow fence, hardware cloth, or chicken wire makes fine circular bins. Eleven feet of fencing will make a bin 3 feet across and 4 feet high. Use the wire ends as self closures. To stabilize, tie or wire to a length of metal pipe sunk into the ground.

■ Slatted wooden shipping pallets make great long-lasting bins and are often free for the taking (check with local factories, grocery stores, hardware stores, garden centers). Drill holes along the edges and tie together at the corners, or drive poles into the ground and slip pallet sides over the poles.

■ Recycle spare pieces of wood into frames to make a four-sided box. Staple wire mesh in place to cover the sides, then attach all the sides together.

■ Stack cinder blocks to make a three-sided bin. Leave 1- to 2-inch gaps between neighboring blocks and stagger the rows to provide ventilation. Four layers of blocks is high enough to house a compost pile.

Accelerated Compost

You can pay up to $13 for a couple pounds of commercial compost activator that claims to speed up activity in the pile so you can get compost sooner. But why deactivate your wallet by spending money on this when there are three free, natural materials that can accelerate a faltering pile? A common cause for a slow pile is a lack of nitrogen. Just add fresh weeds, grass clippings, or manure (all high in nitrogen) to the pile to get things moving again.

Psst . . . Save a Bundle!

Grow Your Own Nitrogen Fertilizer

Legume cover crops, also called green manures, are the best fertilizer bargain around. By growing these plants, then tilling them into the soil, you add rich stores of nitrogen captured from the air by the plants' roots. (See "Cover Crops Cost Only Pennies" on page 195 for a listing of legume cover crops.)

To show you what a bargain these green manures are, compare prices among various nitrogen sources. It costs a couple dollars to buy enough green manure seeds to plant 1,000 square feet of garden space. You'd pay nearly $50 for enough dried blood to cover that same area, and almost $35 for cottonseed meal. Need any more convincing?

Finished Compost for Free

Here's the no-fuss, no-muss way to get compost for your garden. All you supply is the muscle power to collect and haul it.

Check places like corn mills, sawmills, riding stables, hat factories (straw or cotton scraps), rice mills, feedlots, poultry farms, dairies, and places where ground crews are likely to dump fall loads of deciduous leaves. Look for the oldest piles where these organic materials have been sitting for a while and have reduced themselves to black, crumbly humus. (These piles are likely to be found at the rear of the lots.) Dig into the bottom where the oldest material will be found. If you add fresh or undecomposed materials like corn husks, sawdust, and leaves to the soil, you risk causing a nitrogen deficiency.

Free Food for the Garden

It's possible to have the lushest, most productive garden around without spending a single cent on fertilizers. The table "Garden Food" gives you some ideas on where to track down free sources of important plant nutrients.

Feed Bulbs for Less

For years gardeners have been dutifully adding bone meal to their bulbs in the belief that this was the key to better blooms and a longer life for the bulbs. Now it turns out that bone meal isn't a magic bulb elixir.

Studies have shown that bulbs need nitrogen more than they need the phosphorus in bone meal. Also, the current process used to prepare bone meal makes it a less beneficial source of phosphorus than was previously believed. What this means is that you should stop spending money on expensive bags of bone meal and turn instead to the compost pile.

Every fall, top-dress your beds of bulbs with two bushels of compost per 100 square feet (you can also use well-rotted manure). These free fertilizers will provide your bulbs with all the nitrogen and trace elements they need to put on a dazzling display. Apply the compost again in the spring when bulb foliage peeks out 1 inch above the soil.

The Right Rates
for the Backyard Garden

It's not unusual for organic fertilizer rates to be given in rates per acre, but this isn't of much use when you're a backyard gardener with only a fraction of that area. Guesstimates about application rates can cause you to overapply and therefore waste fertilizer. To

Garden Food

MATERIAL	FREE SOURCE	HOW TO USE
Fish waste	Fish tanks	Save water after cleaning tank and use to water garden and houseplants; good nitrogen source
Garden trimmings	Ask friends and neighbors for lawn clippings, hedge trimmings, pine needles, leaves	Compost; green matter; good source of nitrogen
Hay	Farmers may give away spoiled hay the cows won't eat	Add to compost pile; good source of nitrogen and potassium
Human hair	Barbers, beauty shops (provide them with garbage bags and arrange regular pickups)	Add to compost pile; spread under mulch; put in planting holes; excellent source of nitrogen
Kitchen scraps	Restaurants, grocery stores, coffee shops	Add to compost pile (take out bones, meat, and greasy materials)
Manure	County fair stables, racing stables, boarding or renting stables; animal science department at local university; feedlots and dairies; classified ads may list free manure if you haul	Add only well-rotted manure directly to garden during growing season; fresh manure can be applied in fall or added to compost pile; good nitrogen source
Wood ashes	Wood stoves (no outdoor grills or coal-burning stoves)	Potassium rich; best added directly to garden in fall

help give your plants just what they need, here are conversion rates for backyard gardens.

When rate is given as 100 pounds per acre:

> For 1,000 square feet: $2\frac{1}{2}$ pounds or $2\frac{1}{2}$ pints
> 100 square feet: $\frac{1}{4}$ pound or $\frac{1}{2}$ cup
> 1 square yard: $\frac{1}{2}$ ounce or $2\frac{1}{2}$ teaspoons

When rate is given as 1 ton (or 2,000 pounds) per acre:

> For 1,000 square feet: 50 pounds
> 100 square feet: 5 pounds or 5 pints
> 1 square yard: $\frac{1}{2}$ pound or 1 cup

Mulches for the Miserly

Spread the News

Newspapers make a terrific mulch (put a few stones or bricks at the corners to prevent them from blowing away). On garbage night, tour the neighborhood and look for bags loaded with papers. Take the colored sections, too—the colored inks used in today's newspapers are safe for garden use.

Leaves Are Lovely

You'll probably be up to your eyeballs in mulch if you pass the word among friends and neighbors that you want to collect their bagged leaves. Shred before applying them to the garden. Decomposed leaves in a crumbly, brown condition also make a lovely mulch. Visit country friends and scoop bagfuls from the back of their wooded property. City dwellers can check with maintenance departments to find out where leaves are dumped.

Choice Chips

Wood chips are very attractive and often used as mulch in landscape design. They also cost a pretty penny. Check with tree pruning services, or the electric or telephone company to find out where their chipped tree prunings are collected and whether they're free for the taking. Beware of chips from the black walnut. This tree may contain a substance that retards the growth of or even kills susceptible plants.

Clip, Clip, Clip

Don't throw those grass clippings away! They are quite suitable as mulch. If your own lawn doesn't generate enough clippings, check with your neighbors or local landscaping or lawn service companies (be sure no chemicals have been used on the grass). Stop at a job site and talk to the person in charge; you may be able to arrange to have them drop off their load of clippings at the end of the day when they're in the neighborhood. What could be better than free delivery of free mulch?

Municipal Mulch

Some towns have arranged to have tree prunings shredded into wood chips, and other organic matter turned into compost piles. These wonderful mulch materials are free for the hauling. To find out if your town offers free mulch, call the park or street maintenance department or check with the local garden club.

Cart Away the Corn

Shredded or ground corncobs make a good moisture-retaining mulch (apply a nitrogen-rich fertilizer before mulching). Check with a local mill that shells corn; you may be able to take as many cobs as you can carry away. But don't stop at the cobs; shredded cornstalks make great mulch, too. Ask local farmers if you can help yourself to their stalks.

Pine Needles

A plastic bag and a rake are all you need to "harvest" this mulch from beneath pine trees.

Seek Out the Sawdust

Visit local woodworkers, lumber companies, or mills, and ask for sawdust. Add a nitrogen fertilizer to the soil before mulching. (See the warning in "Choice Chips" earlier in this chapter.)

A Word on Weeds

Yes, you can recycle weeds and put them to use as a mulch. Let the weeds dry completely before mulching to keep them from springing to life again. Or, shred and mix with grass clippings. Since weeds are so plentiful but not very sightly, this is a good mulch to use in the orchard, where a lot of mulch is needed but good looks aren't mandatory.

Spread the Wealth

Many gardeners feel that flower beds or other showplace gardens deserve a handsome mulch like cocoa hulls or shredded bark. But buying bag after bag of these mulches, enough to spread at least 1 inch over the garden, can put a dent in anyone's wallet. Here's a money-saving compromise: Lay a 1-inch-thick layer of newspaper over the garden; this free mulch provides the first level of defense against pesky weeds. To add the finishing touch, spread a thin layer of the decorative mulch over the bottom "working" layer. You'll get the dual benefit of a thick but attractive mulch layer at a fraction of the cost.

Unlikely but Likable Mulches

Resourceful gardeners can turn one person's castoffs into garden mulch. Two examples are what we call bed-to-bed carpet and fiberglass underfoot.

Keep your eyes open for any places (hotels, office buildings, homes in your neighborhood) where jute-back carpeting is being removed. Strips of carpet cut to fit between beds or garden rows keep weeds out of sight, don't mold or disintegrate, protect vegetables from mud splatters, and give you a nice place to walk. Roll up the carpet at season's end and you can reuse it year after year.

Even discarded fiberglass roofing panels can make their way to the garden. Panels can be laid across the garden plot, leaving planting strips in between. The fiberglass speeds soil warming and keeps the harvest clean and off the ground. The panels are durable and hold up well under foot traffic.

Stone Your Garden

We're all conditioned to remove stones from the garden, so it's a little surprising to consider bringing them back on purpose. But stones can make an excellent mulch. They're especially good at conserving soil moisture and absorbing heat and are plentiful and dirt cheap in most places!

To use, cultivate the garden plot, work in lots of organic matter, and add a thick layer of chopped leaves on top. Set the stones in rows 2 feet wide, leaving a 1-foot planting strip between rows. Spaces between plants in the planting rows can be mulched with grass clippings, shredded leaves, or any mulch you desire.

Penny-Pinching Pest Controls

Homemade Sprays

Put on your apron and get ready to whip up a home-brewed batch of bug spray. All of these recipes call for ingredients you probably already have on your shelves and will cost you only pennies to make:

■ Soap Spray. Mix 2 tablespoons liquid Ivory soap in a gallon of water. Mist leaves to kill whiteflies, spider mites, mealybugs, cinch bugs, and aphids.
■ Triple-Threat Spray. Chop 1 garlic bulb and 1 small onion, add 1 tablespoon cayenne powder, and mix with 1 quart water. Let steep 1 hour, then add 1 tablespoon liquid Ivory soap. This all-purpose insect spray remains potent for one week.
■ Hot Pepper Spray. Grind some of your most incendiary hot pepper pods, then mix with an equal amount of water. For each quart, add 1 tablespoon liquid Ivory soap. This all-purpose spray keeps a wide range of insects away.
■ Garlic Spray. Use this on wireworms, cutworms, slugs, and whiteflies. Soak 6 tablespoons chopped garlic in 2 teaspoons liq-

uid paraffin for 24 hours. Add 1 pint water and $\frac{1}{4}$ cup liquid Ivory soap. Strain and use within a week.

■ Buttermilk Spray. Fruit trees covered with spider mites will welcome this spray. Mix together 5 pounds white flour, 1 pint buttermilk, and 25 gallons of water. Filter into a sprayer and apply weekly until mite infestation subsides.

Psst . . . Save a Bundle!

Home-Grown Pyrethrum

Pyrethrum is sold as a botanical poison to use against leaf-hoppers, aphids, whiteflies, corn earworms, thrips, and cabbage loopers. It may also deter imported cabbageworms, tomato fruitworms, and beet army-worms. Instead of buying this potent bug killer, spend your money on chrysanthemums for the garden. After you've enjoyed the beauty of the flowers, you can grind them up to make your own bug spray.

Buy plants of *Chrysanthemum cinerariifolium;* this is the only species that contains pyrethrum. Grind several dried flower heads to a fine powder. You can use this dust as is to sprinkle on the garden, or mix it with water to make a spray.

Add enough powder to 1 cup of water to make a paste. Keep adding water until it measures 3 quarts. Filter this solution into the sprayer through several layers of cheesecloth. Don't use either the dust or spray within three to seven days of harvest.

Fight Fungi

Prepare to do battle against the fungi that attack your plants and stored beans, grains, and peanuts by using these homemade mixtures:

■ Plant juice. Put clematis, corn leaves, and the papery layers of a garlic bulb in a blender with enough water to make a thin juice.

Filter and spray on plants until signs of fungi are gone. This works against downy mildew, powdery mildew, rust fungi, and gray mold.

■ Baking soda cure. This is the treatment for black rot that strikes developing grapes. Dissolve 4 teaspoons baking soda in 1 gallon of water. Spray over grape clusters and vines. Apply as fruit begins to appear, then once a week for two months. Reapply after every rain.

■ Spicy blend. This fragrant concoction may help keep your stored beans, grains, and peanuts free from a dangerous fungus. Mix together cinnamon sticks, whole black peppercorns, ground black mustard, and some garlic greens. Tie up in cheesecloth bags and place one bag in each storage container.

Keep the Deer Away

Everyone loves Bambi, but in real life deer are a lot less than lovable when they raid your garden. They can ravage expensive landscape plants and fruit trees and cost you money when you have to replace damaged plantings. Here are two low-cost measures you can use to safeguard your investment in plants:

■ "Eggsellent" deer spray. Mix together two raw eggs and 1 quart of water. Add enough water to make 1 gallon, and blend. Spray on the vegetable garden, fruit trees, grapevines, and cornfield. Respray after a rain.

■ Dangling soap. Deer seem to have an aversion to bars of soap! Protect your orchard and other tender trees by running a wire through a bar of strongly scented deodorant soap. Hang one bar about 3 feet from the ground in every tree. Replace the bars every two months.

Gopherproof Beds

Call a halt to gophers' underground invasions by lining the bottom of garden beds with recycled pieces of aviary mesh or window screening. Dig the beds 1½ feet deep, then line the bottom with wire (if you use two separate pieces, be sure to wire them together). Arrange the wire so it covers the bottom and sides completely. Finish by filling the beds with soil.

Bird Buster

To keep birds away from newly sprouted seeds, push a stake into the ground at both ends of each row. Run a piece of brown or black thread between each pair of stakes, directly above the row of seeds, 2 inches above the soil. The birds can't see the thread against the soil and are tripped up when they come in for a tender green morsel.

Anti-Aphids Attack

Paint a 10 × 10-inch piece of scrap wood with school-bus-yellow paint. Then coat with motor oil or petroleum jelly. Lean the wood against a stake next to infested plants.

Thrifty Traps
for Apple Maggot Flies

Paint $3\frac{1}{2}$-inch wooden balls with deep red paint and coat with Tack Trap. Hang them in the tree. Two balls are enough to protect a dwarf tree (under 9 feet); use six to eight on a full-size tree.

Corner Codling Moths

Hang paper cups filled with two parts vinegar and one part molasses throughout the tree. Clean out trapped moths and replace mixture periodically.

Eradicate Earwigs

Lay pieces of corrugated cardboard near the plants that are being chewed to bits. In a few days, collect the cardboard in the early afternoon and burn to permanently dispose of earwigs napping in the corrugations.

Zap Sap Beetles

Fill a soup can halfway with vinegar and set near the berry, melon, or peach crop that's being bothered. Beetles will crawl in and drown. This also works on fruit flies.

Slugfest in the Garden

Slugs and snails can quickly defoliate a garden. Before you spend money on a box of poisonous slug bait, try a safe do-it-yourself anti-slug campaign. Start by recycling old window screens into individual plant protectors. Cut 8-inch squares, then snip from one edge to the center. At the center point make six cuts. Fold up the sections between the cuts to make a circular opening in the middle of the square. Slip a piece around a plant stem. To increase the protection, remove several lines of wire along the outside edges.

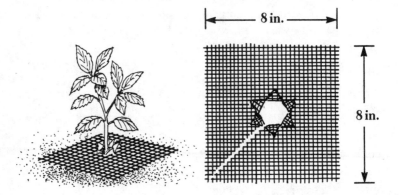

To add to your line of defense, sprinkle a barrier of coarse sand or wood ashes around individual plants, and replenish after every rain. For one-on-one combat, fill a plant mister with half water, half household ammonia. One squirt spells instant death.

Good Help Is Easy to Find

For very little cost and effort on your part, you can encourage nature's own bug patrol to go to work in your backyard. First you need to recognize that birds, frogs, and snakes can help you keep your yard and garden pest-free if you make these hard workers feel welcome. They all need a source of food, water, and a sheltered area they can call home. For more details on how to provide these, see *The Naturalist's Garden* (Rodale Press, 1987).

Good Bugs to Fight the Bad Bugs

You may have read about "beneficial" insects you can purchase for release in the garden. These good bugs then go on to attack the bad bugs. The problem is, often the bugs you buy are gone with the wind—carried away without ever doing any good in *your* garden. Instead of spending money to import good bugs, get naturally occurring predatory insects to stay in your garden by planting the right herbs and flowers.

To lure and keep predatory wasps and flies that attack common garden pests like cabbageworms, grasshoppers, cutworms, aphids, and bean beetles, include some of the following plants in your garden. These flowers and herbs will provide the nectar and pollen the beneficial bugs need:

angelica	Jerusalem artichoke
anise	parsley
black-eyed Susan	parsnip
caraway	Queen Anne's lace
carrot	santolina
coriander	strawflower
daisy	sunflower
dill	yarrow
fennel	

Companion Planting

It seems almost ridiculously simple: How you arrange plants in the garden can help protect them from pests and diseases, and even enhances their growth. And the best part is, it costs you nothing!

For a quick guide to companion plant pairings, see the table "Companions and Allies in Your Garden." For a more in-depth discussion, read *Good Neighbors: Companion Planting for Gardeners* (Rodale Press, 1985).

Don't Buy Weedkillers

Garden pests don't always arrive on wings or furry little feet—they can also invade your garden by runners, shoots, and tenacious tendrils. It is possible to get rid of these uninvited guests—

(continued on page 216)

Companions and Allies
in Your Garden

PLANT	COMPANIONS	ALLIES (AND INSECTS THEY DETER)
Beans	Beets (bush beans only), cabbage family, carrots, celery, chard, corn, cucumbers, eggplants, peas, potatoes, radishes, strawberries	Marigolds (Mexican bean beetles, nematodes), summer savory (bean beetles)
Beets	Bush beans, cabbage family, lettuce, onions	Garlic
Cabbage family	Beans, beets, celery, chard, cucumbers, lettuce, onions, potatoes, spinach	Catnip, chamomile, garlic, hyssop, mint, rosemary, sage and southernwood (cabbage moth); nasturtiums (beetles, aphids); tansy (cabbageworms, cutworms)
Carrots	Beans, lettuce, onions, peas, peppers, radishes, tomatoes	Chives improve growth and flavor; rosemary, sage (carrot flies)
Corn	Beans, cucumbers, melons, parsley, peas, potatoes, pumpkins, squash	Odorless marigolds, white geraniums (Japanese beetles); pigweed raises nutrients from the subsoil to the corn
Cucumbers	Beans, cabbage family, corn, peas, radishes, tomatoes	Marigolds (beetles); nasturtiums (aphids, beetles) improve growth and flavor; oregano (pests in general); tansy (ants, beetles, flying insects)

PLANT	COMPANIONS	ALLIES (AND INSECTS THEY DETER)
Eggplant	Beans, peppers, potatoes	Marigolds (nematodes)
Lettuce	Beets, cabbage family, carrots, onions, radishes, strawberries	Chives, garlic (aphids)
Peas	Beans, carrots, corn, cucumbers, potatoes, radishes, turnips	Chives (aphids); mint improves vigor and flavor
Peppers	Carrots, eggplant, onions, tomatoes	
Potatoes	Beans, cabbage family, corn, eggplant, peas	Horseradish planted at the corners of the potato patch provides general protection; marigolds (beetles)
Pumpkins	Corn, melons, squash	Marigolds, nasturtiums (beetles); oregano provides general pest protection
Radishes	Beans, carrots, cucumbers, lettuce, melons, peas	Chervil and nasturtiums improve growth and flavor
Squash	Celery, corn, melons, pumpkins	Borage (worms), improves growth and flavor; marigolds (beetles); nasturtiums (squash bugs, beetles); oregano provides general pest protection
Strawberries	Beans, lettuce, onions, spinach, thyme	Borage strengthens resistance to insects and disease. Thyme as a border (worms)

(continued)

Companions and Allies in Your Garden—Continued

PLANT	COMPANIONS	ALLIES (AND INSECTS THEY DETER)
Tomatoes	Asparagus, carrots, celery, cucumbers, onions, parsley, peppers	Basil (flies, mosquitoes), improves growth and flavor; bee balm, chives and mint improve health and flavor; dill, until mature, improves growth and vigor; marigolds (nematodes)

NOTE: Companions are plants that have compatible growth habits and share space well; allies are plants that enhance growth and ward off insects.

permanently—without having to buy an arsenal of pricey and potent weedkillers. Below we tell you how to get rid of four nasty pest plants.

Choke Out Wild Jerusalem Artichokes

Wild Jerusalem artichokes aren't called "chokes" for nothing. Give your yard breathing room by smothering the artichoke patch with a layer of black plastic mulch. The artichokes will come up under the plastic, but won't last for long. Eventually, they'll die back completely and no new shoots will emerge.

Cut Back Tree Shoots

Seedling trees can drive you mad by sending up two new shoots for every one you cut off. To end the matter once and for all, cut off the shoot close to the ground. Push a tin can firmly into the ground to cover the stump (a paint can works for larger shoots). After several months under cover, the sprouts should be out of commission for good.

Prune Poison Ivy

The tin can treatment mentioned above for tree shoots works for poison ivy, once you've carefully cut the vines back to the ground. (This is best done in winter when leaves are gone.) The mulch method is another option. Cover the patch with black plastic. Pile on a layer of cardboard or newspaper, and hold that in place with grass clippings or leaves. If you spot new shoots peeking through the mulch or out the sides, cut them off with a shovel blade and pile on more mulch.

Quell Quackgrass

Try the three-prong attack to defeat this plant's invasive rhizomes. First, pull out as much as you can, trying to get at the main clump of roots beneath the leaves. Next, hoe once a week during growing season. Turn up the ground late in fall to expose the rhizomes to freezing temperatures. And last, mulch with at least 6 inches of dense material like leaves, grass, or straw.

Money-Saving Methods

How Much Does Home Preserving Really Save You?

There's no doubt that preserving your own garden harvest gives you a great deal of satisfaction. But are you actually saving any money? And which method of home preservation is the least expensive? Which one costs you the most? The table "The True Cost of Home Food Preservation" can give you some enlightening answers.

Savings by the Square Foot

Are you always faced with a handful of leftover seed packets at the end of the season because you weren't sure how many you

The True Cost of Home Food Preservation

	ENERGY	
METHOD	FUEL	HUMAN EFFORT
Freezing	High	Low
Canning	Moderate	High
Drying	Moderate to high	Moderate
Pickling	Low	Moderate
Storage (not processed)	Low	Moderate (checking/culling)

SOURCE: Prepared by Ruth N. Klippstein of Cornell University.

needed? Do you end up buying or growing more seedlings than you really need? In August, does your garden swamp you with a glut of fresh produce that you have to leave on neighbors' doorsteps under the cover of darkness?

If you answer yes to even one of these questions you are guilty of the sin of wasteful gardening. And wasteful gardening means you're being foolish with your time and money. Return to sanity by practicing square-foot gardening. This method, developed by Mel Bartholomew, allows you to plot out your garden one square foot at a time. You grow just what you need in a very organized and efficient layout. As an extra bonus, your well-tended garden, planted neatly square by square, ends up looking like a million dollars—even though you'll be spending less time and money than when your garden ran amok. With the square-foot method of planting in concentrated spaces, you'll save money on seeds, seedlings, water, fertilizer, and mulch material. For a complete description of this innovative method, see *Square Foot Gardening* (Rodale Press, 1981).

TIME	ON-TABLE DOLLAR COST	QUALITY SATISFACTION
Minimal to low	High	Very high
Moderate	Moderate	Moderate to high
High	Moderate to high	High (special items)
		Low, if only method used
High	Depends on type chosen*	High
Low to moderate	Low	Moderate to high

*Some are quick to make, take little effort, and use inexpensive ingredients. Others such as sweet chunk pickles require prolonged brining over several days plus expensive sugar and other ingredients.

Garden Beds to the Rescue

There's no reason to garden on the flat when you can make the move to raised beds and save time and money and have a more productive garden, to boot.

Raised beds are less expensive to maintain than a ground-level garden that is planted in single rows. You won't need to rotary-till the soil (so there's no tiller to buy or rent), you can concentrate soil amendments and fertilizers exactly where they're needed so you use less (and buy less), and you can easily tend a bedded garden with hand tools instead of more expensive rotary cultivators. To make the switch to garden beds, see *High-Yield Gardening* (Rodale Press, 1986).

Enjoy More Plants for Less Money

Make Your Own

You don't have to be a garden magician to turn one plant into two or three or even more. All it takes is a little plant propagation know-how, which you can easily find in a book like *Plants Plus: A Comprehensive Guide to Successful Propagation of House and Garden Plants* (Rodale Press, 1987). Once you've mastered the basic techniques of dividing, rooting, and layering, you'll be able to get lots of new plants for free. Besides multiplying your own plants, see if friends and neighbors will let you multiply theirs as a way of introducing some exciting new specimens into your yard. Listed in the table "Plant Multiplication" are just a few of the garden and house plants that can be multiplied with little effort.

Plant Multiplication

METHOD	GARDEN PLANTS	HOUSEPLANTS
Dividing	Astilbe, chrysanthemum, coral bells, daylily, iris, phlox, pinks, primrose	African violet, asparagus fern, snake plant, spider plant
Layering	Forsythia, holly, ivy, magnolia, rhododendron	Dieffenbachia, ficus, monstera
Rooting	Forsythia, fuchsia, geranium, ivy, lilac	Begonia, coleus, philodendron, spider plant (babies)

Garden "Swap Meets"

An easy way to get new plants is to organize a swap meet among neighborhood gardeners, where everyone can get together to exchange cuttings, divisions, or extra plants. If you want to go farther afield for your garden trading, subscribe to the newsletter *Gardeners Share* ($15 for six issues, available from P.O. Box 243, Columbus, IN 47202). It's full of money-saving tips on growing all kinds of garden plants, and includes a section where subscribers list and trade seeds, cuttings, and bulbs for free. You'll find just about any kind of plant there, including houseplants, vegetables, annuals, perennials, vines, and wildflowers.

Transplanting Timetable

One of the best sources for free plants is friends and neighbors who are dividing perennials or digging up extra or unwanted bulbs, trees, or shrubs. The question often arises: When is the best time to transplant these to their new home? The timetable below should give you some answers.

PLANT	METHOD
Bulbs	Dig up after flowering when foliage yellows and replant right away; or dry bulbs and store until fall planting time
Berry bushes	Move in early spring before leaves appear or in fall after killing frost has hit and leaves have fallen
Perennials	Most adapt to spring or fall transplanting; in fall, replant at least 8–10 weeks before soil freezes
Trees and shrubs	Early spring transplanting, before new growth appears, is best in places where winters are very cold; early fall is the best time for transplanting in areas where winters are not severe

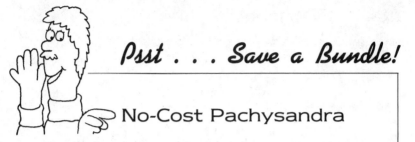

Psst . . . Save a Bundle!

No-Cost Pachysandra

Want a lush bed of pachysandra at absolutely no cost? Find a friend or neighbor with an established bed and ask if you can give the pachysandra a trim. An established bed will burst forth with new growth, and you'll come away with bags full of cuttings to start your own bed—a nice alternative to spending 15 to 20 cents per plant!

The best time to take cuttings is when the new growth snaps crisply. Wet the patch with a hose or wait until after a rain. With a pair of scissors, clip each plant right above the second leaf cluster. Every cutting should contain the top leaf cluster with a good sized length of stem.

The new bed should be dug and raked smooth and freshly watered. Insert each cutting at a 45-degree angle, 3 inches deep. Space plants 4 inches apart and keep constantly moist while plants are rooting.

Cutting Costs in the Flower Garden

Perennials vs. Annuals: Which Are the Best Buy?

It's hard not to notice the difference in price between perennial and annual flowers. You can buy a flat of six annuals for under $2, while a single potted perennial can cost $4 or more. Your first thought might be that the annuals are kindest to your pocketbook, but stop and think about how these plants behave in the garden. The annuals are cheaper initially, but you'll have to spend money to replace them every year. The perennials will cost you more up front, but they'll be around year after year. Plus, most perennials can be divided, so you'll be able to turn one plant into many. For the money-wise gardener, the initial investment in perennials will pay you back in short order.

Fill in the Gaps

If you've got a large flower bed to fill and aren't ready to spend the money it would take to plant it full of perennials, here's a compromise plan that's easier on your wallet. The first year, buy half a dozen perennials, and fill in the empty spaces with masses of inexpensive annuals. The next year, add half a dozen more perennials and fill in with annuals. By the third year you can divide the original perennials, filling in more spaces for free. Buy half a dozen new perennials, and pop annuals into any remaining open spaces. Continue this way, dividing the established perennials, buying a few new ones at a time and using annuals to fill the gaps.

Save with Seeds

If you're willing to grow your own annual and perennial flowers from seed, the savings can be dramatic. For example, geraniums raised from seed cost $.20 per plant, compared to the $2 or more you pay per bedding plant. The savings on perennials is even more impressive. Chrysanthemums from seed can cost as little as $.04 per plant; purchased fully grown, these cost at least several dollars. (But you must be patient—some perennials from seed may take several seasons to bloom.)

Flowers That
Plant Themselves

Some plants have the very endearing trait of popping up season after season from seeds that have scattered from dried flower heads. These eager bloomers include candytuft, California poppy, columbine, cosmos, foxglove, gloriosa daisy, larkspur, stock, and sweet alyssum. To encourage this natural reseeding, let a few flowers dry until they're brown and papery, then sprinkle the seeds over the garden. Come spring, you'll have free flowers!

Winter Guests

Take cuttings of your favorite summer annuals, tend them over the winter, then set them out again in the spring for a whole new round of flowers. Good overwinterers include: coleus, fibrous begonia, fuchsia, geranium, impatiens, and scented geranium.

Bulbs Galore

Double your bulb display without spending a cent by "harvesting" the offsets or tiny corms that grow from the parents. Every few years after the foliage dies back, dig up crocuses, daffodils, and tulips; remove the new growths, and replant. Pull the little corms off gladiolus in the fall, store them over the winter, then plant the following spring.

Best Buys for the Garden

Follow the Sales

Savvy shoppers know that the best buys appear at certain times of the year like January "white sales" and year-end car clearances. There are similar savings waiting for gardeners who pay attention to the calendar. March is an economical time to buy bare-root roses; by June annual plants have been marked down; spring-flowering bulbs go on sale in July; September offers a bonanza in roses, perennials, and spring-blooming bulbs; and October shopping usually brings savings on fruit trees, shade trees, and shrubs.

Annual Savings

When bargain hunting for annuals—both vegetables and flowers—look for short, bushy, well-branched, green plants. Avoid any that look "stretched out" and are dropping lower leaves. Pick the most vigorous-looking specimens; these will weather the rigors of transplanting the best.

The Best Bulbs

Be on the lookout for large, heavy, smooth, firm bulbs. Reject any that have moldy patches and any that are shriveled or soft. Avoid bulbs that have already sprouted.

A Perfect Rose

A healthy rose bush has a round, well-developed root system. Watch out for black or shriveled canes. Leaves should be green and lush, not yellow and dropping from the plant.

Choosing Trees and Shrubs

Look for bright white root tips. Pass by any plants with masses of roots growing out of the container or with roots circling the root ball. Avoid plants with girdling at the base of the trunk. A smaller plant will often recover from transplanting better than a larger one.

Low-Maintenance Plants

One way to reduce the money and time you spend on the plants in your yard is to look for varieties with built-in low-maintenance characteristics. The first thing to watch for is disease resistance. More vegetable and flower varieties appear every year with resistance and tolerance to certain diseases, and sometimes even to certain pests. You won't have to spend a lot of money on powders and sprays to keep these plants healthy. Another useful characteristic is a bushy or compact variety of a normally tall and lanky plant. You won't need to go to great lengths to provide staking and supports. Yet another money-saving trait is tolerance of dry soil; plants that don't need a lot of visits from the garden hose will help you save on your water bill.

Seeds and Seedlings

When It Makes Cents to Start Seeds

Most gardeners assume they're saving lots of money when they start flower and vegetable seeds at home instead of buying plants from the garden center. The rule of thumb is the more plants you need, the more you'll save by starting your own.

Homegrown Seeds for the Garden

Every year the price of a packet of vegetable or flower seeds seems to inch upward. Sidestep this creeping inflation by saving seeds from the plants you grow to start next year's garden. To learn more about home seed saving, consult the excellent guide, *Growing Garden Seeds,* available from Johnny's Selected Seeds, Foss Hill Road, Albion, ME 04910.

Thrifty Seed Starting

You can enhance your savings by being a thrifty seed starter. Mix your own seed-starting soil instead of buying it. (See "Make Your Own Potting Soil" on page 199 and "Homemade Soil Mixes" on page 200.) Be creative in recycling containers for seedlings (see "Cut-Rate Seedling Containers" below) instead of buying pricey peat pellets and other commercial planting trays. Make your own ID labels from wooden Popsicle sticks or strips cut from plastic gallon jugs. Don't succumb to all the seed-starting gimmicks you see advertised in catalogs and magazines. Plants grow just fine from a very humble start in life!

Cut-Rate Seedling Containers

Your kitchen is a great source of recycled seed-starting containers. Line plastic berry baskets with a two-sheet layer of newspaper;

this works especially well for finicky transplanters like squash and cucumbers—just plant the basket along with the seedlings. Cut the tops off plastic milk jugs, leaving 4-inch sides, and punch drainage holes along the bottom. Save grapefruit and orange halves to use as biodegradable containers. Scoop out the pulp before filling and planting. When you're ready to transplant, set the seedling, citrus container and all, into the ground.

Milk Carton Seed Flats

Cardboard milk cartons can be transformed into sturdy seed flats. Staple the mouth shut and lay the carton on its side. Make a lengthwise slit down the center of the side facing up, then cut from corner to corner along the bottom. Bend down the flaps made by the cuts, and staple them to the inside of the carton to reinforce the sides.

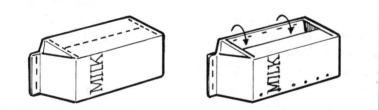

Affordable Seedling Lights

Commercial light units for seedlings can cost as much as $85! There's no need to spend that kind of money when a little ingenuity and some inexpensive materials can illuminate your seedlings for a fraction of the cost.

Attach a fluorescent light fixture to a piece of wood at least 8 inches longer than the light. To support the light, make two stacks of bricks, one for each end of the wood. To raise or lower the light all you do is add or remove bricks to the supporting stacks. Because this light unit is so inexpensive and easy to assemble, you can afford to make several, so you'll always have enough room under lights for all your seedlings.

Bright Lights, Big Savings

You don't need to buy a special (and expensive) grow light for your vegetable and flower seedlings. Regular fluorescent lights are just as effective, cost less, and last longer than fancy grow lights. If you combine one cool white with one warm white fluorescent tube in a standard shop fixture, your plants will thrive.

The Fruit of the Land

Self-Pollinating Fruit

The nice thing about self-fertile fruit trees is that you can buy just *one* plant and it will bear well without a pollen-producing partner. If you're short on funds or space for the home orchard, pick one of the fruit trees listed below. (All berries, with the exception of blueberries, will self-pollinate.)

- Apricots. Most are self-fertile.
- Cherries. All sour cherries are self-fertile; sweet cherries need partners.
- Peaches. Most are self-fertile except for J. H. Hale and June Elberta.
- Plums. European varieties are self-fertile.

Multipurpose Apples

When you're shopping for apple trees, it's smart to buy varieties that are suited for many different uses. For example, Jonathan, Mutsu, Red Stayman, and Winesap apples are equally good when used fresh or in baking, cooking, sauce, or cider; and they store well. Instead of buying a number of different varieties that have limited uses, you can buy fewer of these multipurpose trees and still enjoy the harvest in all its delicious forms.

Bring 'Em Back Alive and Bearing

Before you give up on that old fruitless apple tree, those tangled bushes that don't give you any blueberries, or the jumbled thicket of brambles that's more of an eyesore than a berry producer, try some rejuvenation therapy. A little TLC and some pruning cuts in just the right places can bring fruit back to those branches and save you the cost of new plants. For more guidance on how to prune and care for plants to encourage fruiting, see *Backyard Fruits and Berries* (Rodale Press, 1984).

Tools and Equipment

Tooling Up

The guiding rule in garden tools is that you get what you pay for. If you buy a $4.99 trowel, you'll be lucky to finish the season with it intact. If you purchase a top-of-the-line trowel for $10.00 and take care of it, chances are very good you'll never have to buy another. Garden tools are truly a case where your initial investment in quality pays you back season after season. To help guide your tool purchases, here are some signs of quality:

■ Forged metal blades with solid shank construction—these are sturdier and will last longer than stamped metal blades.
■ A long metal joint between handle shaft and head, to provide the strongest attachment.
■ Grain on a wooden handle that runs straight from the head to the opposite end.

Get a Good Grip

When buying garden tools, stay away form those with painted handles and heads, because the paint will wear off. Avoid most plastic handles; these have a tendency to break. One of the few plastics that has shown reliable durability is True Temper

Super-D. Be sure to test the grip; most gardeners find D-shaped handles are the most comfortable and are the least likely to cause blisters.

Making Tools Last

Once you've invested in quality hand tools, you should treat them well so they'll give you a lifetime of good work. The people at Smith & Hawken recommend sanding the varnish off wooden handles, then rubbing linseed oil into them. Keeping tools indoors, cleaning them after each use, and oiling the metal after cleaning will ensure many seasons in the garden. (Don't use engine oil because this will pit the metal.) If rust should ever appear, remove it with steel wool. Set up a regular schedule to sharpen blades on hoes, spades, trowels, and shears with a flat file.

First Aid for Garden Tools

Bad breaks can happen to any garden tool, but that doesn't always mean you have to go out and buy a replacement. Here's a tip to help fix a handle that has snapped in two. Use epoxy to join the handle pieces, holding them in place with C-clamps. Using heavy, fishing-line quality nylon thread, wrap the break, spacing the thread spirals $\frac{1}{8}$ inch apart (remove the clamps while wrapping, then replace them). Once the adhesive hardens, take off the clamps and wrap the whole joint with friction tape.

Finding the Best Pruners

Why waste your money on pruning equipment that's uncomfortable to use or won't last more than a season or two? Spend your money right the first time and you'll never have to spend it again. Rodale's Product Testing Department has come up with the following pointers to help you with your pruner purchases:

■ The thinner the blade on hand shears, the easier the tool will cut. Teflon coating inflates the price and doesn't stand up in the garden. Look for smooth blades held together with a screw and nut. Forged steel blades or blades made of a different material than the handle are the signs of quality.

■ Lopping shears with handles shorter than 25 to 30 inches won't provide enough leverage. Rough-looking blades and other signs of

poor workmanship mean you'll probably be back in the store buying a new pair in a couple seasons.
■ The best pruning saws have bevel-filed teeth. Cheap saws often
have blades stamped out of metal with teeth that are never sharp-
ened. You can tell these by the slight lip around the edge of the
teeth. Pull-cut saws are easiest to use for pruning; these have
teeth angling back toward the handle.

No-Cost Plant Supports

Six-Pack Trellis

Collect the plastic holders that come with beverage six-packs.
Connect these plastic panels with twist ties until you have enough
surface to support your vining plants. Attach this to the side of the
garage, house, or wherever there are vines to support.

Closet Stakes

Raid the coat closet for extra metal hangers. Using pliers, untwist
the wire and straighten out the bends (leave the hook alone).
Three inches from the top of the hook, bend the wire at a right
angle. Push the straight end of the wire into the ground and use
the hook to loop around the heavy heads of flowers like irises, lil-
ies, and peonies.

Sunflower Tepee

Once the sunflower harvest is over, remove all the leaves, and let
the stalks dry in place for a week or two. Cut them off at the
ground, and stand them in a protected spot for the winter (don't
lay them down or they'll get too wet under the cover of snow).
When spring returns, lash them together with twine to form pea
and bean tepees.

Pea Tree

Instead of discarding the Christmas tree, save it to use as a pea trellis. By spring most of the needles will have fallen off. Drive a stake one foot into the ground, and tie the Christmas tree skeleton to the stake for support. Plant vining peas in a circle around the bottom branches. In time, the vines will climb through the branches and blanket the tree in new greenery.

Economical Equipment

Hot Bargains in Cold Frames

A brand-new cold frame ordered through a catalog can set you back $100. But why spend all that money when you can make one of these season extenders from recycled materials? There's no hard and fast rule about how a cold frame should look. There are just two basic requirements: The sloping top should face south, and there should be good drainage inside.

For the frame, use concrete blocks, spare pieces of $\frac{1}{2}$-inch exterior grade plywood or other scrap wood, or even bales of spoiled hay. For the top, use old storm windows, discarded window sashes, fiberglass panels (avoid the colored kind), or 4- to 6-mil polyethylene.

Hotbed That Heats Itself

Some gardeners may appreciate extra heat inside a cold frame to keep plants going through cold winter days and nights. Electric heating cables are available to hang inside frames, but if you have access to fresh manure, you don't need to plug in to provide the heat.

Dig a 2-foot-deep hole inside the frame. Add enough fresh manure to make an 18-inch layer. Top this off with 6 inches of soil. Once the soil temperature has settled at around 75°F, you can plant. The warmth generated by the decomposing manure should last for about six to eight weeks, during which time you won't have to pay a single cent in heating bills!

Basement Cold Frame

A very resourceful gardener designed a cold frame that attaches to the outside of his basement window. This gives him easy access to the plants and allows him to vent warm air from the house into the frame on very cold days. He framed the basement window with 2 × 4s fastened with concrete nails. Next he made the cold frame base from 20-inch-high panels of discarded window sash. Triangular pieces of plywood were attached to the long sides of the base to make it slope from 32 inches at the back to 20 inches in the front. The whole base was nailed to the 2 × 4 frame on the window, and seams were caulked. The top (a piece of window sash) was attached to the 2 × 4 frame with hinges, and then foam insulation was added all around to keep the cold air from leaking in.

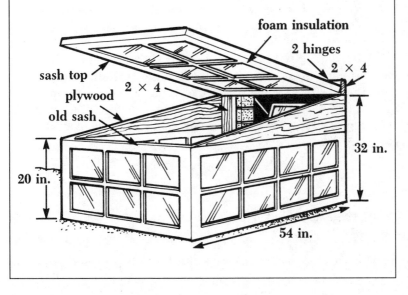

Build Your Own Tunnels

It's easy to extend the growing season on both ends by making some simple, inexpensive tunnels or row covers for the vegetable garden. Kits are sold in garden supply catalogs, but there's no need to pay top dollar when you can make your own for much less.

Here are three different options for making the frame: Use spare pieces of wire mesh (with openings no larger than 2 to 4 inches), wire coat hangers, or forsythia or willow branches. Bend the wire mesh into a semicircle and anchor it to the ground with stakes. Bend coat hangers into U or square shapes, and push the ends into the soil, spacing them every 2 feet along the row. If you use branches, bend them into semicircles, and push the ends 4 inches into the soil, spacing them $2\frac{1}{2}$ feet apart. (To stabilize you may need to lash 1 × 2s to the ends of the semicircles to join them together.)

For the covering, use inexpensive 4-mil polyethylene (4 feet is a convenient width). Stretch the plastic over the frame and hold the ends in place with soil, rocks, or "hairpins" made from bent wire coat hangers.

Old window sashes or screen doors sitting around gathering dust can also be converted readily into tunnels. Hinge a pair of same-size sashes or doors together along the long side to make a row-covering tent. Drape the screening with plastic, and prop scrap pieces of wood against the ends to keep out the cold.

Hot Water Bottles for the Garden

Several years ago clear plastic water-filled rings that protect plants made a big splash in the garden market. These rings absorb heat from the sun during the day and keep plants warm at night, shielding them from frost and speeding their growth. You can take advantage of this same principle without having to purchase any fancy devices. Simply fill plastic gallon jugs, inner tubes, or clear plastic bags with water and position them around the plants you wish to protect.

Cloche Encounters

When you've spent time and effort, not to mention money, planting the spring garden, the last thing you want to do is lose your plants to a sudden frost. Individual plant protectors, called cloches, are quick and easy to make from materials you already have on hand. Try some of these suggestions:

- Scour the kitchen for plastic gallon jugs, coffee cans, 2-liter soft drink bottles, and milk cartons. Remove the bottoms from all of these, and keep the tops open for ventilation.
- Cover tiny seedlings with clear plastic party glasses (poke holes for ventilation).
- Protect taller plants by creating a tepee out of stakes or branches and then draping a plastic drycleaning bag over the structure. Or, set four stakes in a square around a plant and slip a large paper bag over the top.
- Keep medium-size plants cozy under wooden bushel baskets with a few slats removed; a plastic bag over the top adds extra protection.
- If you don't mind what the neighbors think, take the handle off an old, clear plastic, dome-type umbrella and position it over your prized plant (use the pole as an anchor).
- If you have young children, put their energy to use by having them create little plant hats or cones fashioned out of newspaper.

Saving Money Drop by Drop

Drip irrigation brings big savings to the garden; it can reduce water usage by 50 percent. Drip irrigation systems initially cost more to set up than conventional watering systems like sprinklers, but in the long run you will save money.

In its most basic form, a drip system contains a network of hoses and emitters that deliver a slow trickle of water to precise spots throughout the garden. Very simple kits for home gardens start as low as $15 and are available through garden centers, seed catalogs, and drip equipment suppliers like: Urban Farmer Store, 2121 Taraval Street, San Francisco, CA 94116.

For a more extensive, ambitious drip system, you can call upon your local extension agent, irrigation store, or drip system manufacturer to help you design the most efficient layout for your yard and gardens.

Make-Your-Own Drip System

Before you spend money on a commercial drip irrigation system, try making your own. Scour auctions, flea markets, and garage sales for great buys on ⅜-inch garden hose (buy enough feet of hose to reach all the plants to be watered). A trip to the hardware store for end caps and three-way connectors gives you all you need for the system. Use one length of hose to connect the system to the faucet. Using the three-way connectors, lay out the other hoses to reach all the thirsty plants. Once the hoses are in place, use a nail or ice pick to poke a hole all the way through the hose in every spot where you want water to emerge. To create the slow, steady trickle effect, tie 1 × 6-inch strips of old rags around the holes. Before you turn on the water, put the hose end caps in place.

Low-Tech Drip Systems

An even more inexpensive way to enjoy the benefits of drip irrigation is to place containers of water around individual plants and let the water trickle out slowly into the root zone. Unglazed clay pots, with their drainage holes plugged, can be sunk in the garden up to their rims. Water will pass through the porous clay into the surrounding soil. Tin cans with holes poked around the bottom and sunk into the soil will release water slowly and steadily. Plastic gallon milk jugs with holes along the bottom edge can be set next to plants to provide aboveground trickles of water. Whenever you want to give your plants a drink, just fill the containers with water.

Knee Savers

Knees can take a beating in the garden. Be kind to your joints by filling an old hot water bottle with sand or sawdust to make a cushiony kneeling pad. Or, take an old pair of jeans and sew patches over the knees, leaving the top edge open. Before you go out into the garden, stuff the patches with pieces of foam rubber cut to fit. To make a portable kneeler, stuff a 3-inch stack of newspapers inside an old pillowcase or a plastic bag.

Portable Seat

Stooping over to weed can take its toll on your back. Keep aches and pains away by making a handy seat that can travel around the garden with you. It's easy; just take an old gallon paint can, and nail a small piece of wood across one end.

Easy Picking

Fruit trees don't always offer their harvest within easy arm's reach. To pull the branches down to your level, fashion this device. Screw a large utility hook (the kind used to hang bicycles) into the end of a long wooden pole. Another handy device helps you pick fruit. It's made from a plastic 2-liter soda bottle. Cut a hole in the side near the bottom of the bottle large enough to accommodate an apple. On the edge of the hole closest to the bottom, use scissors to cut a V shape. Insert a long pole into the neck of the bottle, and hold it in place with a screw. The point of the V will fit around the stem of the fruit, and a downward tug will drop the fruit into the bottle.

Thrifty Landscaping and Lawn Care

Low Maintenance Means Low Cost

If you can plan and plant your landscape so that you need fewer tools, less fertilizer, and less water, you'll see a corresponding drop in the amount of money you need to spend to keep your yard looking great. Listed here are eight suggestions for a low-maintenance, low-cost landscape:

- Replace labor- and money-intensive lawns with alternatives like interesting brick paving, decks, wildflowers, or groundcovers. If you must have a patch of green, keep it small.
- Seek out disease-resistant or disease-tolerant varieties of trees and flowers.
- Create perennial flower beds to avoid the yearly chore of re-planting.
- Pick "neat" trees and shrubs that you won't have to constantly clean up after. Avoid messy ones, such as mulberry and sweet gum, that drop berries and pods.
- Choose plants native to your area so there's no need to coddle them through winter cold and summer heat.
- Look for slow-growing trees and shrubs; these will require minimal pruning.
- Mulch all the flower beds or use creeping plants as a living mulch.
- Consider using evergreens wherever you can in place of deciduous trees; in the fall there will be no leaves to rake.

Be Your Own Landscaper

It's been estimated that designing and planting your own landscape can save you half of what it would cost to have a professional do it. Of course, this represents a lot of work. But if you spread the work over time and have family members and friends who are willing to pitch in, the undertaking goes from overwhelming to manageable.

First, bone up on landscape design. Local YMCAs and garden centers often offer classes for homeowners. Look through magazines for yards you like. Read a good landscape design book like *The New American Landscape Gardener* (Rodale Press, 1987). Drive around town and note any landscape effects you particularly enjoy. Put *everything* on paper before you buy a single plant or dig a single hole.

You'll save the most money by doing the physical labor yourself. Professionals usually charge a planting fee for everything they stick in the ground. For jobs that are simple but too big to handle alone, hire college or high-school kids. For the really big or complicated jobs, you might find it worth the money to call in the professional landscape contractor, who has the right equipment and know-how.

Double-Duty Landscapes

Nowadays there's a blurring of the lines between the landscape and the vegetable garden and orchard. Edibles that were once relegated to the backyard are being recognized for their beauty and are showing up in prominent spots in ornamental beds and elsewhere throughout the landscape.

This new way of looking at the landscape can save you money. When you incorporate attractive edibles into your yard, you're gaining double benefits for the price of each plant. Instead of buying one kind of tree to give you fruit and another kind to shade the front yard, buy a single tree, such as a peach or cherry, that does both. Instead of erecting a fence or planting a prickly hedge, plant a handsome row of blueberry bushes to mark the boundary of your property year-round, and enjoy the basketfuls of sweet berries in summer.

Landscape Insurance

What do you do when an evergreen mysteriously disappears from your yard one December? Or an automobile sideswipes your well-established rose bed and gouges big ruts in the lawn? Or lightening strikes and damages a giant shade tree? Is your first thought to call your insurance agent? Well, maybe it should be, because most basic homeowners' insurance policies extend outdoors to provide coverage for trees, shrubs, plants, and even the lawn! Filing a claim can cover your out-of-pocket cost of buying a replacement.

You'll want to check your own particular policy for the details, but in general, damage by ice, snow, and wind are *not* covered. Besides the catastrophes mentioned above, damage by fire, explosions, aircraft, vandalism, riots, or civil commotion *are* covered. There will most likely be a dollar limit on the price your insurance will pay per damaged plant.

Psst . . . Save a Bundle!

Free Trees

It's possible to save hundreds of dollars on your landscape by avoiding the local nursery and looking instead for *free* sources of trees and shrubs.

Comb the wooded areas of your yard or that of a friend for small seedling trees to transplant (early spring before leaves appear is the best time). Healthy-looking trees that are not crowded in with others make the best transplants. Dig an ample rootball, replant as soon as possible, and prune lightly. Keep the tree well watered and mulched in its new home.

In early spring take a cutting of a desirable evergreen. Place the cutting in a plastic bag or shoe box filled with equal portions of peat moss and sand. Moisten thoroughly, then close the bag or box. When set in filtered light and kept moist (but not soggy), roots should begin to sprout in a couple weeks. Once they appear, repot the cutting in a richer soil mix and tend it until it reaches transplant size.

For the adventuresome gardener, there is always the option of gathering tree and shrub seeds and starting from scratch. This takes equal measures of skill, patience, and luck, but you can reap a great measure of satisfaction *and* savings from this sort of seed starting. For more on this technique, see *The New Seed-Starters Handbook* by Nancy Bubel (Rodale Press, 1988).

Nursery Savings

Smart shoppers can shave some money off their bill for landscape plants at the nursery by remembering these two rules of thumb.

First, bare-rooted plants cost less than those that are container grown. There shouldn't be any difference in quality, but there is a difference in planting times. Bare-rooted plants must go in the ground while still dormant; container plants can go in during the summer.

Second, size affects price. The younger (and smaller) the plant, the lower the price tag. By choosing smaller trees, shrubs, and other ornamentals for the yard, your patience will be rewarded by noticeable savings.

Don't Waste Your Money on These Trees

Grounds Maintenance magazine compiled a listing of the worst landscape trees for various regions of the country. (See the table "Trees to Avoid" for a listing of these trees.) They all have nasty habits that will soon make you regret you planted them, and may end up costing you more money as you try to get rid of them. The best money-saving advice is not to plant any of these in the first place!

Trees to Avoid	
REGION	TREES (REASON TO AVOID)
Northeast	Horse chestnut (fruit litter), mulberry (fruit litter), sweet gum (fruit litter), willow (roots clog sewers and drains)
Southeast	Box elder (female trees are messy), mimosa (messy), sunburst thornless honeylocust (messy)
Midwest	Poplar (susceptible to eight different pests and diseases), willow (roots clog sewers and drains)
Plains	Plains cottonwood (seeds clog air conditioners and gutters, aggravate allergies; roots are invasive), Lombardy poplar (short-lived, invasive roots), quaking aspen (susceptible to many diseases and insects)

Spend Less
on Construction Materials
for the Yard

When you're shopping for materials to create a garden path or build an arbor or raised beds, there are a few ways to cut costs. The most inexpensive surface materials are gravel, wood chips, and beach stone. Used bricks are another money-saving option that adds an instant touch of class; if you're lucky you can find these for a few pennies apiece through ads in the paper or visits to demolition sites. If you're purchasing new brick, building grade is less expensive than paving brick and is well suited to landscape uses. When shopping for lumber, construction-grade unsurfaced wood is a low-cost choice.

Sidewalk Savings

When you're adding a pathway or sidewalk to the yard, keep in mind that a straight line is the shortest route between two points and will require less material to complete. A cheap and attractive alternative to concrete is a pathway of used bricks set in sand. One resourceful do-it-yourself landscaper recycled an oak tree trunk into a sidewalk that cost her only $5. She obtained the large tree trunk from a builder who had dug it up from a housing site. She cut the trunk into 8-inch slices, weatherproofed these slices, then laid them on the ground to form a pathway. She was able to get a pickup truck full of wood chips for $5 from a local sawmill, which she spread between the oak slabs to keep down weeds.

The Lawn vs. Groundcover
Debate

Over the years, gardeners have stopped at nothing to plant and maintain the Great American Lawn. But now money- and time-conscious gardeners are questioning whether that expanse of fertilized, watered, weeded, mowed, and manicured green is worth it all.

If you're debating whether to go with lawn or groundcover, here's the money-saving point of view. Planting grass seed costs you less up front, but ongoing maintenance of the lawn will be expensive. Covering an area with groundcover will be more expensive initially, but once it's established, you'll probably never need to spend another penny on it.

Significant Savings
on Groundcovers

To help defray the cost of planting a large area of the yard with groundcover, take the do-it-yourself approach, and propagate it from purchased seeds or cuttings or layerings taken from a friend's garden. The groundcovers listed in the table "Propagating Groundcovers" are all excellent lawn substitutes.

Propagating Groundcovers

GROUNDCOVER	HOW TO PROPAGATE
Chamomile	From seed
Common speedwell	Divide
English ivy	Layer
Lily-of-the-valley	Divide
Pachysandra	Cutting
Vinca or creeping myrtle	Divide

Getting the Best Buy
on Grass Seed

If you are and always will be a devotee of green grass, then there are things you can do to cut your costs, starting with the grass seed you select. *Consumer's Research* magazine advises steering away from seed mixes with high percentages of ryegrass or other coarse, annual seeds. These annual grasses die back in the fall, and if you're interested in establishing a good quality, long-lasting lawn, why pay for grass seed that won't give you the lawn you desire?

By simply comparing prices, you may be swayed by the low cost per pound for large bags of mixes with lots of coarse-seeded annual ryegrass. But cost per pound isn't a fair measure. You're better off buying a 1-pound bag of a more expensive, smaller-seeded perennial grass because that will sow a larger area with a permanent, better-quality lawn than the "bargain" 5-pound mix containing coarser ryegrass.

Good Mowing Habits
Save Money

Lawn abuse isn't a crime, but it *is* a waste of money. When you mistreat your lawn you pay dearly for it by having to reseed dead patches, buy sprays and powders to fight weeds, pests, and diseases, and spend even more money on watering than you normally would. To make sure you're not paying the penalty for bad lawn care, follow these rules of good mowing:

- Don't let the grass get too tall between mowings. Infrequent mowings are a shock to the lawn and open invitations to weed invasions. Plus, you have to water more than usual to help the yellowed stubble recover.
- Never remove more than half the height of the lawn in a single mowing. If summer vacation leaves you faced with a junglelike thicket, adjust the mower to cut only half the height of the grass blades. Wait a few days, then cut again to the desired height (this also saves wear and tear on your mower).
- Keep lawn mower blades sharp; check them periodically throughout the mowing season.
- Mow cool-season grasses slightly taller during summer heat waves. This keeps the lawn healthier and reduces the need for watering.

Mow at the Right Height

	COOL WEATHER MOWING HEIGHT (INCHES)	SUMMER HEAT STRESS MOWING HEIGHT (INCHES)
Bluegrass	2	3
Tall fescue	$2\frac{1}{2}$	$3\frac{1}{2}$
Turf-type tall fescue	2	3
Ryegrass	2	$2\frac{1}{2}$–3
Bermudagrass	1–$1\frac{1}{2}$	1–$1\frac{1}{2}$
Buffalograss	2	2
Zoysia	1–$1\frac{1}{2}$	1–$1\frac{1}{2}$

SOURCE: Kansas State University Cooperative Extension Service.

Low-Maintenance Grasses

The good news is that you don't have to look very hard to find low-maintenance grass varieties. All of the named varieties released on the market in the past ten years have wonderful characteristics, such as resistance to diseases and insects, lower fertilizer and water needs, and tolerance of poor growing conditions bred right into them. The bad news is that most gardeners don't know this and keep pumping massive amounts of fertilizer, water, and pest and disease controls into their lawns. The Lawn Institute has some very simple, money-saving advice: Cut out the expensive TLC and let the grass take care of itself. The money you save by watering and feeding the lawn less can go toward some new plants for the garden!

Among the four main groups of grasses, here's how they rank from lowest maintenance needs to highest: tall fescue, fine fescue, Kentucky bluegrass, perennial ryegrass. To find out the names of the newest and best grass varieties for each of these groups, send a self-addressed stamped envelope to: The Lawn Institute, P.O. Box 108, Pleasant Hill, TN 38578.

Five Steps to a Money-Saving, Weed-Free Lawn

A weed-free lawn is every homeowner's dream. You can be the envy of everyone on the block and save money on weed killers at the same time by establishing a thick stand of grass that repels weed invasions. Follow these five steps for a weed-free lawn:

1. Select the right type of grass for your growing conditions. If your lawn area is partially shaded, make sure you get a seed mix blended for low light levels.
2. Once you've got the right kind of grass in place, encourage nice lush growth with timely fertilizing. A thick mat of grass denies weeds the light and space they need to gain a foothold.
3. Take the necessary steps to control insect damage and disease. A healthy lawn is better able to defend itself against weed attack.
4. Take it easy on the watering. A lawn that gets *too much* water is ripe for weed problems.
5. Don't clip the grass too short. (See "Good Mowing Habits Save Money" on the previous page.)

CUTTING COSTS
ON KIDS

You wouldn't trade your children for anything in the world. But children are as expensive as they are priceless. You'll spend $111,548 to raise a child from birth to age 18, according to the U.S. Department of Agriculture. Is it worth it? Of course! A baby is the most rewarding investment anyone can make. Still, $100,000-plus is an unnerving thought. Before you begin to sweat and tremble, take heart. You *can* save money in child rearing. In this chapter, we'll help you cut corners in buying food, clothing, and equipment, and in seeking medical and child care.

Children as Chowhounds

Nature's Formula for Savings

Sometimes, Mother Nature knows best. Breast-feeding a baby will not only save money but also give you a special, loving time with a child who will grow up all too fast.

But let's talk practical: the savings. If you breast-feed a new-born instead of offering ready-to-serve liquid formula, you'll save several dollars a day. Infants can put away up to 32 ounces daily, which translates to nearly $120 a month in formula. Concentrated formula that you mix with water costs less, but the monthly bill still may come to more than $50.

Super Snack Savings

When your child acquires more sophisticated tastes—we're talking yogurt here—you still need to shop smart. Individually packaged snacks are real budget busters. There's no loss of convenience in doling out a portion of yogurt, pudding, or fruit slush from a family-size container.

The same goes for sliced cheese. Separately wrapped servings cost twice as much per pound as cheese from the deli. Ditto for microwavable popcorn packages versus the bags of loose kernels you pop in a pan on the stove or in a popper. If you have a snack-hungry youngster, buy in bulk and save.

Psst . . . Save a Bundle!

Homemade Baby Food

When the family's newest member is ready for solid food, it can really pay to be a smart shopper. Take a hard look at jars of processed baby food. You'll pay a dollar or more—per pound—for such lowly things as peas and carrots. A 2.5-ounce jar of baby applesauce costs a quarter; it's no different from store-brand applesauce that costs 50 cents for a jar ten times that size. The story on meats is even worse! So do your food budget a favor—skip the baby food aisle and process your own concoctions.

Use a blender, food processor, or baby-food mill to puree or mince meals according to the baby's needs. Feed whatever's on the menu that night, or prepare several servings ahead of time. Freeze extras in ice cube trays, then pop the frozen cubes into plastic bags. Reheat as needed.

A handy and inexpensive guide that gives pointers on home baby-food preparation, as well as fast and easy recipes is *The Complete New Guide to Preparing Baby Foods* by Sue Castle (Bantam Books, 1983).

Bargain Baby Gear

Car Seats:
Safety with Real Savings

Car seats are not cheap. And safety is certainly not something you want to skimp on. But there are a couple ways to save some money on buckling up your baby without shortchanging safety.

There are two distinct stages in a child's safety-seat life: infancy (up to 20 pounds) and toddlerhood (20 to 40 pounds). Over 40 pounds, a child is considered ready for seat belts. Manufacturers sell car seats for infants, seats for toddlers, and convertible seats that can accommodate both. Buying one safety seat that suits your child as both infant and toddler cuts your purchases in half. (Be sure you read the directions carefully and position the seat correctly for your child's weight.)

Another way to sidestep buying both an infant's *and* a toddler's car seat is to lease an infant seat. Hospitals, parenting organizations, or automobile clubs often offer these seats for rent. You'll have to put down a refundable deposit, and maybe pay $1 a month for the lease, but these costs are certainly less than the price of a new infant seat.

Baby Needs New Clothes

Who says they need to be new? If there's one thing children do with predictability, it's outgrow their clothes. You can save big by buying everything from newborn undershirts to size 6 overalls secondhand at garage sales, thrift shops, or consignment stores.

Begin shopping before baby comes home from the hospital. Newborns are especially easy on clothes, which makes it simple to find unstained, almost-good-as-new outfits. Look for bargains in very slightly used layettes, bibs, and one-piece shirts. There's just one thing you won't find in a secondhand shop, and that's disposable diapers. Those you'll have to buy new!

Secondhand play clothes—those that take wear and tear—are great bargains. Keep your eyes open for jeans, sweaters, T-shirts, and other hard-knocking clothes.

If you have a lot of children, or if you're shopping with friends' youngsters in mind, keep a list of sizes in your purse. It's hard to memorize these ever-changing dimensions.

Don't be bashful about frequenting children's clothing consignment shops. These are surprisingly classy affairs. Owners only accept clean, pressed, in-style clothes in need of no repair, which are then racked according to size and sex. These days, as families tend to be smaller, there may be no one in the upcoming ranks to hand down clothes to. So you'll be getting good stuff, not threadbare rags. Good buys at such shops are snowsuits, dress coats, and other big-ticket items that don't get much wear before they're outgrown.

Baby Needs New Digs

The same advice for clothes shopping applies to outfitting baby's room: Shop secondhand for terrific bargains. Spend a few weekends making the rounds of garage sales and used furniture shops for such things as cribs, playpens, strollers, rompers, high chairs, changing tables, and carriages. There are still other things to keep in mind as you search for good buys on infant furnishings.

Buy unfinished furniture. Paint, stain, and decorate with decals to suit your nursery decor. Resist the temptation to buy a deluxe suite of matching dressers. Time enough for that when the child is a teenager and old enough to appreciate fine furniture.

That first year can be a cruncher. You'll need more equipment for a baby than at any other time of his or her life. If possible to do so tactfully, urge friends to go together on big-ticket items for the baby shower. Or borrow things like bassinets, which are only used for a short time.

Compare models not only for price but also for such things as ease of assembly. Babies travel with an incredible amount of luggage, so be sure his or her accessories are simple to dismantle for the car.

Don't try to pinch pennies on essentials like safety gates, however. Buy top-quality products when your child's well-being is at stake.

Buy for the Future

When buying children's clothes or other necessities, keep an eye to the future. As your kids grow, so will their needs. If you come across a bargain—be it a tricycle or overalls—buy it. Even if Junior's still in diapers, a good deal won't be any cheaper in years to come. Choose clothing in several sizes and colors when you see articles you know you'll need later. If you think the price is too good to pass up, it probably is.

Taking the Sting out of Medical Care

Shots for Free

Free shots still hurt but at least they're free. Many county health departments offer free immunizations for children. Shots include vaccines for diphtheria, pertussis, tetanus, measles, mumps, rubella, polio, and hemophilus influenza type b diseases. Many of these immunizations are required before children start school. The health department will give you cards to keep track of who got what when. The free clinics usually are for children ages 2 months to 18 years. Although the clinics are walk-in, parents are urged to call before coming to avoid waiting in line.

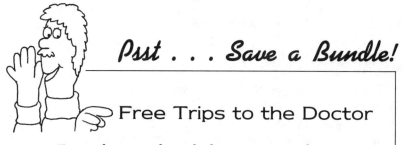

Psst . . . Save a Bundle!

Free Trips to the Doctor

Free or low-cost physicals, hearing tests, and eye exams are available for children whose families meet financial eligibility criteria set by the government. You need not be on public assistance. There's a sliding scale of fees for lower- and middle-class families. Contact your county's health department for information on eligibility and appointments. (You'll find the health department's number in the blue pages of the phone book.)

Who's Minding the Kids?

Basic Child Care Math

Of the three factors that determine what type of care a parent chooses—convenience, age of the child, and cost—cost is most likely to make the difference.

You must weigh more than your take-home pay to decide if paying for child care is worth going to work. Does your job offer benefits such as medical insurance? Is the opportunity for advancement (meaning greater pay) sufficient inducement for working now? Or is your income, combined with your spouse's, putting you in a higher tax bracket? Factor in the federal government's income tax credit for child care costs before you make the decision to return to work. If you see it will cost you more to work than to care for your child yourself, put off reentering the job world until your child is in school.

The other factors involved in looking for child care—convenience and age of the child—relate to the price you'll pay. You may find a lovely center, staffed by caring professionals, but it's a 45-minute drive. Or you may have a first-grader who needs care only a few hours a day. You'll have to examine all of these factors very carefully to make sure your child is getting the kind of care you're comfortable with at a price you can afford.

Full Time for Less

Full-time baby-sitters who use their own homes can be real bargains. Some charge as little as $10 a day and include lunch and snacks. They might watch a half-dozen children in addition to their own. "I couldn't afford to send my own children to a baby-sitter if I worked, so I stayed home and accepted a few others to take care of," says one rural sitter. "I'm affordable for other parents, and I make a little money for myself."

Go for the Group Rates

Group care centers spread the cost of child care among many parents. You can use a family center or one that's professionally oper-

Sitters' Fees: 4 Ways to Save

If "you get what you pay for," as the adage goes, you'd never leave your children with a baby-sitter. For $2 an hour, you're not going to entice a Ph.D. in adolescent development to your home.

Luckily, baby-sitters are an American institution that for generations have proven the adage wrong. These parental godsends are happy to bathe your toddlers, lure them into jammies, and pack them off to bed—without demanding combat pay. However, sitters expect—and earn—bonuses for staying past midnight, working on holidays, or caring for more than two children. Rates increase, too, as the neighborhood demands. A Pennsylvania teen might ask $2.50 an hour, while her pal in Connecticut commands $4.00.

While the sitter is likely to be the least expensive item on the tab for a night on the town, there are ways to cut even that cash outlay:

- Barter professional services with a teen. Exchange two hours of babysitting for lessons in driving, playing tennis, cooking, woodworking, braiding hair.
- Break in a first-timer at a reduced rate. And don't overlook boys as potential sitters.
- "Baby-pool" when going out with another couple. Have a single sitter hold down the fort at one home. One couple can pick up the sitter, the other can provide the return trip, and you can split the sitter's fee.
- If dependable teens are as hard to come by as nights out, enlist your neighbors. Baby-sit for friends on a Friday night and ask them to reciprocate on Saturday.

ated. Family day care ranges from $30 to $160 a week, and day care centers range from $30 to $150, according to a 1988 survey. Call around in your area, and see which form of group care offers the best rates. Shop for the best price, but know that openings are few in the nicest centers. You may not want to compromise on such things as adult/child ratio, cleanliness, and activities.

After-School Care

Sometimes you need to find a program that will watch your child for just a few hours, the time between when school ends and you get home from work. Places with reasonable fees include churches, the YMCA, or even the child's grade school. One in five schools offers a supervised after-school play program. The average cost per week is $29.

Some Creative Ways
to Save Money

Resourcefulness and ingenuity can go a long way in helping defray some child care costs. Ask your employer for flexible hours. Perhaps you can work through your lunch period so you can leave earlier. Or work Saturdays instead of Mondays, when your spouse can watch the child, to cut center costs by one day a week.

Consider part-time employment. Be careful here, though. Part-timers may not be eligible for job benefits. And you may find yourself turning over a huge chunk of your paycheck for child care even at 20 hours a week. One way to cut back on child care costs is to form a cooperative babysitting pool with several other parents who also work part time.

Get the Boss to Pay

Day care is front-page news these days. Proposals for making child care a bona fide employment benefit are becoming reality. More than 3,000 companies already provide support to workers. Says financial analyst Jane Bryant Quinn, "Just as company-paid medical plans were created to help men meet their family responsibilities, child care will become *the* benefit for the female work force on which this country now depends."

Look to these innovative programs to give your company ideas:

■ Discounts. Employers can subsidize a percentage of child care costs, either directly to the provider or to the parent.
■ Networks. Companies can find and recommend providers.
■ On-the-job care. Both blue-collar and white-collar workers enjoy on-site child care in many companies. Leading the way is

the Senate and House of Representatives, which maintain centers for members of Congress and their staffs.

■ Flexible benefits. With this program, workers who need child care can substitute that benefit for another. Childless employees, then, are not forced to subsidize their coworkers. Options include a temporary pay reduction, or a tax-free subsidy for child care costs.

9

HIGHER EDUCATION, LOWER TUITION

The best time to begin planning for your child's college education is P.B.: Pre-Baby. But alas, you may be paying off your own college loans as you start your family. So let's assume you're a typical American, meaning you've procrastinated. Your child is now in high school. College looms just a few years away. Before you begin figuring *how* to come up with the cash, let's look at *how much*. Tuition has been increasing by 6 to 7 percent a year for the past few years. The increase for public and two-year schools has been less; for private schools, more.

"The money that you and your family pay toward college costs may well represent the single biggest financial investment that you make in your lifetime (next to buying a home, perhaps)," according to the College Entrance Examination Board. Whether it's a sound investment, only you and your child—and time—can tell. But it's a fact: Today's job market demands higher educational standards of its work force. In this chapter, we'll help you take the squeeze off financing a college education.

Figuring Out
Financial Aid

Reduce Your Share

Financial aid officers like to think they look at the big picture before they draw upon you to contribute. They'll examine such things as parental income, student earnings, family net assets, and family expenses. It's up to you to paint the picture black; within legal limits, of course. Be sure to point out unusual circumstances, like heavy medical bills, a retired or disabled parent, or siblings in college at the same time. Now's the time to protect personal assets in things like individual retirement accounts. Join a salary reduction plan at work—such as a 401(k) investment—to cut what the college considers available income. Enlist a tax planner long before you take on the financial aid office to further reduce expected family contribution.

Savvy College Shopping

Here are two don'ts to keep in mind when looking at schools. Don't let your child apply to every school that strikes his fancy. Applications are costly! Have him study brochures in the high school guidance office or public library to narrow his choices. Don't rule out expensive colleges. Some may be richly endowed, which means they can offer a fat financial aid package.

The Two Types of Aid

Planning helps you do two things: Squeeze the most out of your own resources and heighten the chances of getting the right kind of aid. To help with your planning you should know that financial aid comes in two forms. The first is *gift aid*, which you don't pay back. This includes grants and scholarships. The second form is *self-help aid*, which you repay. Loans and work-study fall into this category.

Aid sources include the federal and state government, colleges themselves, and private organizations such as banks. Aid may be awarded based on achievement, either scholastically or athletically, but most times it's based on need. Rarely is a student given a full scholarship with no strings attached.

Look for Aid
from Private Sources

In addition to seeking aid from the college and government, you should investigate aid from private sources. Start by looking here:

- Parents' and students' employers or labor unions may have educational programs. Check to see if your child is eligible for scholarships, grants, or low-interest loans.
- Canvass social organizations that you belong to, be it religious or civic, to get aid. Likely prospects include 4-H clubs, Kiwanis and Jaycees, Girl and Boy Scouts, American Legion chapters, YMCAs and YWCAs, and chambers of commerce.
- If your daughter is set on becoming a journalist, doctor, or lawyer, petition those particular associations.
- If you are a military veteran, or the child of one, investigate benefits from the Veterans Administration.
- Hole up in the public library to do your own scholarship search

for scholarships that may be little known but right up your alley. Do not pay for this service from a private computerized search firm; you'll be charged dearly for information you can find yourself with a little digging.

Free Number for Federal Aid Info

If you have questions about applying for federal student aid, call the Federal Student Aid Information Center at 1-800-333-INFO. Counselors can explain eligibility requirements, offer forms, check on your application, or correct a report.

Aid from the Federal Government

Pell Grants

Think of Pells as the cornerstone of financial aid. Other federal aid is dependent in large part on whether you're accepted or rejected for a Pell. Eligibility is determined by a need formula that produces a Student Aid Index number. If you're eligible for a Pell Grant, lovely. If not, there is no appeal. The formula is a complex one, passed into law by Congress, and there's no manipulating the number once it's determined. The financial aid officer of the school you wish to attend is the person best qualified to lead you through the complexities of Pell Grants. Federal regulations allow professional judgment in these matters, so it pays to ask the pro.

Supplemental Educational Opportunity Grants

SEOGs are for students with exceptional need. You should apply for federal aid promptly, because each college gets only a set amount of money for SEOGs.

College Work-Study

The student is paid at least minimum wage for work on or off campus. Typical jobs are as assistants in the library, cafeteria, or laboratories. If your child is given a work-study "award," the amount he earns can't exceed what the college sets.

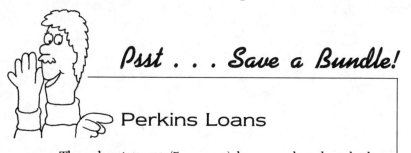

Psst . . . Save a Bundle!

Perkins Loans

These low-interest (5 percent) loans are based on both need and availability of funds at the college your child has chosen. If she qualifies, she'll have up to ten years to repay these loans. And there's a bonus: Your child can have all or part of her Perkins loan canceled after graduation by teaching handicapped or low-income children, volunteering in the Peace Corps or VISTA, or enlisting in the Army Reserves or National Guard.

Guaranteed Student Loans

These loans are insured by the guarantee agency in your state and are reinsured by the federal government. The rate is 8 percent for the first four years of repayment and 10 percent thereafter.

More Low-Interest Loans

PLUS

PLUS stands for Parent Loans for Undergraduate Students. These loans are offered by banks and are interest-subsidized by the federal government. Parents can borrow up to $4,000 per child per year for college. Pay over ten years, and defer repayment of principal until after graduation if you like. PLUS loans have a variable interest rate and are based on the government's Treasury bill rate plus 3.25 percent.

SLS

Supplemental Loans for Students are for independent (meaning self-supporting) or graduate students. They may borrow up to $4,000 a year with a variable interest rate. If your child has trouble finding a lender for a PLUS or SLS, contact your state's guarantee agency. (You can find the number, usually toll-free, by calling the student loan department of a local bank.) Banks and other lenders participate in these programs voluntarily; you may have to shop around to find an institution that will lend you money.

Making the Most of Your Money

The Gift of Education

Regardless of your success in cornering federal aid, you'll have to pay *some* of the college bill out of pocket. Here we offer a few ideas to make those pockets a little deeper.

Stash money into a custodial account under the Uniform Gifts to Minors Act. Invest that money in a sound, insured vehicle such as a long-term certificate of deposit. Stagger maturity dates on several certificates of deposit (CDs) to coincide with tuition payments. A financial advisor can help you set up the account.

Tax consequences: The first $500 of interest income is not taxed. The next $500 is taxed at the child's federal rate, which is marginal. But when the interest amounts to more than $1,000 a year, the account will be taxed at the parents' rate. Once the child turns 14, the income again is taxed at the child's own rate.

Don't gnash your teeth at the government, however. In realistic terms, if you invest the money at 7 percent, your child's account can amass more than $14,000 before the interest income exceeds $1,000.

Let Your Home Pay for School

Set up a home-equity line of credit to pay for college. Equity is the difference between the value of your home and what you still owe on it. Because your line of credit is secured by the equity in your home, the interest rate may be lower than that of commercial loans.

A bonus: Depending on your financial situation, you might be able to fully deduct the interest payments on a home-equity loan. Be sure to talk with a tax advisor to see whether you qualify for tax savings.

An idea to consider: Some lines of credit can be changed to a fixed-term installment loan. This may be to your advantage, depending on how long you want to take to pay off college debts. Ask if you have this option, and at what interest rate. It might be worth doing if you're unable to deduct interest.

Buy U.S. Savings Bonds

Buy U.S. Savings Bonds regularly, staggering them to mature in time for each semester's tuition payment. These bonds yield a variable rate, averaged at maturity or redemption. When you cash them in, you're taxed on the earnings. But since you can buy them for much less than face value, they're a painless, sure way to put away money for college.

You can purchase Series EE bonds in amounts as small as $25 or up to $5,000, for maturities of $50 and $10,000, respectively. You are taxed (federally only) on the interest, which is the difference between the purchase price and the redemption value.

Zero-Coupons Add Up to a Lot

You buy zeros at a big discount. They're called zero-coupons because there are no semiannual interest payments, so there are no coupons to exchange for that interest. The interest rate is locked in, and interest is paid in one sum when the bond matures at face value. Since you know how much you'll get when the bond matures, you can coincide redemption with tuition payments.

Zeros are taxable; you pay tax on accrued interest even

though you don't receive that interest each year. Attractive ones are issued by the U.S. Treasury. But look into municipal zero-coupon bonds; they're tax-free. Unfortunately, zeros issued by state or local governments often can be called early, which means you would not get the yield you planned.

Special Bond Issues

Several states are planning to follow the example set by Illinois in offering tax-exempt college savings bonds. These issues are quickly sold out, so keep on top of what your state is doing. Illinois' 1988 offering of zero-coupon bonds cost $1,000 minimum and mature at $5,000. If used at an Illinois institution of higher learning, investors get a bonus of $100 to $400.

Other Ways to Make the Government Pay

Psst . . . Save a Bundle!

You're in the Army Now

Sock away $25,200 for college by enlisting in the Army for four years. You can use the G.I. Bill plus the Army College Fund to painlessly save for school. The program works this way: You pay $100 a month for a year in payroll deductions. That's $1,200 out of your pocket. The government adds up to $9,600 from its G.I. Bill. The Army College Fund contributes another $14,400.

If you enlist for only three years, the total you can earn for college is $22,800. Enlist for two years, and you'll earn up to $17,000. For information, call 1-800-USA-ARMY.

ROTC: Your Best Foot Forward May Be in a Boot

Picture yourself graduating from college free of debt. Now picture yourself in uniform. The military can offer an all-expenses-paid education with a service commitment that's not as lengthy as you might think. In fact, scholarship students in the Army Reserve Officers Training Corps (ROTC) need never serve on active duty. The contract calls for eight years in the Reserves or National Guard if that's what you prefer.

It would be hard to find a more attractive scholarship. Army ROTC awards $7,000 or 80 percent a year for tuition, whichever amount is greater; all or part of the cost of books; all academically related fees; plus a $100-a-month stipend, up to $1,000 a year. And some schools offer free room and board to students on ROTC scholarships.

The Ultimate in Planning

Prepaid Tuition Plans

Pay now, enroll later. Much, much later, in fact. Prepaid tuition plans are one way to bankroll your youngster's college education. Some call for a lump sum payment; others, for installment payments. The idea is to freeze costs at today's prices for tomorrow's students. The concept is great but there are a few catches to beware of:

- Such plans don't guarantee admission to the college you've paid for. Your child will have to meet academic and other standards.
- There's no telling if your child will *want* to attend the college you've so carefully selected.
- The Internal Revenue Service has gotten in on the action. Prepaid tuition plans are not always tax-free.

Two States to Watch

Several states are exploring prepaid tuition plans. Among them is Michigan, with the Michigan Education Trust for tuition at a state college or university. You make a one-time investment for an infant that guarantees tuition for four years. Students will be taxed on the difference between the tuition the state pays and their parents' original contribution.

Massachusetts is looking into the College Opportunity Program for tuition at public and private schools in the state. Parents would buy certificates, financed by state-issued bonds (making them tax-free), to redeem for a set percentage of tuition.

Weigh the Options

Before you plunk down cash in a prepayment plan, consider that you may be smarter to invest that money elsewhere. If tuition continues to rise at 6 percent, you may well get a better rate in another investment.

More Loan Sources

SHARE with Nellie Mae

If your family doesn't qualify for federal loans or needs extra help, there are some other student loan organizations you should know about. One of these is Nellie Mae, the New England Education Loan Marketing Association. It lends up to $20,000 a year, with up to 20 years to repay. Select monthly variable interest rates, which are not to exceed the prime rate plus 2 percent. Or choose a one-year renewable interest rate, not to exceed prime plus 3 to 4 percent.

Thirty schools cooperate in Nellie Mae's loan program (called SHARE), including Barnard, Columbia, Dartmouth, Massachusetts Institute of Technology, Princeton, and Yale. You must be enrolled in a member institution to qualify for this loan.

SHARE loans up to $80,000 also may be borrowed to cover four years of college under a formal tuition prepayment plan or tuition stabilization plan. For more information, call Nellie Mae at 1-800-634-9308.

Hello, Sallie Mae

While Nellie Mae loans restrict where you can go to school, Sallie Mae loans let you enroll anywhere you like. Sallie Mae stands for Student Loan Marketing Association. Sallie Mae provides PLUS and SLS loans, and also their version, which is called FamilyEd Financing.

Before you apply for these or other consumer loans, check to see if you've got a shot at borrowing under a lower-interest program such as one that's government sponsored. FamilyEd loans from Sallie Mae, for instance, charge according to the rate of Treasury bills plus 3.5 percentage points.

Consumer loans are approved based on whether you look like you can repay. Government loans are approved based on whether you need the money. There's as big a difference in interest rates as there is in philosophy. Still, Sallie Mae and similar programs can bail out middle-class Americans who planned for college, but not well enough.

For more information, call Sallie Mae at 1-800-831-LOAN.

Be ConSerned

Pardon our spelling. ConSern is the Consortium for Supplemental Educational Resource Needs. With this program you can borrow up to $25,000 per year at variable interest rates based on the commercial paper rate, plus 3.6 points. You'll have up to 15 years to repay, and as with many similar loans, you can defer payment of principal until after graduation. For information on ConSern, call 1-800-338-7196.

Cutting Costs in College

Budget Savers 101

It doesn't take a Phi Beta Kappa to figure out that college costs include much more than tuition. As a student you should budget for each category: books, housing, food, and so on. These are places where you can cut costs, because many of these factors depend on your lifestyle. And once you've made that budget, stick to it!

Bargain Books and Supplies

Each semester, used texts come up for sale. Obtain a list of required reading for each course, and scout for these books from students who took the course the semester before. As for supplies, the college bookstore may not be a bargain. Load up on notebooks and pencils at discount stores like K-mart.

Home Away from Home

Some colleges require students to live on campus the first year or two. If you can get around this, rent an apartment with other students. Spartan is the key word here. There will be time enough for high living after graduation, when you have a job. If it's possible to commute, do so—provided you're close enough to take advantage of after-class activities and to get full use of the library. Weigh the cost of keeping a car, or paying for bus or train commuting, against the isolation commuters may feel.

Chow Time

If you pay for the college meal plan, *use it*. Many students get into the habit of buying fast-food instead of adhering to scheduled meal times in the cafeteria.

Curing What Ails You

You may be covered under your parents' health insurance. Check the policy before paying infirmary bills for the inevitable colds and flu that strike students in droves.

Fun and Games

Ah, here's the biggest bugaboo. Allot only so much for movies, parties, and other nonessentials that are, of course, essential in the life of a college student. Don't exceed that monthly spending limit, and don't be tempted to borrow from friends to get by. You're learning lessons for life here!

Other Smart Strategies

There's Savings in Numbers

If you have several children, or if you'd like to complete your own education, by all means plan to have as many family members as possible in college at the same time. You may qualify for heaps of financial aid that way. A financial aid officer can help you determine this.

Ask Grandparents for Help

Get grandparents in on the action. If they're planning their estates, urge them to give tax-free gifts each year to students to reduce their estate taxes later. They can give up to $10,000 a year to an individual without being subject to the gift tax.

Pay for Education, Not Reputation

Be a big fish in a small pond rather than a minnow at an ivy-covered institution. Less prestigious colleges may offer honors programs—and attractive financial aid—that can look mighty good to an outstanding student who may not qualify for as much aid at a big-name school.

Tuition as a Fringe Benefit

If you're a parent in need of work, knock on a college's doors. Many schools offer employees free tuition for themselves and their children. The pay may not be great, but the fringe benefits can add up!

Fast-Track Savings

Earning a degree in less time can save on tuition. Taking a heavier course load, attending summer semesters, using advanced placement or academic credit testing can shorten the time needed to complete an education.

Start Locally

A student can begin at an inexpensive community college to reduce costs, then transfer to another institution to complete her studies.

One Semester On, One Semester Off

Alternate semesters of full-time studies with full-time work. Some colleges have cooperative education programs that allow students to work in their chosen fields. You can even earn academic credit while you're earning money.

Work First, Study Later

Another option may be to defer enrollment. A student can work for a semester or a full year to save money before matriculating. Be sure, however, this will not affect the financial aid package adversely.

Let the Boss Pay

Many companies encourage employees to further their education. You may be reimbursed for part or all of your tuition, fees, and books, depending on how well you do in school. You'll work full time and attend classes part time. Beware of a catch-22, though: It's hard to get jobs with such progressive companies unless you have a college education! This plan may work best for employees looking to earn a master's or doctorate.

It Never Hurts to Ask

Explore tuition and/or fee waivers based on circumstances: If you're the child of an alumnus, a minority or adult student, one of several family members enrolled simultaneously, or a child of an unemployed worker, you may be eligible for special status. It can't hurt to ask; you have nothing to lose and everything to gain.

Installment Plan

Ask for tuition budgeting. Like everything else, you can pay for college on the installment plan. Spreading out payments may cost more in the long run—because of interest and service charges—but this can solve a cash crunch problem. Insurance companies also sometimes offer tuition budgeting plans. Parents make monthly payments to the company, not the college. Depending on the plan, the insurance company may continue to make payments if a parent dies.

10

TAKE OFF
TO TRAVEL
BARGAINS

It's time to face facts: Have your vacations over the years been exhilarating and refreshing—or boring? If you're like most people, vacations mean trips to visit old friends, holiday jaunts to see Grandma, or maybe a long weekend at one of the big theme parks. All that hectic packing and driving—and all that money spent—can make you feel cheated when your time's up.

Travel doesn't have to be humdrum or harried, or even expensive. Not when you know the ropes. The key to an exciting vacation lies in getting not only your money's worth, but your *time's* worth. If you have just a week or two of vacation time, make those days count. To do that takes planning.

Planning, not coincidentally, is also the way to stretch travel dollars. Let's take a look at how you can get the most for your money and have a great time doing it.

Getting Around

You're Up in the Air

The flight may be the most expensive part of your trip. To cut corners, you have to know how airlines operate. Here are some tips:

- Pay for your ticket when you make the reservations. If you don't, the quoted price may go up.
- Beware of penalties if you change your plans. Discounted fares often are subject to hefty penalties if you ask to change flights.
- Be flexible about when you can leave or return. You can save hundreds of dollars simply by staying over on a Saturday night, for example.
- Discount tickets tend to be nonrefundable. That means just what it says. But first class and coach tickets purchased at full fare should be completely refundable. Ask before you pay. The safest bet, of course, is to be 100 percent sure of your travel arrangements.

Psst . . . Save a Bundle!

Parking Savvy

Airport parking lots have been known to charge an arm and a leg for the privilege of keeping your car while you're on vacation. Even outer lot parking (meaning you can barely see the airport) is expensive. Consider a shuttle service instead. These offer a remote parking lot, usually a few miles away from the airport, and lots of amenities. You park your car in their lot, they shuttle you to the airport in their vehicle, and while you're away they guard your car (and even sometimes wash it). Pick up a coupon for discounts the next time you use the service. And keep your eye peeled for shuttle specials in the business and travel sections of newspapers.

Park and Sleep

Another way to avoid the airport parking blues is to stay overnight in an airport hotel. Many offer cut rates in conjunction with package flight-tours. By starting your vacation a night ahead of time, you can splash in the pool, bask in the sauna, take in a cable-TV movie, and park all week for free in the hotel's lot. The service includes a shuttle to the airport.

Get into Training

Clickety-clack has been replaced by whoooshhh on today's trains, but rail travel remains an economical way to see the country. Amtrak, the National Railroad Passenger Corporation, operates 500 stations in 42 states and Canada, covering over 24,000 miles.

Look into discounts for senior citizens, military personnel, and the handicapped, at 25 percent off regular one-way fares. Or select a family discount, in which the head of the household pays full one-way coach fare, the spouse pays half, children 12 to 21 pay half, and children 2 to 11 pay a fourth.

Better yet, get "All Aboard America." This Amtrak program divides the country into three regions. Tickets for each allow travel for a single fare with three stopovers. This single rate works out to be much cheaper than individual city-to-city fares. For information on Amtrak routes and fares, call 1-800-USA-RAIL.

Home Away
from Home on Wheels

There are people who will tell you the only way to travel is in an RV with a CB, AC, PS, and BR. If you're new at this and don't recognize the alphabet soup, an RV is a recreational vehicle, motorized or towed. Recs, as they're also known, come with such features as citizens band radios (CBs), air-conditioning (AC), power steering (PS), and bathrooms (BR). These kings of the road can pay for themselves in a few years if you travel a lot. Factor in the price of gas, campground fees, and insurance on the expense side, and weigh against savings on hotels and meals. Chances are you'll come up with a good argument for hitting the trail in one of these behemoths.

One estimate says vacationing in an RV costs 52 percent less than a car/hotel trip, 68 percent less than a bus or train/hotel trip, and 78 percent less than an air/hotel trip.

But before you buy, try. Rent an RV to see if you really don't mind sleeping on a kitchen table that converts to a bed, or chugging up mountainsides at a crawl. Renting also lets you see how much machine you need for your money. You can rent an RV for $200 to $1,000 a week. For the price of admission, an RV show is a great place to compare options and prices, and to find dealers in your area.

If you're game, but not sure you want to commit the money for a lifestyle that may not appeal to you later, buy a used RV. They hold their value well, which helps if you want to trade up or get out of the genre altogether someday.

For free information about RV types (travel trailers, tent trailers, van conversions, and motor homes), and a list of RV shows, write to the following:

Recreation Vehicle Dealers
  Association
3251 Old Lee Highway
Suite 500
Fairfax, VA 22030

Recreation Vehicle Industry
  Association
P.O. Box 2999
Reston, VA 22090

Car Rental Cautions

Be firm on two things when you prepare to rent a car. Get the car you want (subcompact, air-conditioning, whatever), and *never* pay full price.

Rates vary according to such things as time (midweek, weekend, number of days), mileage, and whether you'll return the car to the original location. When you're quoted a price, ask for a better deal. If the Big Three—Avis, Hertz, and National—can't do business with you, check other major firms such as Dollar, Alamo, Budget, or Thrifty. Call local car rental firms, as well as auto dealerships; they often have surprisingly low prices.

Know if your own auto insurance will cover rental cars; if so, don't pay extra charges. If you're traveling on business, your company may have a policy that covers rental car insurance. Be sure to check if your policy covers rental car theft. Some rental companies are replacing their collision/damage waiver with a loss/damage waiver. If you decline the option, you're responsible should the car be stolen.

Lodging for Less

My House Is Your House

If you've got a touch of the horse trader in you, swap houses with a stranger. Home-exchange companies can match you with agreeable folks for an unusual vacation. You go to a Vail condominium for a winter skiing holiday; the Colorado contingent goes to your beachfront house in Venice, Florida, for sun and surf.

Such companies charge a fee to list your home in a directory. Two to try are the following:

International Home Exchange Service P.O. Box 3975 San Francisco, CA 94119	Vacation Exchange Club, Inc. 12006 111th Ave. Unit 12 Youngtown, AZ 85363

If you'd just like to rent your home—or homes—for a short time while you're away, check with your accountant. Rental income is tax-free only if you rent fewer than 15 days a year.

Free Overnight Stops

Perhaps you're in a hurry and on a budget. You planned to drive straight through, but now you find yourself getting too tired to go on. Most highway rest stops don't allow you to sleep, but there are several alternatives.

■ Police stations. Ask the desk sergeant if you can pull into the lot for a few hours. You'll be safe, that's for sure!

■ 24-hour convenience stores. Let the manager know you're not a holdup man, just a weary traveler. Be sure to buy coffee and doughnuts there in the morning.

■ Truck stops. They are loud and full of fumes, but are close to the road and with a bathroom to boot.

■ Churches. Look for one with a parsonage and ask for permission.

Wherever you pull over, lock your car doors and hide valuables under the seat. Don't park in shadows; try to stay under a street light.

Bed and Breakfast Bargains

Tired of thin blankets, even thinner bath towels and noisy halls? Get out of the hotel rut and indulge in a bed and breakfast. But be forewarned. What was once a quaint well-kept secret is now a booming business, often with prices to match. Rooms in a B and B can cost well over $100 a night, and you might find yourself sharing a bathroom! But quite a few B and Bs charge under $50 for a double room and some even charge under $30, depending on the season. For the best bargains, inquire about off-season rates.

Many B and Bs are located near terrific fishing spots, or are romantic hideaways for honeymooners. Some are vacations in themselves, so you needn't spend money on sightseeing. You can hole up in a log home in Alaska, or take the children for a weekend on a dairy farm in Wisconsin.

A good place to start your search for the perfect resting place is with a B and B guide, available in paperback in libraries and bookstores. These guides are updated annually and include information on Reservation Service Organizations (RSOs) that can find lodging for you in a private home, which can often prove to be a very economical way to spend the night in pleasant surroundings.

Take a Hike and You'll Save Money

Enjoy hiking but hate toting all that gear? Put up for the night at a hostel. You'll get the lowest in low-cost lodging (try $5 a night!), with friendly house parents offering tips on what to do and see the next day.

American Youth Hostels (AYH) maintains about 280 hostels in this country and more than 5,000 in the world. Don't let the name fool you—there's no age limit to membership.

AYH also sponsors low-cost tours in the United States and abroad. You can hike, bike, raft, or journey by train with companions your own age.

Membership in AYH costs $20 for adults ($30 for two years) and $30 for a family (this includes children under age 18). Members receive a quarterly newsletter and handbook. For more information, write to: American Youth Hostels, 1017 K Street NW, Washington, DC 20001.

Hotels: Rest for the Weary

Some of today's hotels look more like resorts than sleeping spots. You'll find pools, nightclubs, exercise spas, gift shops. Don't pay for these amenities if you're simply in need of a night's rest. Patronize budget hotels. They may surprise you (one man's budget is another man's luxury).

The larger hotel chains now have varying levels of luxury, meaning expense. The Quality Inn chain, for instance, offers low-priced Comfort Inns, moderate Quality Inns, and luxury Quality Royales.

Make reservations as far in advance as you can to get special rates. Ask for, but don't expect, discounts for high-occupancy periods such as Kentucky Derby Day in Louisville, or Mardi Gras in New Orleans. When you register, confirm the discount. Discounts could be for senior citizens, commercial, military, family, or car club membership; try whichever ones are applicable. When you check out, remind the clerk of the discount *before* the bill is totaled.

Bargains in Vacationland

Ready, Set, Go

If you're footloose, pack your bags and call a discount travel service. These firms cater to those who can be out the door on short notice. They typically offer unsold space and tickets on cruise lines, charter flights, and tours at savings up to 67 percent or even more as departure nears.

These are not standbys; reservations are guaranteed. If you deal with an established discount travel company, you won't have to worry about "you pays your money and takes your chances."

Such firms usually charge an annual membership fee ($30 to $45), but folks with the get-up-and-go spirit will find the fee more than offset by the discounts. Two companies to consider: Stand-Buys (1-800-255-0200) and Vacations to Go (1-800-624-7338).

To Club or Not to Club

Travel clubs can be a godsend, or a nightmare. Pluses include savings on flights, car rentals, hotels, cruises, and tours. Minuses include fine print such as "subject to availability." That means the vacation you want can't be had right now, but for a little more money another one is all yours.

No matter how good an offer sounds, never sign on the dotted line without investigating the club first. Insist upon a clause-by-clause explanation of benefits. If a club presents incredible deals, keep your checkbook closed. Those too-good-to-be-true offers probably are just that.

Before you pay a membership fee, ask for information on the following items: First, ask for a list of participating hotels and airlines. "All of the big ones" is *not* a good answer. Second, ask the size of the discounts. You might be able to wrangle a bigger discount on your own, especially if you're a senior citizen. Third, ask about the method of payment. If you give your credit card number over the phone, you may lose consumer protection rights offered to those who do business in writing. Finally, ask for the total cost. Related, optional, and service charges can pad the price of a discount vacation.

Who benefits most from a travel club? Anyone whose schedule can be rearranged to take advantage of special trips throughout the year. If you're locked into a particular time for vacation, you probably can scout a better deal by yourself.

Club fees range from $30 to $60 typically and include brochures or hotlines explaining upcoming trips. Some firms that have been in business for many years include: Encore (1-800-638-0930); Sears Discount Travel Club (1-800-331-0257); and Montgomery Ward Travel Club (1-800-621-5505).

Dial-a-Vacation

Now that postage costs a quarter, phoning for information makes more sense than ever. Always use toll-free phone numbers to make reservations, to check on fares, and to ask for tourist information. If you don't have a number on hand, call toll-free information (1-800-555-1212) to see if the company you're trying to reach maintains a free line. Most state bureaus of tourism and travel have toll-free numbers, as do the convention and visitors' bureaus of large cities.

Places to Go for Cheap

Short but Sweet

The trend these days is for shorter vacations, taken more often. Families have to juggle work schedules and other commitments, which make two- and three-week getaways impractical. Look for money-saving "shorties" to take advantage of long weekends or abbreviated holidays.

City excursion packages are cooked up by hotels to book rooms during low-occupancy periods. Spend two days and a night on a mini-vacation that includes room, champagne welcome, continental breakfast or picnic lunch, and valet parking. Pay for a deluxe package—just a few dollars more—and get a guided tour of the city, dinner, a rental car, and theater tickets.

Take a romantic cruise, but only for half a week. Cruise lines are responding to the trend with packages short on time but long on value. Sail on a ship to nowhere and enjoy the great food and fun activities.

A Capital Idea

Washington, D.C., is the country's best-kept vacation secret. Nearly all of the sights in the nation's capital are free. Now, doesn't that stir your patriotic spirit?

Your family could spend a week, easily, touring the FBI, the Federal Reserve Board, the Lincoln Memorial, the Washington Monument, and the Library of Congress. The best bargain, though, is the Smithsonian Institution. The Smithsonian is the world's largest museum complex, covering 14 museums and the National Zoo. For more information write to: Visitor Information and Associates' Reception Center, Smithsonian Institution, 1000 Jefferson Drive SW, Washington, DC 20560.

To plan your visit to the capital, write to the Washington, D.C. Convention and Visitors Association, 1575 I Street NW, Suite 250, Washington, DC 20005.

More Money-Wise Travel Tips

Age before All Else

Adults have the travel game won. Join a senior citizen organization—membership can begin as young as 40 in some—to get discounts on plane, bus, and train travel; hotel and restaurants; entertainment; tourist attractions; and car rentals.

The travel industry knows seniors have the time and money to travel. But not all businesses automatically offer discounts. You have to ask, and sometimes, you have to have clout. That's why membership in an organization is your passport to savings. Three to consider are:

The American Association of
  Retired Persons (for those
  over 50)
1090 K St. NW
Washington, DC 20049

Mature Outlook (for those
  over 40)
P.O. Box 3096
Arlington Heights,
  IL 60006

The National Council of
  Senior Citizens (for those
  over 55)
925 15th St. NW
Washington, DC 20005

When Is a Discount Not a Discount?

Use that senior savvy before you get out your wallet. Sometimes senior discounts are not as substantial as other discounts. Shop for the best price by asking about discounts for weekend travel, off-peak hours, package deals, or one-time specials.

Got Credit? Flaunt It!

Credit cards can be a traveler's best friend. Dig out the literature that comes with your bill every month or so, and study it to see if you're entitled to free accident insurance, lost baggage coverage, rental car and hotel discounts, and bonus points in frequent flyer programs. All these and more are little-known—and little-used—offerings in the increasingly competitive world of credit card companies.

One caution, though: Be prepared to pay the bills quickly. Don't let the cost of credit (in finance charges) bog you down. And another thing: Never give your credit card number over the phone to a firm you've not dealt with before. Unscrupulous travel operators—the kind who call unsolicited, offering unbelievable deals—can rack up charges you never authorized.

11

"TWOFERS" AND OTHER ENTERTAINMENT TREATS

So when are you going to start living the good life? You can play the lottery regularly (not a bad idea; after all, somebody has to win those millions), or you can make do with what financial advisors seriously call disposable income.

That's the cash left over after housing, food, cars, medical expenses, utilities, and all other necessities are paid. With the help of this book, you can learn to shave a neat sum off of each category. That leaves you more money than ever with which to play.

But don't be silly about it. The biggest lesson *Cut Your Bills in Half* teaches is smart shopping. Whether you're in the mood for a ten-speed bicycle or tickets to a Broadway show, this chapter explores ways to stretch that disposable income. Budget for leisure and entertainment just as you do for groceries and the phone bill. Whether you're left with $5 or $500 each month for play, make it count. Don't be timid about asking for discounts; it's a buyer's market out there. You're a valued customer no matter how much you pay.

Dining
with Dollars to Spare

Seniors, Speak Up

If you're a senior citizen making the rounds of restaurants, ask for discounts. Special prices may be noted on the menu or they may not. Always inquire before ordering; you'll be pleasantly surprised more often than not. Some establishments even have separate menus for seniors. Family dining and fast-food chains are most likely to offer senior discounts; gourmet restaurants are least likely.

Early Birds Get More
Than Just Desserts

Restaurants don't like customers to wait in line any more than the customers like waiting. That's why many dining places offer early bird specials. While it's difficult for working families to beat the clock, retirees may be able to use these discounts during the week. And on weekends, everyone can take advantage. Typically, these dinner specials are offered until 5:30 P.M., or during off-peak hours. You'll save on complete dinners, drinks, and desserts. Sometimes restaurants require coupons for these specials, so check the newspaper for them before you go. If you try a new place and like it, ask the waitress about specials for return visits.

Be a Smart Tipper

Tipping Do's and Don'ts

There is no mystery to sensible tipping. A few rules are all you need to get you through any situation you might encounter.

A smart tipper always:

- Gives a tip when service is good or excellent
- Carries dollar bills and a few quarters when traveling or dining out (that way you won't "pay" more because you don't have change)

A smart tipper never:

- Tips the owner of a restaurant
- Adds an additional tip to a service charge (usually 15%)
- Overtips
- Tips if service is poor (you should not pay for what you don't receive)

Help for Chronic Overtippers

If you can't control your tipping, carry the handy "15% Tip Table" in your wallet. This credit-card-size plastic card gives you at a glance the exact 15 percent tip for amounts from $1 to $100. If you tend to overtip, this card can force you to "pay" the correct amount. For less than a dollar, this card is available from Target Promotions, Inc., P.O. Box 1693, Santa Monica, CA 90406-1693 (213) 458-2152, as well as from book and novelty stores.

Who Gets What and When?

PERSON	SERVICE	TIP
Cars or taxis		
Car parking attendant	On returning car	50¢ to $1
Parking valet	On returning car	50¢ to $1
Taxi driver		15% but 50¢ minimum
In hotels		
Bellhop	From front desk to room; from room to car or taxi	$1 per bag
	Picks up bags at desk, loads into car or taxi	$1 per bag
	Checks bags for any length of time	$1 per bag
Chambermaid	Makes up room	$1 to $2 per day
Doorman	Opens car or taxi door on arrival	Smile and a thank you
	Takes bag(s) to front door only	Smile and a thank you
	Takes bag(s) to check-in desk	$1 per bag
	Hails taxi; opens door	$1
Room service	Tip not included in bill	15 to 20%
	Tip included:	
	Small order	$1
	Big order	$2 to $5
Restaurants		
Bathroom attendant		50¢
Cloak room		50¢ to $1 per article

PERSON	SERVICE	TIP
Cocktail waitress	Drinks only	15% but 50¢ minimum
Maître d'hôtel	Directs you to captain or table	Smile and a thank you
Waitress/ waiter	Brings the food	15 to 20% of pretax check; more if extra service provided
Wine steward	Opens bottle at table	10% minimum of cost of wine

It's Showtime!

The ABCs of VCRs

Videocassette recorders (VCRs) come in three formats, all of which are incompatible with each other: VHS, Beta, or 8 mm. Your best bet may be VHS; the other formats are not common when it comes to buying or renting tapes.

Select a VCR according to what you'll do most with it. A survey by *Consumer Reports* magazine shows most owners use recorders for time-shifting. This means they tape shows for later viewing. If this is your thing, buy a model that's easy to program.

If you're planning to play back prerecorded (rental) tapes most times, a basic, stripped-down model will suit you instead. Look for one with a good picture and sound.

Users who want a VCR to show home movies taken on a camcorder, however, should select a full-featured model. Be prepared to pay more for VCRs that allow editing and dubbing.

VCRs can be bought for as little as $150 or as much as five times that. Consider carefully what your family needs and wants. Don't underbuy. Better to lay out for a midrange device from the start rather than a budget model. Don't plan on "trading up" later. You'll find used equipment has little resale value. That, however, can work on your side if you buy used equipment.

Be a Vid Whiz

Feeding a video-viewing habit can get pricey unless you shop around for the best bargain in video clubs. Erol's, the number one video rental store (ranked as such by *Video Store Magazine* in 1987 and 1986), offers a wide selection in movies, multiple rentals (up to six at a time), no deposit, and a free magazine mailed monthly.

Search for low membership fees and rental charges. Erol's charges $9.95 to join and $2.00 per tape. Many minimarts and supermarkets lend videos for less with no membership fees, but the selection may not be as great. The key to saving money is in the convenience in picking up and dropping off tapes. If you have to drive far out of your way after shopping or work, that $1.00 tape may be no bargain compared to the $2.00 one that's from a nearby outlet.

Rent, Don't Buy

Unless you plan to set a record for most viewings of a movie, never buy a video. You may think you could stand to watch *Citizen Kane* every week, but chances are you won't get your money's worth from the purchase. Rent, rent, rent; at $1 a shot, you can't go wrong. There's no worry about maintenance, no worry about storage.

You Ought to Be in Pictures

Some movies just have to be seen on the big screen. Or maybe you simply enjoy a night out of the house. Here are some ways to enjoy the big screen without spending big bucks:

■ Every theater offers discounts for selected showings. Check listings for matinees or twilight shows, or sometimes late-night ones. Local (unfranchised) theaters may hold "date nights," two-for-one deals on slow weekday viewings.

■ Ask for senior citizen discounts, and investigate whether your favorite theater offers booklets of discounted tickets.

■ Another money-saving way to see movies: Get on the mailing list of your local colleges. Film societies often invite the public to screenings of foreign films, classics, and comedies. Your community library, too, may sponsor such screenings.

■ Check listings at the drive-in, that fast-disappearing bit of Americana. Drive-ins often combine first-run movies with one or two other films that were hits a while ago. You might find the latest Clint Eastwood flick showing with two others from his past, all for one price. Plus, you can bring your own refreshments to a drive-in to save big on drinks and popcorn.

Psst . . . Save a Bundle!

Free Movies

The best bargain in town is likely to be at your public library. Many offer movies on cassettes for their patrons. Just check them out the same way you would a book. Often local public libraries are part of a statewide system, which means that a wide variety of movies are available, even classic movies from years gone by.

Step Right Up for Tickets

A night at the theater is a night to remember—in more ways than one. Tickets, cab fare, and dinner can total well over $100 for two, twice that if it's a hot show. Investigate ticket discounts to halve that part of the tab. Slash-rate tickets for same-day shows are available in not only New York's Broadway district but also in most major cities. Call the tourist bureau in each for the location of discount ticket booths.

In New York, check out TKTS, located at both Broadway (47th Street) and Wall Street (at 2 World Trade Center). There you'll pay half price, plus a small service fee for that day's shows. Don't count on getting discounts to the most popular shows, which may be booked for a year. Still, you'll be able to see big-name stars in long-running productions. A word of caution: Lines form at these booths, so arrive long before showtime. Or take a chance (if you're in town for sightseeing), and drop in at a booth 15 minutes before curtain time. Be prepared to hoof it quickly to the theater.

Another option is a "twofer." These are 30 percent discount coupons that let you buy one or two tickets in advance. You can choose seat locations for the show of your choice. Get twofer coupons from: New York City Convention and Visitors Bureau, 90 East 42d Street, New York, NY 10017.

Tune In to Cable

Cable television programming offers much more than movies. You'll get sports, home shopping channels, foreign language shows, aviation weather, and reruns of old hits. Cable-TV makes sense for families who have time to enjoy the offerings, or who have a videocassette recorder to tape selective shows.

Watch for promotions to get reduced installation charges and a free trial for premium channels like HBO or Cinemax. You'll get a better deal in areas that have cable competition; check both companies for rates. The national average for basic cable in 1987 was $13.11 a month. Industry deregulation in recent times has meant higher rates for cable service but a decrease in the charge for extras like pay movie channels. Sign up only for what you know you'll use.

Music to Your Ears

The Sound and the Fury

Consumers have been known to go haywire in their search for the perfect sound. Be prudent when shopping for a big-ticket item, such as a stereo or compact disc player. Compromise on what you need and what you want for the best deal. Watch newspaper ads for bargains on good-quality items, but don't pay more for quality you really don't need. Be honest: Can you really tell the difference between the sound of a $500 device and one that's $1,000? Don't look to salespeople for help here. They're out to sell oversized speakers and consoles that look as if they belong in an airplane hangar.

Window-shop in large specialty and department stores, taking note of models that appeal to you. Narrow down your selection. When you've settled on one, go to a small, privately owned shop. Ask the manager to special-order that model for you at wholesale price, and let him add on a few dollars for himself. If he's willing to do this—remind him he doesn't have to stock it or advertise it—you'll still save money.

Shop Smart

Here are a few other savvy consumer tips to save money shopping for audio equipment:

- Do not spend more than you've budgeted. Installment buying is no deal, even with such sales inducements as "no money down" or "no payments until January."
- Ask about floor models, those on display. They may show a little wear, scratches or such, which means you can dicker on price.
- Scan classified ads for used equipment. Be alert for people buying up; you can get an especially good deal on just the model you're looking for when a self-styled audiophile is ready to unload his old stereo.

Read First for No Regrets

An hour in the library can save you hours of driving from store to store later. When you're in the market for a home entertainment gadget, check the latest *Consumer Reports Buying Guide* issue. It's an inexpensive paperback that rates products by brand name. Get the lowdown on VCRs, CD players, boom boxes, TV sets, and cameras. The annually updated guide looks for such things as ease of use and reliability, and rates according to value for price.

Best Bets for Bargains

Be an Old Hand at Secondhand

Attitude is important when it comes to buying secondhand anything. It's either "broken in just right" or it's "beat to the max," as teens say. But whenever you're shopping for leisure equipment—bikes, birdcages, or books—think about buying it from someone who already paid top dollar.

Good places to look: classified ads, under articles for sale, or the particular listing if it's something specialized like a camera. Check garage sale listings, too, for descriptions of items for sale. Don't overlook classifieds in local throwaway papers and announcements on supermarket bulletin boards.

Peek in occasionally at thrift shops run by charities such as Salvation Army, Goodwill, and St. Vincent dePaul, as well as those operated by hospital auxiliaries. These places stock clothes more than anything else but may offer other items from time to time.

Should you find your heart's desire, don't hesitate to bargain. If that item's been taking up space for a while, the manager may well be open to offers.

Try Repair Shops

Pop into repair shops if you're looking for a quality item at a secondhand price. These shops sometimes sell unclaimed—and completely reconditioned—articles, such as bicycles, lawn mowers, and pianos. You can buy with confidence, since many shop owners will offer a guarantee on their work. If you have time to wait, put in a standing order. When the proprietor comes across the goods, he'll give you a call.

Rent First, Buy Later

"Bandwagon" purchases often wind up in the garage. You know what we're talking about here; that personal computer or ten-speed racing bike that everybody else has and you just had to buy, too. A few weekends later, the fun fizzled out. If you even suspect the novelty of a new item may wear off, rent, don't buy.

Renting allows you to try out different features. When or if you decide you really will get your money's worth from the Jet Ski or snowmobile or what have you, that's the time to buy.

Look for items at rental shops and also specialty retailers. Often these items are for sale, too, so if you fall in love with the guitar you've rented, you may keep it.

What's Mine Is Yours

If your neighborhood is one big happy family, consider joint ownership of big-ticket items like pools, boats, even barbecue grills. Enlist relatives and friends for help in buying expensive goodies. Make clear arrangements for maintenance and use, however, to stave off arguments.

Sales Smarts

Comparison-shop not only for price but also for service. Check different types of stores—specialty, discount, department—and go with the place that offers the best deal in maintenance or instruction, as well as cost.

Ask for cash discounts. Deal with the store owner or an experienced salesperson, and "flash the cash" for a reduced price. If you reach an impasse, agree to the price but ask for something else to sweeten the deal: a free roll of paper with the computer printer, or free film with the camera. "No" is not a forever word; be pleasant, be polite, but be insistent.

Practice bargaining techniques. Ask, "Can you do better on this price?" Or say with regret, "I'd really like to buy it, but it's more than I can spend." Chances are good a merchant in a near-deserted store will strike a bargain.

Sell, Don't Toss

When you're in need of a little extra cash, say to purchase a fun item for the family, consider selling some of your possessions. Nothing essential, like the bed. We're talking about coats you no longer like, boots that never fit right, drapes that were too short. Hold a garage sale, run a classified ad, or pack the whole lot off to a consignment shop. Depending on how quickly you need the money, a consignment shop is the easiest option. Figure on giving 30 to 50 percent to the shopkeeper, who will mail you the check when your items are sold.

Be a Bookworm

Psst . . . Save a Bundle!

Check Out a Library Card

So you never bothered to get a library card. Who wants to spend his leisure time in a stuffy room with little old ladies, right? Well, if that's what you think, you're missing out on the best bargain in town. Today's public libraries offer film shows, music workshops, antique exhibits, poetry readings, lectures, and more—all for free.

Many offer computers for public use, albums and cassettes for loan, and holiday programs for children. They may even tie in with local museum and art center shows by offering "read more about it" book selections.

But if you'd prefer to read in the comfort of your home, peruse the stacks for a best-seller. Take home an impressive coffee table book to enjoy for several weeks. Check out an armful of spicy paperbacks to take along on vacation. Or save money on magazine subscriptions by borrowing issues.

Some libraries offer their services for free while others charge a nominal fee for a library card; either way you'll save a bundle if you love to read.

The Postman Bringeth Books

If you're an inveterate reader of cookbooks, gardening guides, poetry, or romance novels, there's a book club for you. First, exhaust all that your public library has to offer. (Don't forget to check for additional books offered by branches.)

Then join a specialty book club. *Never* buy books at a regular bookstore unless they're heavily discounted. Book clubs always discount, and what's more, you can earn bonuses redeemable for free or half-price books.

Take advantage of the one-time joining offer, in which you might receive several books for $1. You'll be shopping by mail, which means you save on gas and time. To look for specialty book clubs, peruse magazines on the subject of interest (in the library, naturally), and photocopy the address and offerings in ads.

A typical plan calls for you to buy just six books within two years. Some clubs apply a special savings option when you join, in which you buy your first book at a cut-rate price. This is a terrific way to shop for Christmas gift books, by the way.

Cut-Rate Fitness

Sports for Seniors

Be a card-carrying member of a senior citizens' organization. Membership can begin as early as age 40 in some. You'll be entitled to discounts at many resorts and sports centers. The National Senior Sports Association (NSSA) is for golfers, bowlers, and tennis buffs over 50. Write for information from the following: National Senior Sports Association, 10560 Main Street, Suite 205, Fairfax, VA 22030.

Their golf card allows you to play two times on 1,200 U.S. courses with no greens fees. Or you can get a 10 percent discount at any Brunswick Bowling Center.

Ask for discounts at ski resorts, too. Many don't advertise—but do offer—special rates or even free skiing at special times for seniors.

Timing Is Everything

From miniature golf to roller skating, you'll play at a discount if your timing is right. Many sports and games establishments entice customers with reduced-rate admission for periods that are slow.

Amusement parks are real bargains when it comes to timing. Go before Memorial Day or after Labor Day if you can, to beat the vacation crowds. While there's no real slow time at Disney World in sunny Florida, theme parks in the rest of the country have off-peak months. If you don't mind battling crowds in summer, you still can enjoy lower ticket prices by arriving for twilight sessions.

Y Not Join the Y?

Your county may have a family YMCA or YWCA that offers a pool, weight room, tennis, racquetball, and aerobics classes. Many have indoor tracks, too. Membership rates differ for youth, seniors, couples, and families, and are far lower than private health clubs. The Y won't turn away people who can't pay; apply for financial assistance for low-cost membership. There are special rates for single-parent families, for instance.

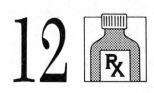

12

IN SICKNESS
AND IN HEALTH

Only a few years ago, few of us felt compelled to ask, "How can I save money on health care?" As long as our hospital and doctor bills were paid by group insurance plans or by Uncle Sam, we had little incentive to economize on medicine. We may have been thrifty when buying food, clothes, and automobiles, but when it came to purchasing medical care, money was no object. Why? Because third-party insurers were picking up the tab.

Today, however, the party is over. In response to the soaring costs of medicine, corporations that once provided generous health benefits have begun to "share" some of their insurance costs with their employees. As a result, those of us who once took health care for granted are now paying higher deductibles and copayments. Suddenly, everyone is asking, "How can I save money on health care?"

Fortunately, there are plenty of opportunities to economize. By choosing home health care over hospitalization, by taking advantage of the free care available from government agencies, by staying healthy, by becoming as consumer-minded about medicine as we are about groceries and cars, and by the dozens of other strategies outlined here, we can reduce our health care costs without sacrificing our good health.

Hospital Bills

Audit Your Hospital Bills

Banks make errors in their own favor, and so do hospitals. You could save yourself hundreds of dollars simply by auditing your hospital bill carefully. The larger the bill and the longer your hospital stay, the more likely it is that the bill will contain an error or two. In one case reported in the journal *Zenith Healthcare*, a patient was billed for $1,120 for two days of intensive care that she never received. In another case, a pregnant woman was charged for an $850 tubal ligation that never took place. Always ask for an itemized bill when you check out of the hospital, and study it for services or supplies that weren't given to you. If you find a mis-

take, call your employer or your insurer. Some companies offer
cash rewards to employees who spot errors on hospital bills.

Don't Check In on Friday

Friday is the most expensive day to check into the hospital. Why?
Hospital labs usually close for the weekend, and you may waste
two and a half days—and several hundred dollars—just waiting
for the labs to open on Monday. If possible, wait until Tuesday to
check into the hospital. By that time, the staff will have gotten
over the Monday blahs. Also, find out in advance what time of day
billing begins. If billing begins at noon, for instance, don't check
in at 11:00 A.M. You may be charged for the previous day.

Emergencies Only

It's a Saturday afternoon, and your child has come down with an
excruciating earache. You feel that he needs immediate medical
attention, but you're not sure where to take him. Your family physician isn't available. You must choose between the hospital emergency room and one of the new no-appointment "emergi-centers"
that have sprung up in many communities.

In most cases, it will be less expensive to go to the emergi-
center. You will probably be charged a flat fee there—$30, for
instance—when a doctor examines your child. At the hospital
emergency room, you might be billed twice—once by the hospital and once by the doctor. Fees vary from town to town, but in
many cases, the emergency room will be substantially more
costly. In both cases, additional fees will be charged for x-rays or
laboratory tests. If you have diagnostic coverage, insurance will
pay for this.

Avoid emergency facilities unless you've got an actual emergency on your hands. Your insurance carrier may refuse to cover
the costs of emergency treatment. As a rule, you should call your
family doctor first in time of crisis. If he or she isn't available, use
an emergi-center before the hospital emergency room.

One Doctor,
One Consultation

When the doctor who admits you to the hospital is puzzled by
your symptoms, he may ask a colleague or specialist to study your

chart or examine you. This can be of critical value to your swift recovery, but it may also be expensive. Some group insurance plans limit their coverage to only one consultation per consultant during any given hospital stay. In other words, if your doctor huddles with the same colleague twice, you may wind up paying for that second conversation.

Outpatient Surgery Is "In"

Tonsillectomies, hernia repair, and cataract removal used to require at least one night in the hospital. Today, such minor surgeries are just as likely to be performed in an outpatient clinic at only a fraction of the cost. The cost of an average day in the hospital can be as much as $700 more than the cost of an average outpatient visit.

If you opt for inpatient care, you could end up footing part of the hospital bill. Some insurance companies now provide 100 percent coverage for outpatient care, but require a 20 percent copayment when the same procedure includes an overnight stay in the hospital. This could cost you hundreds of dollars. Also, your insurance carrier might audit your medical bills, and if they find that you've spent $2,500 for an operation that might have cost only $250 as an outpatient, they may reject your claim. In that case, you might have to pay the extra $2,250. Avoid the hospital if you can.

Use Home Health Care

If you're paying any portion of your own hospital or nursing home bills, you could save hundreds or even thousands of dollars by convalescing at home instead of in an institution. Even if you don't realize any direct savings, you'll recuperate faster in the comfort of your own home than in the alien and often germy environment of a hospital.

There are at least three basic kinds of home health care, and their prices and services vary widely. In order of expense, from least to most costly, they include: subsidized homemaker services; Medicare-certified, Blue Cross-participating home health care; and private, or "proprietary," home health care.

Subsidized homemaker services: In many communities, a publicly funded health aide/homemaker agency sends health aides into the homes of people who are unable to cook, clean, or care for themselves. Medicaid or other insurance typically does not cover these services, and fees are based on ability to pay. If you are elderly and living alone on a small fixed income, you would be eligible for this kind of low-cost care.

Medicare-certified, Blue Cross-participating home health care: There are many nonprofit agencies, such as Visiting Nurses of America, that send licensed nurses into homes to provide intermittent, medically necessary assistance to people who have been discharged from hospitals to recuperate at home. If you and your family are covered by Blue Cross and Blue Shield, you could qualify for this type of home care. Check to see if this service is covered in your agreement.

Private, or proprietary, home health care: This is the Cadillac of home health services, and it is typically not covered by group insurance. Since you're paying for this yourself, your choice of services is limited only by how much you decide to pay. Private home health companies can bring all of the services of a nursing home into your home.

Home Health Care by Jo-Ann Friedman (W. W. Norton, 1986) is an excellent reference book for anyone preparing for home care.

Consider Hospice Care

When a relative is dying, saving money on health care is the farthest thing from your mind. But it's useful to remember that the cost of hospice care during the final months or weeks of life can be thousands of dollars less—and usually more personal—than expensive care in a nursing home or hospital.

What are hospices? They are organizations that provide pain relief, counseling, and help with daily living to people who are terminally ill. Hospice care is usually provided at home and is delivered by a team consisting of doctors, nurses, trained volunteers, social workers, and/or clergy, in cooperation with the dying person's family. The first American hospice was founded in 1974.

A study conducted by the Health Care Financing Administration recently showed that hospice care saves between $585 and $2,221 in Medicare expenses during the last year of life. Even if your relative's health care bills are fully covered by Medicare or private insurance, you could reduce the overall burden of health care on the nation and, indirectly, your own burden—by using hospice care.

To find out more about hospices, ask your doctor, or contact the National Hospice Organization, 1901 North Fort Myer Drive, Suite 307, Arlington, VA 22209 (703) 243-5900.

A Living Will

In 1968, an organization named Concern for Dying developed the concept of the living will: a legal document that establishes a terminally ill person's wish not to have his or her life artificially prolonged by life-support systems or medication, especially when that person is no longer capable of making a decision for himself or herself. The document allows physicians to withhold heroic treatments when death is imminent. It also spares the patient and his or her family needless suffering and expense.

For more information about living wills, write to: Concern for Dying, 250 West 57th Street, Room 831, New York, NY 10107 (212) 246-6962.

Shop Around

Like motels, hospitals vary widely in their daily costs, even when their basic services are pretty much the same. If your doctor has admitting privileges at more than one hospital, find out if you can be admitted to the one that's less expensive. It could save you a bundle, especially if you're footing part of the bill.

Teaching hospitals, because they offer the most sophisticated treatment with the most modern equipment, tend to charge the highest rates. (If you have a simple problem, such as a tonsillectomy, there's no sense paying for technology that you'll never need.) And keep in mind that hospitals operated by nonprofit foundations are usually cheaper than investor-owned, for-profit hospitals. Studies conducted by the National Academy of Sciences and Johns Hopkins University have shown that rates at for-profit hospitals are 15 to 24 percent higher than rates at nonprofit hospitals.

To find out how much your local hospitals charge, ask your doctor or employer. Some states, such as Maryland, have Health Services Cost Review Commissions, which compile such data.

Uncle Sam May Lend
You a Hand

In the admissions offices and emergency rooms of many American hospitals, there's a little sign on the wall that says "NOTICE—Medical Care for Those Who Cannot Afford to Pay." This sign indicates that the hospital provides free or subsidized care for low-income families. In 1946, the United States Congress distributed millions of dollars to hospitals and other health care facilities for expansion and modernization. In return, these hospitals agreed to provide a "reasonable volume" of free services. This is known as the Hill-Burton program.

To receive care under Hill-Burton, you must file an application at a participating hospital and present proof of your income. Families earning below the federal poverty line automatically qualify for free care, but some hospitals also provide subsidized care for families earning up to twice the poverty level. A family of four with an income below $11,200 would be sure to qualify, for instance, but so might a similar family making up to $22,400.

On the downside, not all hospitals participate in Hill-Burton, and not all services are covered. The program only pays hospital bills, not doctor bills. If you have other forms of health insurance, you may be ineligible. For more information on the program and a list of participating hospitals in your area, call toll-free 1-800-638-0742; in Maryland, 1-800-492-0359.

A Roommate Is Cheaper

Unless you have a passion for privacy that's as strong as Greta Garbo's, don't bother asking for a private hospital room. If you do, you'll probably have to pay for it yourself. Your insurance carrier will reimburse you for the cost of a semiprivate room, but ask you to make up the difference. That difference varies from hospital to hospital, and can range from $15 to $39 per day. For a ten-day hospital stay, the cost of privacy might be as much as $390.

Forget the TV

If you're a standard Blue Cross subscriber, your insurance may not cover the added cost of having a personal telephone or television in your hospital room. It's not unusual for a telephone to cost $.50 to $1.50 a day, while the cost of a television might vary from

$3.00 to $5.00 a day. Of course, if you plan to make five or six phone calls a day, a private phone would be cheaper than pumping quarters into the pay phone down the hall.

Is That Trip Necessary?

No matter how good your insurance coverage is, a trip to the hospital is going to cost you and your family money. Whether it's in the form of a 20 percent copayment, or merely the price of delivering a bouquet of roses, hospitalization will inevitably perform a surgical strike on your pocketbook. But many hospitalizations, it turns out, are unnecessary.

In a study of 1,132 hospital patients conducted by the Rand Corporation, 60 percent of all hospital admissions were considered appropriate, 17 percent could have been avoided by the use of ambulatory surgery, and a full 23 percent were entirely inappropriate. The study, which was published in the *New England Journal of Medicine* on November 13, 1986, also shows that roughly one-third of all inpatient days are unnecessary.

How can you tell if hospitalization is appropriate or not? In the Rand study, admissions were judged inappropriate if there were "no acute services required or rendered during the first 24 to 48 hours." Hospitalization was deemed necessary if a patient was experiencing a medical crisis, such as a heart attack, paralysis, massive bleeding, or a loss of consciousness. It was also considered necessary if the patient had to be hooked up to a cardiac monitor, an intravenous (IV) bottle, or a chemotherapy drip, or was being prepared for next-day surgery. Unless these conditions were met, the hospitalization was ruled unnecessary.

Dealing with Doctors

Get a Second Opinion out of Town

Believe it or not, your chance of undergoing an expensive and painful surgery might depend simply on where you happen to live. Statistics show that the rate of certain medical procedures varies widely from town to town. For instance, residents of New Haven, Connecticut, are twice as likely to undergo a coronary by-pass operation as residents of Boston, Massachusetts. At the same time, residents of Boston are twice as likely to undergo surgery for removal of a blood clot from the carotid artery.

Why? John E. Wennberg, M.D., M.P.H., of the Dartmouth Medical School, whose studies of geographic variations in surgery rates have shattered traditional notions about the necessity of medical procedures, says that certain operations are simply more fashionable in some cities than in others. What does this mean for you, the medical consumer? If you plan to get a second opinion prior to surgery—and you definitely should—consider going to a specialist in another city. Or, if possible, find out what the surgery rates are in different cities in your region. Some states, like Maine, now keep that kind of information on computer. If you have difficulty finding a second-opinion doctor, call the U.S. government's toll-free second-opinion hotline: 1-800-638-6833; in Maryland, 1-800-492-6603.

Don't Pay Double for a Second Opinion

If you plan to seek a second opinion, ask your doctor to send copies of your medical records, x-rays, and lab tests to the second-opinion doctor. That way you'll be sure not to get stuck with a bill for the duplicate tests, and it will help you get your second opinion that much faster.

Haggle with Your Surgeon

Haggling, to most Americans, is something they do only when visiting a flea market or a Middle Eastern bazaar. Even then, it's more for sport than for financial profit. But Dr. Eugene McArthy, the director of the Health Benefits Research Unit at Cornell University, has found that negotiating with a surgeon over a big-ticket operation—like coronary bypass surgery—can often result in a 25 to 35 percent fee reduction.

How does a consumer bargain with a doctor? Simply by insisting on a second opinion, and threatening to seek a better deal somewhere else. In a study by the Cornell group, prospective

surgery patients were furnished with lists of second-opinion surgeons. If the first surgeon refused to perform the operation for a
reasonable fee—a fee that about 80 percent of the other surgeons
in the community would accept—the patient kept shopping.

Surprisingly, in the Cornell study, four out of five surgeons
agreed to lower their price. In a typical case, one surgeon's fee for
a gall bladder operation was reduced to $2,750 from $3,500. Of
course, haggling with one's surgeon isn't easy. It requires a will-
ingness to switch doctors if necessary, which can be scary. And it
requires a list of potential second-opinion physicians. Your employer may be able to furnish you with such a list, or call the government's toll-free second-opinion hotline (see "Get a Second
Opinion out of Town" on page 304).

Take Your Dental X-Rays with You

When you become a new dental patient, your dentist will probably want to take a new set of x-rays of your teeth and gums. These
new x-rays can cost between $20 for the bitewings and $50 for the
whole mouth. You may be able to eliminate these costs, however,
by asking your previous dentist to send your most recent x-rays to
your new dentist. The better you take care of your teeth by
brushing and flossing, the less need there will be for x-rays. If patients practice good oral hygiene and have regular checkups,
many dentists suggest bitewing x-rays every two years and whole-
mouth x-rays every three to five years.

Avoid Specialists

Would you hire Michelangelo to paint the ceiling in your living
room when a house painter could do just as workmanlike a job for
a fraction of the cost? Of course not. The same holds true for medical specialists. A good rule of thumb: To save money, find the
most competent but least specialized doctor for your problem.

Consider, for example, the removal of a minor skin growth.
You can choose to have it removed by a dermatologist, a general
surgeon, or a plastic surgeon. All three can do the job, but the
plastic surgeon will probably charge you at least $100 more than
the dermatologist will, with the general surgeon's fee being somewhere in between.

Psst . . . Save a Bundle!

Low-Cost Counseling

If you've ever shopped around for the services of a psychiatrist, you know that their soaring rates alone could give you a nervous breakdown. In large cities, psychiatrists routinely charge as much as $100 for a 50-minute session. Even in small cities, the going rate can be $65 or more, and psychologists' fees aren't very far behind. These prices may make long-term therapy financially impossible for the average family, and few insurance plans provide extended coverage for outpatient therapy.

Many states, however, sponsor mental health clinics where qualified psychologists and psychiatrists offer short-term counseling at prices that are based on an individual's ability to pay. For instance, you might be asked to pay as little as $23 a month for four counseling sessions, with the difference paid by the state. In most instances, a psychiatrist conducts an initial evaluation of your needs, and then a psychologist or social worker provides weekly therapy for 12 to 15 weeks. To find out more about these services, contact your city or county social services agency.

Pregnancy and Birth

Free Contraception Services

Free or subsidized gynecological and contraceptive services are available in most communities through the local affiliate of the

Planned Parenthood office. These services are free to those receiving birth control care. Girls under 18 can receive a free physical exam and a free pelvic exam, as well as Pap smears and tests for sexually transmitted diseases (STDs). Contraceptives—birth control pills, condoms, sponges, foams, and diaphragms—are also free to teenage girls. For women over 18, fees for these services are charged on a sliding scale, based on ability to pay. (Those who earn less than $112 a week receive free services.) Planned Parenthood offices also serve men—providing condoms at low cost and free testing and treatment for STDs as well as counseling. Nurse practitioners working under the supervision of a doctor usually provide the services. To find your local office, just look under Planned Parenthood in the white pages of your telephone book.

Don't Smoke during Pregnancy

The costs of delivering an infant prematurely are astronomically higher than the costs of a normal full-term delivery—ten times higher, according to one estimate. The increased costs cover the need for special incubators, heart monitors, and respirators. Children born prematurely also require more health care during early childhood as well. Many premature deliveries are caused by cigarette smoking during pregnancy. So if you're pregnant and you smoke, quit now. You'll reduce your risk of premature delivery and the high costs it incurs.

See a Midwife

Regardless of how much you or your insurance company pays for your maternity care, chances are that you will receive more hours of prenatal counseling for your money from a certified nurse-midwife than you will from an obstetrician. Expectant mothers often find that midwives schedule 45-minute weekly consultations with expectant mothers, while a doctor's consultation may only be for 15 minutes. Those extra minutes or hours of reassurance can make a big difference in a woman's mental outlook during pregnancy. Choosing a midwife for maternity care can save you money, and it will pay you a hefty dividend in terms of time spent in counseling. Birth centers normally cost one-third to one-half what hospitals charge for deliveries and for aftercare.

Avoid a Cesarean Delivery

Delivering a newborn by surgery—also known as a cesarean or C-section—adds greatly to the cost of giving birth. According to one estimate, a C-section adds an average of 2.3 days to the length of hospitalization and 20 to 40 percent to the obstetrician's fee, as well as lengthening the mother's recuperation time. If your insurance policy requires a hospital copayment, you could save $100 to $150 by avoiding an unnecessary C-section. The Public Citizen Health Research Group claims that as many as one-half of the one million C-sections performed in the United States in 1987 were unnecessary. To avoid an unneeded C-section, look for a doctor and a hospital with a low cesarean rate. The C-section rate for deliveries by midwives is 4 to 10 percent, whereas the rate for deliveries by physicians is 20 to 25 percent.

Skip Circumcision

For years, it was considered medically necessary for a male child to have his foreskin circumcised at birth. After several years of debate and indecision, Blue Cross and Blue Shield recently ruled that "routine neonatal circumcision" is nonessential and will no longer be covered by its maternity benefits. Unless the physician decides that circumcision is needed to ensure the health of your newborn son, you may have to pay for the procedure yourself. In one small city, the price charged by the average pediatrician for a routine circumcision in 1988 was $135.

Despite all of this, the decision to skip a circumcision is not merely financial. The Centers for Disease Control says not being circumcised increases the risk of acquiring AIDS. The American Academy of Pediatrics says the chances of bladder problems developing, as well as urinary tract infections, increases in uncircumcised males.

Bank Your Sperm

Every year, about 300,000 American men in their 30s and 40s undergo a vasectomy that surgically sterilizes them. It's estimated that roughly 10 percent—or 30,000 of these men—will eventually change their minds and wish that they could undo the vasectomy and sire additional children. They can choose a vasectomy reversal, or vasovasectomy, in an attempt to regain their fertility. Such an operation costs anywhere from $2,500 to $10,000.

The expense of a vasovasectomy can be avoided, however, if a man stores samples of his semen in a human semen cryo-bank, or sperm bank, prior to his vasectomy. It costs about $300 to deposit five samples of semen in one of the 80 or so recognized sperm banks in the United States, and long-term storage costs anywhere from $12 to over $200. A lower charge is *not* indicative of quality or experience. Artificial insemination with the thawed sperm costs about $100 per insemination, and its rate of success in producing pregnancy is high.

Be wary of banks that don't offer insurance. Most sperm banks don't offer long-term insurance because they don't want to be involved with legal problems.

To find a semen cryo-bank, write or call:

The American Association of
Tissue Banks
1350 Beverly Rd.
Suite 220-A
McLean, VA 22101
(703) 827-9582

The American Fertility
Society
2140 11th Ave. S
No. 200
Birmingham, AL
35205-2800
(205) 933-8494

Health Care for Seniors

Join a Health Cooperative

Senior citizens can cut their health care costs significantly by banding together into health cooperatives. In a number of American cities, senior citizens have already done so. The 100,000 members of the Minnesota Senior Federation, for instance, can receive 20 percent discounts on purchases of dental care and chiropractic therapy, and a 10 to 15 percent discount on drugs. The federation has also convinced local doctors and hospitals to accept Medicare payments as full payments for the low-income elderly. In Milwaukee, the Allied Council of Senior Citizens of Wisconsin,

Inc. persuaded six hospitals to waive Medicare deductibles and
copayments for seniors earning less than $14,000 a year. In Wash-
ington, D.C., the United Seniors Health Cooperative offers its
members 15 to 25 percent discounts on home health care, eye
and ear care, podiatric services, and medical equipment.

If there is a senior citizen health cooperative in your town,
you might benefit by joining it. If there isn't one, consider starting
one. For information about senior cooperatives, write to the
United Seniors Health Cooperative, 1334 G Street NW, Suite
500, Washington, DC 20005.

The (Pharmaceutical) World according to AARP

Through its mail-order pharmacy program, the American Association of Retired Persons (AARP) offers its 28 million members
wholesale prices on prescription drugs, over-the-counter drugs,
and medical supplies like elastic stockings, walkers, canes, and
such. AARP members simply mail their prescriptions to any of
the 12 AARP-affiliated pharmacies nationwide instead of taking it
to their local drugstore. The only disadvantage is the delay: It
takes eight to ten days to receive the prescription. AARP doesn't
guarantee that its drugs will always cost less than they do at your
pharmacy, but the organization tries to deliver discounts whenever possible. To join AARP, which also offers discounts on travel
services and health insurance, write to: AARP, Membership Di-
vision, 1909 K Street NW, Washington, DC 20049.

Share a Home

In Katonah, New York; East Rutherford, New Jersey; and about
200 other cities and towns across the United States, groups of 4 to
14 or more senior citizens have chosen to share large homes as an
alternative to living in nursing homes. Each resident maintains a
private bedroom, and residents share large family rooms, bathrooms, and the kitchen. They cook and clean together, and each
contributes as much toward the rent as he or she can afford to.

The advantages to this communal living are manifold: It is
cheaper and often more dignified than nursing home care, it pre-
vents loneliness, and it allows people to maintain a sense of inde-

pendence. The group homes are often sponsored by a community housing authority or a nonprofit corporation.

To find out more about group living for the elderly, write or call:

American Association of
    Retired Persons
Consumer Affairs
1909 K St. NW
Washington, DC 20049
(202) 728-4355

National Shared Housing
    Resource Center
6344 Greene St.
Philadelphia, PA 19144
(215) 848-1220

Try Adult Day Care

Inexpensive adult "day care" often provides the extra margin of assistance that can allow an older person to continue living at home instead of in a nursing home. In many cities, private non-profit senior centers provide a variety of services. This includes social activities, nutrition programs, free health screening, and dental and hearing checkups. Transportation is provided from the home to the center only. These centers accept donations, but no one is turned away because of inability to pay. For example, the Federal Nutrition Agency provides meals and craft programs but no transportation. This program is by donation only. Metro Plus offers reduced rates for seniors who need transportation to medical appointments. Day Care, run through private agencies and the Area Agency on Aging, provides care in the home based on a sliding scale. For the elderly who are unable to leave their homes, the Meals on Wheels program delivers hot meals to the home. The cost is based on a sliding fee. To find out more about these subsidized social programs, contact your community social services agencies.

Be Aware of
Your Medicare Obligations

If you're an elderly American, the more you know about your Medicare benefits, the more opportunities you'll have to save money within the health care system. When you shop for medical care, be as frugal as if you were paying for it yourself—because you are.

As of 1989, Medicare has increased its coverage of catastrophic illness, but has pushed up its premiums by $4 a month. For hospital bills, Medicare recipients pay no more than the annual deductible of $564 per year, thus being spared the $135-per-day copayment that was charged for the 61st to 90th days of in-patient care in 1988. For doctors' bills, Medicare patients will still have to pay the $75 deductible and 20 percent copayment, but as of 1990, they will not have to pay more than $1,370 a year. Partial coverage of prescription drug costs will also begin for the first time in 1990.

Find a Doctor
Who Accepts Medicare

If you're covered by Medicare, you can minimize your out-of-pocket expenses by finding a doctor who agrees to accept Medicare's payment, along with your 20 percent copayment, as payment in full for his or her services. For instance, Medicare rules might indicate that a certain procedure should cost $125. The government will pay 80 percent of that fee, or $100, and you must pay 20 percent, or $25. If, however, a non-Medicare-participating doctor charges $185 for the procedure, Medicare still pays only $100, and you must pay the $85. That's a difference that comes out of your pocket.

You'll save time as well as money by finding a doctor who participates in Medicare. In many cases, participating doctors will submit the Medicare claim for you and handle all of the paperwork. If you go to a nonparticipating doctor, you'll have to file the claim yourself.

File an Appeal

In the event that your Medicare reimbursement falls far short of the doctor's bill—leaving you to pay the difference—you don't have to accept the assignment without a fight. You can appeal to Medicare and possibly have your reimbursement increased. In 1986, more than half of Medicare recipients in Maryland who filed appeals received more money from the government. When it comes to Medicare, being a squeaky wheel can pay off. To file an appeal, call your local Social Security Administration office for the proper forms, which you must file with your insurance carrier.

Know What Isn't Covered

Don't make the mistake of thinking that Medicare will subsidize all of your health care expenses, or you'll find yourself overcommitted to steep medical bills. What doesn't Medicare pay for? In general, it won't cover incidentals like prescription drugs, vitamins, first-aid kits, dentures, or Meals on Wheels. In 1991, though, Medicare will cover outpatient prescription drugs (there will be an annual deductible of $600 in addition to a monthly premium as well as copayments). In 1991 Medicare will cover 50 percent of expenses over $600 and in 1992, 60 percent of expenses over $652. And it won't cover elective cosmetic surgery or routine care for your eyes, feet, or teeth. Many people are unaware that Medicare doesn't cover nursing home or long-term nursing services for custodial care, but it will cover skilled nursing care in the home. If you do need these services, make sure you can pay for them yourself or with other forms of insurance.

Get a Wheelchair Prescription

Elderly people who need wheelchairs or hospital beds can save hundreds of dollars in out-of-pocket medical costs simply by asking their doctors to prescribe this medical equipment for 2 years rather than 6 months. How so? If the doctor prescribes the chair or bed for 6 months only, Medicare might cover 6 months of rental, then charge the patient for any future rental fees. If the doctor prescribes the equipment for 24 months, however, Medicare will purchase the equipment outright, and the patient will have it for the rest of his or her life. This can mean tremendous savings, since rentals for wheelchairs and hospital beds can cost several hundred dollars a month. [Editor's note: When this book went to press, this was accurate information. However, it is likely this will change. The new policy might mean the first time you rent an item, rental will be limited to 15 months. Thereafter, a doctor must recertify the need for the equipment.]

The medical supply house that works with your doctor may already act as your advocate in these cases. But it doesn't hurt for you or your family to speak up and ask the doctor to prescribe the equipment for a longer length of time, thus ensuring the outright purchase.

Medical Suppliers
That Give Discounts

To stay competitive, some medical supply houses offer reduced rates to people over age 65. If you happen to be purchasing equipment that *isn't* covered by Medicare, such as bathroom handrails, shower seats, or transfer benches, these discounts can save you a bundle. So look for a supplier who offers discounts to seniors.

When you purchase equipment that *is* covered by Medicare, make sure you get the most out of your Medicare dollars. For example, if Medicare pays $400 for a wheelchair, make sure your medical supply house gives you a $400 wheelchair, not a $250 one. Also, find a supplier who provides free delivery and installation of your equipment. You'll get more bang for your insurance buck by shopping around.

Unneeded Medical Gizmos

Senior citizens are sometimes approached by door-to-door salespeople trying to sell them medical equipment they don't need, like electronic nerve stimulators and hemaflow pumps. The salespeople, sometimes accompanied by a doctor, are merely looking for a pretext to write up a Medicare insurance claim. Typically, these sales are so profitable that the flimflam men offer to waive the 20 percent copayment that a Medicare subscriber would usually pay for such equipment. But take no chances. Protect yourself from being lured into such a sale. If salespeople turn up at your door with medical gadgets of dubious value, send them packing. If you are tempted to buy, discuss this with your doctor first.

The Low-Cost/No-Cost
Road to Health

Buy a Family Medical Guide

Buying a family medical guide can be a good investment. These reference books often offer clear advice on when your symptoms demand the skills of a doctor, and when they don't. They can save you a lot of unnecessary worry, hassle, and expense.

Take Care of Yourself: The Consumer's Guide to Medical Care by Donald Vickery, M.D., and James Fries, M.D. (Addison-Wesley, 1986) is one such book. Others are *The People's Medical Manual* by Howard R. and Martha E. Lewis (Doubleday, 1986); *Your Good Health: How to Stay Well, and What to Do When You're Not*, edited by William I. Bennett, M.D., et al. (Harvard University Press, 1987); and *Listen to Your Body* by Ellen Michaud, Lila L. Anastas, and the editors of *Prevention* magazine (Rodale Press, 1988).

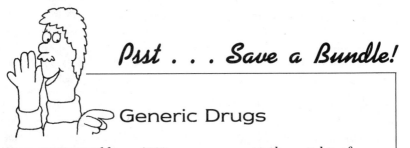

Psst . . . Save a Bundle!

Generic Drugs

You could save $100 or more a year just by switching from a name-brand prescription drug to its generic equivalent. Generic drugs are usually significantly cheaper than the original. But are generics as effective? Yes. All generic drugs must pass tests for potency established by the Food and Drug Administration. So why are they cheaper? Simply because their manufacturer doesn't have to pay for the drug's development. Once the patent runs out on a brand-name drug, anybody can produce and sell it without repeating the expensive process of inventing it.

If you decide to use the generic, be sure to speak up and ask for it. Don't rely on your doctor or your pharmacist to give you the generic automatically. (Your doctor may lean toward a particular brand out of habit, but your right to the generic equivalent is guaranteed by law in every state.)

Also—and this is important—remember that the price of the generic may vary widely from one drugstore to another. Simply buying generic doesn't guarantee you the lowest possible price. Some pharmacists don't bother to pass their savings on to you. So shop around to find the drugstore with the lowest price.

Get a Free Checkup

Many community organizations and hospitals throughout the country, for reasons of public health and public relations, now conduct annual, one-day health fairs in which they invite the public to a park or a gymnasium for cholesterol and blood pressure screening, colon cancer tests, health risk assessment, and computerized diet evaluations—all at no cost to the consumer. Such fairs can be entertaining and educational, especially for children. And since preventive health checkups are seldom covered by group health insurance, the tests will save you the cost of a trip to the doctor.

Do-It-Yourself Medical Testing

Americans are expected to spend $736 million on home medical tests in 1989. There are tests for blood sugar levels, venereal disease, pregnancy and ovulation, urinary tract infections, blood pressure, and vision problems, to name only a few.

Medical tests can save you money by helping you detect a health problem early, when it is still inexpensive and easy to treat. Fecal blood tests, for instance, can detect the first symptoms of bowel cancer. Home medical tests can also help you avoid an unnecessary visit to a doctor for a checkup that may not be covered by group health insurance or for a checkup for a condition that you can effectively monitor yourself. For example, blood glucose tests can help diabetics control a chronic health condition. Self-care equipment, especially used under the care of a physician, can help you make day-to-day health care decisions and can help you decide when to see the doctor. You can save money by borrowing some forms of testing equipment (such as blood pressure cuffs) from a home-health organization, or you may be able to rent it from a pharmacy.

Buy Over-the-Counter Reading Glasses

If you're in need of new eyeglasses for close work or reading, you can easily go to an optometrist or ophthalmologist and pay anywhere from $60 to $400 for an eye exam, custom-ground lenses, and frames. But in all 50 states, you have the option of buying over-the-counter reading glasses for as little as $5 or $10.

These nonprescription glasses are usually recommended for people over age 40 who do not need glasses for seeing at a distance but who need magnification lenses for reading. How do you find such glasses? Go to a pharmacy or department store that sells nonprescription glasses, and try several on while looking at test cards. Start with the weakest lenses first, and choose the glasses that enable you to read the test cards at a natural reading distance.

Free Government Health Advice

You can get free informational booklets from the U.S. government on just about any health care topic simply by writing to the Consumer Information Center in Pueblo, Colorado. You name it, the government's General Services Administration publishes a booklet on the subject. Interested in the use of ultrasound during pregnancy, or the latest in cures for arthritis? Concerned about high blood pressure, stroke, or bone loss? Just write to Uncle Sam.

Booklets on these subjects are yours for not much more than the price of postage. In all, the government offers several dozen pamphlets on nutrition, medical problems, mental health topics, drugs, exercise, and weight control. To receive a catalog of these items, just drop a note to Consumer Information Center-E, P.O. Box 100, Pueblo, CO 81009. And don't say the government never gave you anything.

Let Your Fingers
Do the Walking

You can avoid an expensive trip to the doctor's office by calling for advice before you decide to go in for a visit. Many times, whatever's bothering you or a family member can be handled over the phone. In some cases, a nurse will be able to advise you. If the nurse can't make an adequate decision, she or he will put the doctor on the line. On the basis of your symptoms, the doctor will decide whether there's a need to see you in person. Some doctors' offices designate certain hours of the day when they will be free to field your call.

Toll-Free
Health Care Hotlines

Do you have a question about hearing aids, cancer, or Alzheimer's disease? The U.S. government maintains a large number of toll-free hotlines to help you find the information you need. You might be put on hold for a while, but eventually someone will assist you and send you an information packet. For instance, hearing aids: 1-800-521-5247; cancer: 1-800-422-6237; Alzheimer's disease: 1-800-621-0379. For information on other health topics, call the National Health Information Center at 1-800-336-4797; in Maryland (301) 565-4167.

Floss or Face Tooth Loss

Periodontal disease is the most common—and can become the most expensive—dental problem among American adults. This ailment, which is a bacterial infection of the gums caused by failure to remove plaque from the teeth, affects three-quarters of all American adults to some degree. The first sign of periodontal disease is bleeding and/or sensitive gums. If untreated, it becomes painful and is the leading cause of tooth loss among people over 35. The oral surgery required to repair the damage to the gums can cost as much as $6,000 and with additional care $10,000, and many dental insurance plans don't cover it. To prevent periodontal disease, practice good oral hygiene. Brush and floss your teeth every day (brushing too hard can push back the gum line and accelerate the disease process, however), eat fresh fruits and vegetables that are high in vitamin C, and don't smoke cigarettes.

Maintain Ideal Body Weight
and Live Longer

You can lower your risk of a heart attack simply by reducing your weight. According to statistics from the National Heart, Blood and Lung Institute, a 40-year-old man who is 5 feet, 9 inches tall and weighs 178 pounds has a greater risk of developing coronary heart disease than if he weighed 148 pounds. Similarly, a 40-year-old woman who is 5 feet 4 inches tall and weighs 148 pounds has a greater risk of heart disease than if she weighed 124 pounds. Losing weight is probably the cheapest way to prevent a very expensive heart attack.

Psst . . . Save a Bundle!

Free Weight-Loss Programs

Every year Americans spend billions of dollars trying to lose weight. That money goes for books, franchise diet centers, the costs of specially prepared foods, and seminars on the psychology of weight loss. You can save yourself the $50 a week or more that these programs could cost by indulging in the simplest, most effective form of weight loss: regular exercise. By riding a bicycle or walking for a half hour, four or five days a week, you'll lose half a pound a week, or two pounds a month. By cutting only a few high-calorie foods out of your diet—ice cream, cake, beer, and so on—you'll lose weight even faster. At the same time, you'll feel better, look better, and have a better mental outlook.

Go on a Low-Fat Diet

Eliminating foods that are high in saturated fats is one way to prevent heart disease and "cut out the fat" in your weekly grocery bill. Potato chips cooked in coconut oil or lard, processed meats, packaged cakes and pies, and ice cream are all more expensive than low-fat foods such as vegetables, fruits, chicken, and fish. Lowering the amount of saturated fat in your diet will also prevent the buildup of cholesterol and plaque on the walls of your arteries, thus keeping your blood pressure down and reducing your risk of heart attacks.

Limit Alcohol

Every year, alcoholism costs our society billions of dollars in terms of lost productivity, damage to property, and avoidable medical treatment. Heavy drinking has been associated with a number of serious and expensive diseases, including cancer, heart disease, cirrhosis of the liver, and pancreatitis.

No one knows exactly how much alcohol you have to consume in order to damage your health, but some physicians feel that two ounces of alcohol a day—the amount contained in two cans of beer or two martinis—marks the absolute upper limit of safe drinking. Other physicians say that even this small amount can have ill effects. To protect yourself from expensive medical treatment, limit your alcohol consumption to a maximum of two drinks a day.

Prevent Back Injuries

Every year millions of Americans injure their backs and consequently miss millions of workdays. In fact, among people under 65, back injuries are second only to childbirth as a cause of hospitalization. Eight out of every ten Americans, it's been estimated, will suffer some form of back pain during their lives. Workers in the steel, mining, and construction industries, along with long-haul truckers and aircraft flight attendants, are those most likely to strain their backs. You can save hundreds or even thousands of dollars' worth of chiropractic treatment, lumbar pillows, and pain relievers by avoiding back injury. Here's how:

- Bend at the knees when you lift a heavy object.
- Use a pillow for low-back (lumbar) support when driving long distances or sitting for extended periods of time.
- Don't do straight-leg sit-ups. Instead, keep your knees bent and your arms across your chest, and curl up partway so your lower back is still on the floor.
- Last, but definitely not least, keep within the recommended weight range for your height and build. A protruding tummy puts strain on your back.

Join a Self-Help Group

The least expensive and most effective balm for many medical and/or emotional afflictions often comes not from physicians but from one's own peers—particularly those peers who suffer from the same problem. Spouses of alcoholics, parents of retarded children, dialysis patients, and others have all found strength in numbers by joining self-help groups that are tailored to their special needs. Membership in such groups costs little or nothing.

An estimated 15,000,000 people participate in 500,000 self-help groups in the United States each year. There are groups for the families of alcoholics, and for victims of diabetes, impotence, and cancer. There are groups for battered wives, veterans of Vietnam, compulsive gamblers, and countless more. Members of these groups offer free services that no doctor could ever provide, at any price. They call each other late at night, share books and insights, and extend to each other the love and empathy that often makes the most intractable medical problem bearable.

A number of self-help clearinghouses are scattered about the United States, and any of them can direct you toward the information you need to find the right group in your area. For instance, the Illinois Self Help Center, 1600 Dodge Avenue, Suite S-122, Evanston, IL 60201 (312) 328-0470, maintains the addresses of 75 self-help clearinghouses. To reach the National Self-Help Clearinghouse in New York, phone (212) 840-1259.

Do-It-Yourself Therapy

Psychotherapy costs as much as $100 an hour, and health insurance coverage for such therapy is usually limited. But you can save money by becoming your own therapist. Almost anyone can learn to avert emotional or mental crises by mastering a few simple relaxation techniques and applying them in times of stress.

While there are dozens of theories and methods of stress reduction, most of them consist of two simple steps. The first step is to recognize your own symptoms of negative arousal, such as tension, anger, or an urge to flee. The second step is to train yourself to respond to these symptoms by breathing deeply and relaxing your muscles. In fact, much of the stress of daily living can be resolved through relaxation techniques, and by understanding that it's useless to worry about events that are beyond one's control.

Make a Federal Case out of Your Illness

Every year, the National Institutes of Health (NIH) conducts hundreds of different research programs on a variety of illnesses.

Heart disease, multiple sclerosis, cancer, and herpes are only a few examples. If you or your doctor believes that you have an illness that qualifies you to participate in one of these research programs, you may be eligible for free treatment. Your doctor can recommend you as a candidate for an NIH program by calling the Warren Grant Magnuson Clinical Center's Patient Referral Services Unit at (301) 496-4891, or writing to John L. Decker, M.D., the director of the Clinical Center, Building 10, Room 2C128, National Institutes of Health, Bethesda, MD 20892.

Pharmaceutical Freebies

Doctors are constantly receiving free samples of medication from pharmaceutical salespeople, and many doctors are happy to pass along these free samples to their patients. If you only need a small supply of something—a small tube of ointment for an infant's rash, 10 or 12 tranquilizers during a time of family upheaval, a short course of antibiotics—chances are your doctor may be able to save you a few dollars on the prescription.

Free Trials for Hearing Aids

Hearing aids range in price from $450 to $1,000 for each ear, making them one of the largest single out-of-pocket expenses that people will ever have to face. Purchasing one can be confusing as well as nerve-wracking, since the cost of a hearing aid is rarely, if ever, covered by health insurance, and a high price doesn't necessarily guarantee high quality. Consequently, a hearing aid customer must become a savvy consumer.

Before signing a contract to purchase a hearing aid, make sure that the company you are buying it from has a license from the state. Forty-five states regulate hearing aid sales; the exceptions are New York, Massachusetts, Alaska, Colorado, and Vermont. Always ask for a 30-day trial period, and make sure that the contract spells out the exact terms under which you can exchange the device or return it for a refund. Keep in mind that you should see a doctor about your hearing problems—hearing loss might be a symptom of a hidden ailment.

For more consumer information about hearing aids, contact the National Hearing Aid Society in Livonia, Michigan, at 1-800-521-5247.

Keep Your Own
Medical Records

Few people have more than a sketchy recollection of what illnesses they've been treated for, what lab tests they've undergone, what medications and immunizations they've received, and what health insurance claims they've filed. In effect, they've committed the costly error of not keeping their own medical records. Why costly? Because keeping a personal medical history can prevent you from duplicating treatments and missing out on insurance reimbursements. In fact, it makes just as much sense to keep your own medical records as it does to balance your checkbook every month.

The People's Medical Society (PMS), a nonprofit consumer advocacy group, advises its members to record every medical condition they and their immediate family members have had; every visit to a physician or dentist; all medications taken, with dosages and side effects noted; all hospitalizations and lab tests; and the names and phone numbers of doctors, crisis centers, local police and fire departments, and ambulance services. For a sample medical record format, contact People's Medical Society, 462 Walnut Street, Allentown, PA 18102 (215) 770-1670. The form costs $3 for PMS members and $4 for nonmembers.

Barter for Medical Care

Are you a carpenter? An electrician? A caterer? An accountant? A golf pro? Chances are that your dentist, optometrist, or massage therapist might consider swapping his or her professional services for yours. Not every health practitioner will accept in-kind payments, of course, but such barter transactions are far from unusual. More than one plumber has traded the services of his wrench for his children's dental care. Your health practitioner might turn down your offer, but it can't hurt to ask.

Health Care
at Your Fingertips

No matter what disease or disorder you might have questions about, you will probably find the answers through *Health Care U.S.A.*, by Jean Carper (Prentice Hall Press, 1987), a massive 650-page paperback compendium of names, addresses, and telephone numbers of medical experts, research centers, and foundations all across America. Each chapter of this valuable book contains a state-by-state directory of specialists in a given disease, and at the end of each chapter there's a list of sources of free or low-cost information or materials on that disorder. By offering instant access to expert information, this book can save the average medical consumer time as well as money.

Home, Safe Home

Every year, far more people are killed in accidents right in their own homes than are killed on the nation's highways. A small investment in accident prevention can save thousands of dollars associated with an injury or fatality. To prevent falls, make sure stairways are adequately lit, with nonskid stair surfaces and handrails. Bathtubs should have nonslip surfaces or bath mats, and rugs on the bathroom floor should have nonskid backings. Area rugs throughout the house should have nonskid backings or should be anchored to the floor with double-sided masking tape.

To prevent fires, have smoke detectors on each floor and in the hallway, 10 feet from bedroom doors. Never store gasoline or other highly flammable liquids inside your house, and keep a fire extinguisher on every floor. Take care in the use of space heaters. To prevent poisonings, keep medicines and cleaning chemicals where children can't reach them. Keep all medications in their original containers, and don't give prescription drugs to anyone other than the person they were prescribed for.

Free Safety Items

Children seem to have an inborn radar that directs them toward uncovered electrical sockets and cabinets full of cleaning fluids. Consequently, all new parents face the challenge of child-proofing their homes. You may be able to defray the costs of child-proofing by obtaining free materials from your local municipal health bureau.

In Allentown, Pennsylvania, families with children age six or younger are eligible for a free home safety inspection by a member of the health bureau. The inspector identifies risks and hazards around the house, and provides a variety of free safety items. These include smoke detectors and batteries, "Mr. Yuk" stickers for medicine or soap containers, syrup of ipecac to induce vomiting, electrical outlet inserts, cabinet safety locks, and "Tot Finder" stickers that direct firemen to a child's bedroom.

The health bureau also rents infant and toddler car safety seats—which can cost $60 or more when purchased—for only $.50 a month. Check to see if the health bureau in your area provides similar services.

The Shriners Can Help

Every year, thousands of young Americans under the age of 18 receive free treatment for serious burns and orthopedic injuries at one of the 22 pediatric hospitals (19 of the 22 are orthopedic centers and 3 are burn centers) funded by the Shriners of North America, the well-known service organization. In 1987, 14,981 children were treated at the Shriners' hospitals.

Families are accepted for medical care on the basis of financial need. To qualify for free care, the patient must be under 18, and must be suffering from a severe burn or musculoskeletal injury. To find out if a child you know qualifies, call 1-800-237-5055 for an application form.

Know Your Local
Poison Control Center

Your two-year-old toddles into the living room with a big smile on his face and a small tin ant trap in his hand. You have no idea whether he has ingested the ant poison or not. Or your elderly aunt takes a dose of calamine lotion instead of Pepto-Bismol in a dimly lit bathroom one night. What do you do? You could rush to the emergency room or to your doctor's office. But you could also save time and money by calling your local poison control center first. No matter where you live, you probably have access to such a center, and the phone number should be at the front of your telephone directory. Of course, the best way to prevent poisonings is to keep all insecticides, detergents, and drugs away from small children, and be sure all medications are clearly labeled and never taken in the dark. But if someone in your family does consume a potentially toxic substance, you can call the poison control center for instant, free advice or reassurance.

Save a Life for $10
or Less

By learning cardiopulmonary resuscitation (CPR), you might be able to save a life. To find out when and where you can attend a CPR class, call your local chapter of the American Red Cross or the American Heart Association. The Red Cross charges $10 or so for the class. If your employer decides to sponsor a class, your out-of-pocket cost might be even less.

Donate Blood

By donating blood to your local blood bank, you can sometimes ensure that your entire family—including your children, parents, grandparents, and even your in-laws—will receive blood at a cut-rate price if they ever need it.

In one city, for instance, a blood bank ordinarily charges $35 for lab costs plus a $35 nonreplacement fee for a pint of blood. The lab costs are covered by health insurance, and the patient is billed for the nonreplacement fee. But the blood bank waives that fee for donors and their families.

This protocol is called the split fee system. It is an incentive dreamed up by blood banks and insurers to boost blood donations. If your insurance plan covers 100 percent of your blood costs, but the blood bank doesn't use the split fee system, then it won't matter whether you donate blood or not.

Apply for Medicaid

Through its Medicaid programs, the federal government provides financial assistance to the millions of families who can't pay for their own medical care. Families with a gross monthly income of $200 to $1,000 can qualify for Medicaid's Blue Medical Card, with which they can purchase almost any medical service. Families with net monthly incomes of $392 to $1,100 (after deducting taxes, transportation costs, and other necessities) can qualify for Medicaid's Green Medical Card, which pays for all medical care except dentistry and prescription drugs.

Medicaid requires the families to make a copayment if they are able, and the government won't pay for the services of doctors who choose not to participate in the program. Keep in mind that a family does not have to be chronically poor to qualify for Medicaid benefits. If family income falls below the eligibility level during a month when a family member incurs large medical bills, Medicaid may pay for that care, even though family income at other times surpasses the eligibility limit. For more information about Medicaid, call your state department of public welfare.

13

TELEPHONES: DIALING FOR DOLLARS

Saving on telephone service is easy, but it's not simple. That's because there are more options, allowing more savings, but making things more complicated.

Where once "the phone company" owned everything, now there are phone compan*ies*, not just one. Most people are choosing to buy equipment, from wiring to telephones, rather than rent. Telephone consumers are signing up for competing long-distance services, or they're exercising their option of equal access to all services each time they make a long-distance call. They're eschewing traditionally expensive services, such as collect calls, by charging calls on credit cards—all without operator assistance. Even local callers are finding options that let them slash the fees they pay for these calls. If you're not seeing savings in your phone bill, read on.

Services You Probably Don't Need

Call Waiting

Call waiting allows you to interrupt one call to take another. Recent TV ads imply that without call waiting, you won't get an emergency phone call. But the truth is that in a real emergency situation, the person trying to get through to a busy line can call an operator and ask the operator to cut in. So don't be fooled into thinking that you need call waiting to take emergency calls. Unless you take a lot of business calls at home, or you like interrupting your phone conversations with friends to tell other friends that you're already on the line, call waiting is probably a frill. Decline call waiting and save $36 a year.

Three-Way Calls

Another business-beneficial service, three-way calls allow you to talk to two people at once. But do you really need—or want—to talk to your brother in Peoria and your sister in Cleveland at the same time? Decline three-way calls and save $36 a year.

Call Forwarding

You must be away from home an awful lot, and you must expect some very important phone calls if you pay to have each incoming call to your empty house automatically patched through to wherever you are. Why not give the phone number of where you'll be to the people you're expecting calls from? Or buy yourself an answering machine with a remote function that allows you to call in to your machine from wherever you are and hear your messages. Decline call forwarding and save $36 a year.

Unlisted Number

This service can eliminate calls from people who know your name, but it won't screen out those unwanted sales calls, which increasingly are made by computer dialing (the computer is programmed to dial telephone numbers in every possible combination). Decline an unlisted number and save $21 a year.

Touch-Tone

If you've got three rotary dial phones in very good shape (especially old AT&T phones, which seem capable of surviving nuclear attack), but you need a touch-tone line for long-distance service, consider buying a touch-tone simulator. Available at Radio Shack or other stores with phone accessories, the $5 palm-size boxes beep into a receiver, fooling it into thinking the phone is a touch-tone for long-distance service. Decline touch-tone and save $12 per year.

Speed Dialing

By punching two programmed numbers, you can quickly dial frequently called numbers, including long-distance numbers. Bell offers a 30-number service and a cheaper 8-number service. But ask yourself if it's really worth the fee to punch two digits instead of seven. If it is, you may want to buy a phone with programmable dialing or a box that works with your phone. You'll pay no monthly fee to use them. Decline speed dialing and save $21 to $30 a year.

Inside Wiring
Maintenance Agreements

Your local telephone service supplier will offer you a contract to maintain and repair your lines. Don't bother. You're better off pocketing the $2 to $3 a month this protection will cost. If you do have a line problem you can't solve, you can call for service and pay the one-time bill. It won't be cheap, but service needs on simple wiring are rare. (When's the last time you needed wire service?)

900 Numbers

Callers to 900 numbers are willing to pay a fee for a service received over the phone, and often at a far higher price than they could pay elsewhere. The services offer such information as weather, traffic, or sports scores and usually carry a $.50 to $1 fee.

These calls can really add up. If you depend on a 900 number to give you the weather every day, you'll be paying $10 or more by the end of the month. For less money, you could have bought a daily newspaper—and gotten the sports scores, too.

Gab Lines

The most costly 900 services are gab lines aimed at singles and teenagers. Ranging in price from about $.25 to more than $1 a minute, these lines allow conversations among several people. But teenagers—never known to be shy of the telephone—have run up bills as high as $4,000 a month on these lines!

Check to see if your phone company offers a blocking service that prohibits calls to these lines. In some areas, the service is free. In others, it costs about $5 a month—a fee that could save you hundreds.

Cheaper by the Dozen

Bell allows a discount when more than one service is purchased at one time. But it charges a hookup fee—about $5—each time a service is added singly.

Long-Distance Details

Get a Card

The cheapest way to place a call is direct dial. But what about those times when you're in a phone booth or placing a long-distance call from someone else's home? You'd probably opt for a collect call or a third-number billing—the most expensive calls you can place. Instead, apply for and use a long-distance charge card. It eliminates the need for collect calls, and the $.50 or $1 fee you pay for each charge card use is far below the collect call rate.

You Can Restrict Card Calls

Don't pay high-priced rates for collect calls when your son or daughter calls home from college or camp. Instead, get him or her a restricted calling card. With a restricted card, you can specify which phone numbers can be called with the card, and these calls will be billed to you. You won't have to worry about your kid calling all over the world on the calling card—just have it restricted to your home number and perhaps to a few other numbers you both agree on.

Watch the Clock

When you place a call is just as important as how you place a call in determining your rate. From cheapest to most expensive, the billing periods are:

Weekends, from Friday at 11:00 P.M. to Sunday at 5:00 P.M.
Holidays, which generally follow weekend rates
Nights, from 11:00 P.M. to 8:00 A.M.

Evenings, from 5:00 P.M. to 11:00 P.M.
Days, from 8:00 A.M. to 5:00 P.M.

Use the discount periods to your best advantage. If you have to call a West Coast business during business hours, and you live on the East Coast, call after 5:00 P.M. your time; it will be three hours earlier on the West Coast, but you'll get the lower evening rate. If you're a West Coast resident who has to phone an eastern business, do the opposite: Phone before 8:00 A.M. your time, when it will be three hours later on the East Coast. You'll get the lowest nighttime rate for the call.

Use the same trick for calling friends or relatives if you can't wait for the weekend to make the call. Judicious timing of long-distance calls can save hundreds of dollars a year if you're a frequent caller.

To hold down the length of your call, use a subtle alarm: a silent hourglass, an alarm wristwatch, or the next interval of chimes on your wall or mantel clock, for instance. You may also want to try putting a copy of last month's long-distance bill near the phone!

Psst . . . Save a Bundle!

800 Numbers = Free Calls!

Thousands of businesses offer toll-free numbers for customers. The numbers are called by dialing 1-800 plus the number. Public libraries usually carry directories listing toll-free numbers. You can often find the number you want by calling the reference section of the library, or by using the book there.

If you want the 800 number of a particular company, or if you want to know if a particular company has an 800 number, call 1-800-555-1212.

Choosing
a Long-Distance Company

The Savings Game

The time may be past for saving big simply by picking one long-distance company over another. Rates vary, but by much less than they did in the mid-1980s. Your savings may depend on:

- Where you live. Not all services are available to all locations.
- Where you call. Some services have bigger discounts on inter-state calls but smaller ones on same-state calls.
- When you call. All companies offer similar discounts for evenings, and bigger discounts for nights, weekends, and holidays. But some companies offer only the evening rate for weekday holidays instead of the cheaper night rate.

Shop Around

Pricing long-distance companies is easy. Each has a toll-free number. Call and ask each company to give you basic price information right over the phone. In addition, ask them to mail you a rate card so you can compare. The companies are:

Allnet: 1-800-982-8888
AT&T: 1-800-222-0300
ITT: 1-800-526-3000
MCI: 1-800-333-4000

Mid-American:
  1-800-328-8555
U.S. Sprint: 1-800-521-4949
  or 1-800-531-4686

Compare Services

Not all companies offer exactly the same services or exactly the same discounts. With some companies, you earn a volume discount. It may not pay to jockey from service to service in any given month in an effort to get more favorable rates for certain cities or certain times. If doing so loses you the volume discount, you may sacrifice a 1 to 10 percent savings.

    Some services require a touch-tone line. Others allow you to use a rotary-dial line by calling a toll-free number to get an operator, who will place the call for you. Charge card fees vary. Some are twice as high as others per call.

If you want to change your primary company, your local company will charge a fee—up to $15 in some areas. Check with the company you want to make the switch to; while some will credit the fee to your first bill, others will not.

Submit a Bill

You can find out which long-distance company is cheapest by submitting a typical bill to the various companies and asking what it would cost if you were their customer.

Or, if you want the opinion of a disinterested party, you can contact: Telecommunications Research and Action Center (TRAC), P.O. Box 12038, Washington, DC 20005.

For $35, TRAC will custom-analyze the cost of 30 interstate direct-dial calls that you specify (you can give them a sample of your usual phone bill or create a list of your commonly called numbers) under six long-distance companies. It includes several rate structures. TRAC also provides, for $1, a chart called Tele-Tips that compares standard groups of long-distance calls under eight companies. This may give you some idea of what your costs would be, but unless the specific cities that you call are listed, it may not be very helpful.

Trial Use

Equal access laws enable you to try any phone company you want that is available in your area. These laws also require you to choose a service that you access automatically at home by dialing 1 plus the area code and number. You are allowed to name an "alternate," for which you are given a five-digit access code. The fact is, though, that you can use any of the others by dialing their individual access codes and then the area code and number. You will be billed on your regular monthly bill from your local service.

The access codes also allow you to use other services if you can't get through on your regular service during busy periods—typically, holidays and prime business hours. The access codes are:

Allnet: 10444 or 10666   Mid-American: 10801 or
AT&T: 10288   10001
ITT: 10488   U.S. Sprint: 10777 or 10333
MCI: 10222

Local Calls

Take an Allowance

Sprawling suburbs and expanding commuting patterns have rede-
fined our localities, and many people end up frequently calling
areas that are not served by free calls. Local calling options are an
answer to these small but mounting fees for toll calls to outlying
local areas.

Your monthly local service fee probably allows four to eight
of these local toll calls (more at night and on weekends). By paying
a higher monthly fee, you can increase the number of local toll
calls you can make. A still higher fee will give you unlimited local
calls.

To determine how much you should pay, you'll have to figure how many calls you make and multiply that times the local
toll—typically 2 to 8 cents per call—and subtract your lowest local
monthly flat fee. If that figure is greater than the accumulation of
individual fees, stick with billing by the call. If that figure is
smaller, pay the higher monthly fee and forgo billing by the call.
As with long-distance service, you pay higher rates for daytime,
weekday calls than for evening and weekend calls.

Equipment Decisions

Which Brand Should You Buy?

You want to get the most for your money when you buy a telephone. Many brands perform well, so your choice may come
down to price and features—you want a combination of both.
Brands with similar features can vary in price by as much as 100
percent.

AT&T phones are the standard for transmission of sound and durability, but they are expensive. Other, less expensive, phones performed as well—even better—in tests by consumer magazines.

The simplest push-button phones can be bought for as little as $10 at discount stores. But phones with the most accessories and functions can cost $120 or more. Never pay list; competition is fierce, and discounts of 30 percent or more are common, so be sure to shop around.

Money-Saving Features

Some telephone features may cost more up front but can save you money in the long run:

- Phones with programmed quick dialing can save you a monthly fee to your phone company—perhaps $36 per year.
- Push-button phones that switch to pulse dialing can save you a monthly touch-tone fee, saving $15 per year or more.
- Some phones are easily adaptable to wall mounting, so they can be moved from room to room.
- Cordless phones, although more expensive feature for feature, can save you from having to run additional wiring.

Some phones have convenience features that are hard to put a price tag on, such as adaptability to hearing aids, compatibility with answering machines, and memory retention for programmed dialing when moved to a new location.

It's All in the Sound

Regardless of features, don't settle for a phone that doesn't receive or send voices well. These operations are critical, and some cheaper phones just don't, or won't, perform up to par under heavy use.

Do-It-Yourself Installation

Wiring Is Simple

Installing phone wiring and telephones can be quite simple, and it will save you a lot of money. Simply getting the phone company to send a serviceperson to your house costs about $30 these days, and that's before he or she does anything! Jacks and plugs are standard, and adapters are readily—and inexpensively—available for conversion to the new standards from the old standards. Since telephone wiring is low voltage, you can be free of fear from shocks.

Stores that carry telephone wiring equipment also carry do-it-yourself instruction booklets with detailed illustrations. Often, the wiring itself includes instructions with enough detail that even inexperienced do-it-yourselfers can follow. Wiring from one floor to another is a bit complicated—you'll have to fish the wire through a wall or closet—but still a definite DIY project.

Just remember that your own wiring becomes your responsibility. A quick check of plugs at the jack will usually turn up the cause of a silent phone line, and a reinserted plug usually solves the problem. If not, be prepared to pay big bucks to have a phone serviceperson take a look.

Tools of the Trade

To do your own telephone wiring, you'll need basic tools:

slotted screwdriver
power drill
drill bits that will make a hole big enough to pass a
    standard phone plug through (about $\frac{3}{8}$ inch)

Three jacks and wiring could easily be installed for less than $30 if the materials are purchased at discount stores. Wiring accessories sold in discount stores are often the same brands sold for 20 to 40 percent more in electronics stores. These devices are simple; there's not much that can malfunction, so go for the cheaper ones.

Postage Power

Learn to write letters again.

Remember pen pals? Notes from home amid the box of cookies sent to your college dorm? Love letters? (Nobody has immortalized love phone calls in the sand, right?)

The advent of cheap telephone service has made letter-writing a lost art—an irony in an age when families and friends are scattered far and wide. A ten-page letter can cost far less than a 10-minute long-distance call, and you'll get to say so much more.

You can, of course, use the mail for purely pragmatic purposes: to give directions, file complaints, or shop by mail (much cheaper than ordering by phone, unless there's a toll-free number).

Extend Yourself

If your house has telephone wiring and you simply want a telephone in another part of a room or another part of the house, you may be able to do it with a simple extension phone cord that couples to your existing cord. Such an extension may cost as little as $2 to $4. The phone company would charge up to ten times that just to come to your house; the wiring would cost even more.

14

TAKING THE BITE OUT OF TAXES

Congress will fiddle with the tax laws this year. Congress, after all, fiddles with the tax laws every year. Another thing that is certain about taxes is that you'll have to pay them. The trick, of course, is to pay as little as possible. To do that, you need a good knowledge of the laws—and the loopholes. If your taxes are really complicated, the price you will pay for a good accountant will be repaid through savings on your taxes. In this chapter we give hints on ways to cut your taxes and tips for the best way to prepare them.

All about Deductions

Saving on Interest

Deductions for nonmortgage-related consumer interest—on credit cards, auto loans, bill-consolidation loans, personal loans, revolving charge accounts, and such—will phase out into 1990, then disappear. This makes the cost of borrowing more expensive. To avoid running up interest, consider:

- Paying cash. This is always the cheapest way to buy. Sometimes it even earns a discount. If you can't pay cash, consider saving until you can.
- Rediscovering layaway. Some merchants will set aside products and allow monthly payments at no interest until the item is paid for, with delivery on final payment.
- Ninety days same-as-cash. Some stores allow customers— usually, familiar customers—to break cash payments into three installments without interest charges. If you're bargaining with your merchant, remind him that it also costs him less if you don't use your bank charge card. (The store pays a fee every time it allows an item to be charged.)
- Paying your balance in full. Most cards allow you 30 days interest-free. Paying your bill as close to the 30-day limit as you can without being overdue not only allows you to avoid an interest charge but also allows you to use the bank's money while your own cash earns you interest.

Control Credit Cards

It's tempting to cut credit cards in half, but don't. You may need a credit card when you go to rent a car or a hotel room, or in some stores, to get a check approved. Instead, discipline yourself not to use them. If you must, lock them in a safe place.

Prepay Deductible Items

Under current tax laws, not as many costs are deductible. But of those that are, prepaying them before the close of the current tax year will lower your tax bill. This is especially useful if you have unusually high income for the current year—from overtime, perhaps, or a temporary second job—and need an extra tax break, but don't want to increase your total bills.

Although you cannot prepay interest on several months' worth of next year's mortgage payments to give yourself a tax break this year, you *can* prepay the January interest payment in December because that interest is a charge that accrued in December. So suppose you have a mortgage payment, of which $500 is interest, due on January 1. By paying the $500 interest in December—perhaps just a week early—you'll have an extra $500 to deduct from your current-year taxable income. In January, you will have to pay the principal due on your mortgage, but not the interest (which you've already paid).

Give in December

Ever wonder why you hear from your old alma mater and lots of other charities right around holiday time? They're not hoping to cash in on Christmas cheer, but, instead, they're banking on the fact that savvy taxpayers improve their current-year tax picture by prepaying the coming year's charitable contributions in December. So give to your favorite charity in December, and lower your tax bill in April.

The Down Side to Prepaying

Prepaying interest has one disadvantage: It will reduce the deductible interest you can claim the *following* year. If you have reduced income the following year, don't prepay.

Pay It Next Year

Sometimes you don't have enough of a deductible expense to be able to deduct in any one year. In medical costs, for instance, you may run up large bills, but not more than the 7.5 percent of adjusted gross income you need to deduct the costs. Try to group two years' worth of bills into one year. For instance, let's say it's November or December and you have a large bill to pay. If you pay it right away, you won't have enough in medical costs to deduct. But you also know that high medical bills will continue through the coming year. Arrange with your doctor to pay the current-year bills in January. That way, you can combine them with all the bills of the following year and possibly have enough to deduct at that time. Your doctor may be happy to do it if he or she has higher than anticipated income for the current year and wants to defer some of the income to the next. You both save.

Tax Advice for Business Owners

Buy at the End of the Year

If you have a business—even part time—that earns you a profit through your active participation, you can cut your tax bill by buying equipment in December rather than after the first of the year. For instance, a writer who buys a computer for business use on the last day of the year can write off the whole cost in the current year. (The IRS allows you up to $10,000 capitalization a year, outside of auto and real estate spending.) Or, if you do woodworking on the side and earn a profit, you can buy a power tool as late as the last day of December and write off the whole cost in the current year.

Avoid the Hobby Tax

It's hard to write off all hobby expenses under the new tax laws. To do so, your activity has to be a business, not a hobby. And to achieve business status, you must make a profit in three years out of five. Otherwise, you may write off expenses only to the point that they equal earnings on the activity.

With good planning, you can achieve business status. There are certain steps you can take to even out your hobby's cash flow:

- In good years, when a profit is assured, defer late-year billing so that some of the revenue arrives in the following year. It will give you a head start on making a profit the following year and, therefore, in writing off next year's expenses.
- Time your business purchases so that no one year has too much targeted as a deductible. If profits are up, consider moving up a purchase to year-end. If profits are slim but you expect better profits the next year, delay the purchase to the following year.
- If you're confident of meeting the three-years-out-of-five profitability requirement, or already have, don't juggle spending or billing; take the loss and use it to offset other income.
- Set up separate accounts for your business expenditures. Unlike consumer interest, business interest is totally deductible (as a business expense).

Health Insurance Know-How

If you're self-employed, you can deduct 25 percent of your health insurance premiums as a business expense. You may itemize the other 75 percent as a medical cost, as everyone may, but only if your medical bills total at least 7.5 percent of adjusted gross income.

Business Cars Can Make Sense

If you use a car more than 50 percent for business, you may depreciate it up to $12,800 over six years: 20 percent the first year (up to $2,560), 32 percent the second year (up to $4,100), and varying amounts through the next four. If you sell a car for less than the amount you've depreciated, you can deduct the difference.

You may not depreciate a car in the current year if it is bought within the last three months and does not total more than 40 percent of your total purchases during the year. You can still get the $2,560 write-off, however, if you expense up to 20 percent or $2,560 of the car's cost under the $10,000-per-year capital expenses rule.

The Advantages of Home Offices

The IRS lets you write off parts of many home expenses—utilities, telephone, homeowner's insurance, and mortgage interest payments—if you maintain a *legitimate* home office for business. You also may depreciate that part of your house that is used as an office.

But think carefully before you declare a home office. If you sell your house, you must immediately pay capital gains on the portion of your house used as a business. You may not defer that profit by buying another house within two years, as you can with capital gains on a residence. That could cost you far more than you were able to save in reduced taxes.

The Paper Chase

Do It Yourself

If your tax forms are relatively simple, you may want to do them yourself and save the cost of hiring a tax preparer. Tax instructions are complicated, but the IRS will help you by phone or in person at a branch office, if one is nearby. (Check the blue pages of your telephone directory or look under U.S. Government.)

Your library is likely to have all the forms you need and a wealth of printed information. If you're reasonably intelligent and organized, you can do your own taxes in a few hours. You can even deal with the most complicated information that most of us face on our tax forms—itemizing, the child care form, a home-equity loan, an IRA, dividends, and part-time self-employment income.

Records are most important. File all your relevant receipts in one place. Look at the forms early so you know what to expect and what information to gather.

Hiring a Pro

If you decide to hire a professional to do your taxes for you, you'll choose from tax preparers and certified public accountants. Trained preparers are cheaper. They are paid to know the rules and fill out the forms properly. Simple returns without itemized deductions may cost $25 to $35. Itemized tax returns with earnings, interest income, dividends, child care credit, and an IRA may cost you $50 to $75. The more forms you have, the more you will pay. The same holds true for the amount of income sources you have.

An accountant will cost you more but is a good investment if your finances are more complicated. Your accountant is a counselor who will advise you through the year on your tax status. Fees can vary by location and experience, but $50 to $75 an hour wouldn't be unreasonable. Your accountant will bill you in parts of an hour—in one-tenth increments, for instance. You have a right to an itemized bill.

Tax Breaks

IRAs

Although not as beneficial for many as they used to be, Individual Retirement Accounts (IRAs) can still cut taxes for millions. For some people, they can reduce taxable income in the year in which a contribution is made by deferring taxes on the amount contributed, up to $2,000 a year. And for any IRA holder, they can shelter thousands of dollars of investment earnings from taxes as they accumulate. In each case, you don't pay taxes on the money until the money is withdrawn in retirement, when your income and tax bracket will be lower. That's a lot of money in your pocket over the years.

For you to qualify for a full deferment, you must meet two criteria:

■ Neither you nor your spouse is covered by a pension plan at work.

- If neither of you is covered, your combined adjusted gross income is no greater than $40,000 a year. If you are single, your adjusted gross income must be $25,000 or less.

If you qualify only for a partial IRA write-off, consider taking it. You'll get the same kind of tax breaks, but for smaller amounts. For partial deferment, the same rules on qualified pension plan at work apply, and your combined adjusted gross income can be no greater than $50,000 ($35,000 single). The allowable $2,000 deferment shrinks for you on a sliding scale to as little as $200 a year at the $50,000 income cutoff.

Tax-Free IRA Savings

If your income is more than $50,000 a year and you qualify for an employee pension plan, you cannot defer current-year earnings on an IRA contribution. But consider an IRA anyway. You can still maintain an IRA if you work by investing up to $2,000 of your after-tax income yearly. Although you may not adjust your taxable income downward by that amount, the interest your IRA earns will go tax-free until you withdraw it in retirement. It's a good deal that can save you thousands of dollars. If you can afford to do it, place as much of the money as you can in high-yield but safe savings vehicles, such as guaranteed mutual funds or insured certificates of deposit.

If you are a nonworking spouse or earn $250 a year or less, you may contribute up to $250 to an IRA, tax-deferred. So, if you're a qualifying couple with one income, your deferred IRA contribution can total $2,250.

To avoid taking a big loss, leave your IRA alone. Don't withdraw anything before you are 59½ years old or totally disabled. To violate that limit lands you a 10 percent penalty and a tax payment on the deferred income you have withdrawn.

Keogh Plans

Keogh Plans are, in essence, IRAs for the self-employed. The limits on Keogh contributions are more favorable, however. Keogh contributions are not limited by spousal qualification in a pension plan, for instance. And with a Keogh, contributions can go as high as $30,000 a year—but no more than 20 percent of annual income. As with IRAs, earnings on Keoghs escape tax until they are withdrawn in retirement. Since income is likely to put you in a lower bracket at that time, you'll pay far less in taxes when the money is withdrawn.

Higher contributions can be made under certain kinds of plans. A Defined Goal Keogh raises the limits for contributions to meet that savings goal over a specified period of time. As with IRAs, Keoghs carry a penalty for early withdrawal, so it pays to leave your funds invested until age $59\frac{1}{2}$ or longer.

Pensions

Pensions, like other retirement plans, accumulate interest tax-free—until the funds are withdrawn in retirement. Pension funds are made up of these parts: employer contributions, employee contributions, and earnings on contributions. You'll have to pay taxes on any part of that on which you haven't paid taxes already—your employer's contribution and the earnings. You've probably contributed from after-tax income, so that prorated part of your pension income will be tax-free.

Although some plans may allow early withdrawal, it's best to avoid withdrawal until retirement, when your income and tax rate will be lowest. You'll also avoid any penalties associated with early withdrawal.

You cannot escape the taxes owed on pensions by passing the pension on to a spouse as part of your estate. The spouse will have to pay taxes on any amount that you would—but at his or her rate, not yours.

Give Money Away

Giving too much money away will bring a tax on the giver. The IRS allows you to give away up to $10,000 a year to any one person, including your children, and up to $600,000 during your lifetime. Look for ways to stretch the limit:

■ If you want to give more than $10,000 and avoid taxes, and you are married, declare up to $10,000 as a gift from just one of you and the next $10,000 as a gift from the other spouse. Both spouses must agree to this.

■ If you intend to pay tuition or medical expenses, pay them directly, rather than giving the money to your child and having him

Psst . . . Save a Bundle!

401(k)s:
Something for Nothing

The benefits of an employer-sponsored 401(k) plan are so good they seem illegal. But they're not. They are in fact one of the best savings devices under the federal tax laws. Under a 401(k), which is named for the section of the tax law describing it, you build retirement savings, cut your current-year income taxes, get a partial matching contribution from your employer, and earn tax-deferred interest on your account.

Here's how it works: The IRS allows you to reduce your taxable income up to 6 percent (or up to a certain dollar amount that changes yearly) by putting the money into your 401(k) account. Many employers contribute a partial match—typically 25 to 50 percent—of the employee's contribution (the employer match is *not* a requirement). A 50 percent employer-paid contribution is tantamount to 50 percent interest: It's money you would never get were you not in the plan. As with the earnings you set aside, you pay no federal income tax on the employer contribution or the interest until the money is withdrawn in retirement (in other words, the payment of tax is deferred). By then, you'll likely be in a lower tax bracket.

See the table "401(k) Savings and Payroll Reductions," which shows how much you can save per week with a 401(k).

The big disadvantage to a 401(k) is limited access to your money. You will be able to withdraw your money only for reasons of hardship: to buy a first home, to pay uninsured medical costs, or to finance higher education. If you do withdraw it before retirement, you'll have to pay income tax on the amount withdrawn, as well as a 10 percent penalty.

or her write the tuition check. Direct medical and educational payments are exempt from gift taxes.

■ If you want to give away a large sum or valuable property without paying estate taxes, consider an irrevocable trust. The assets will pass to whomever you designate without becoming part of your estate, but only if you forfeit all control of the trust. You will never again own this property. This not only cuts estate taxes, it speeds up passing on the property to your heirs. A trust does incur fees to the trustee or administrator, however, which will come out of the trust fund.

401(k) Savings and Payroll Reductions

GROSS WEEKLY PAY	$200	$300	$500
Pretax contribution (6%)	12	18	30
Employer's contribution (3%)	6	9	15
Total weekly savings	18	27	45
Weekly payroll reduction*	10	15	22

NOTE: These examples show the amount you can save if you contribute 6 percent on a pretax basis together with an employer's matching 3 percent contribution (50 percent of 6 percent). The examples also estimate the amount that would be deducted from your pay, taking into account your reduced taxes using 1987 tax tables. The employer's contribution is not a requirement of a 401(k), although this is done by many companies.

*This amount shows the estimated effect on pay for a single employee with one exemption, taking into account reduced federal income tax withholdings only, based on 1987 tax rates. In some locations, state and local taxes will also be reduced.

Children and Taxes

A Grand Investment Idea

Children can supply more tax breaks than their deductions as your dependents. One way to save on taxes is to shift some income to your children. Investment income earned by children under 14 will be taxed at the parent's rate—except for the first $500 a year, which isn't taxed at all, and the next $500, which is taxed at a child's lower rate.

Your Child's Uncle Sam

U.S. Savings Bonds are a great instrument for saving two ways on taxes. Interest earned on the bonds is not taxed until the bonds are redeemed. So, instead of buying bonds in your name, put them in your child's name. Have the child wait until age 14 or older to cash them in, and you'll not only defer paying taxes on the interest, you'll also shift the income earned on them into the child's lower tax bracket.

Growing Up with Stocks

You can save for your child and lower your tax bill through growth stocks that don't pay dividends, or tax-exempt securities, such as municipal bonds. If you buy stocks that do pay dividends and put them in your child's name, that income will be taxed at your rate until your child is 14, and the child's rate after that.

The $10,000 Giveaway

You can direct up to $10,000 a year in income to a child without paying gift taxes.

A Trusty Investment

Consider setting up a minor's trust. It is taxed at the child's 15 percent rate, rather than your likely 28 percent rate, even when the child is under 14. You can structure the trust so that the child gets none of the assets or earnings until he or she is 21.

Hire Your Child

If you are self-employed, consider hiring your child and paying him or her wages. The wages will become a deductible business expense for you and taxable to your child at the child's lower rate.

15

BEATING HIGH
INSURANCE RATES

Buying insurance, like a lot of things, is something you do "just in case." Most just-in-case decisions cost very little, if anything: Preparing for a trip, you check your spare tire—just in case. Not sure of your growing nephew's size, you get the bigger sweater—just in case. So what? The tire costs you dirty hands, and the sweater will fit next year.

But what about buying insurance? That just-in-case decision can cost you thousands in unneeded premiums. Or it can cost you and your family tens of thousands in very needed benefits. Insurance comes in as many varieties and with as many options as any other consumer product. The big difference is that it's a product you may never use. If you need it only once, though, you'd better hope the decisions you made were good ones.

To help you make good decisions, here are some tips on gauging your insurance needs, comparing products, and saving on premiums.

Buying Health Insurance

Group Rates Save Big

The cheapest way to buy health insurance is through a group plan. Often, your employer pays all or part of the premium. Even if the total premium is deducted from your pay, it will be lower in a group plan than through an individual purchase.

Once you're in a group plan, you will have an opportunity to buy the insurance at individual rates without getting a physical examination if you resign or are fired. But you'll see quickly just how expensive health insurance can be. Family coverage is likely to run from $150 to $300 a month, depending on where you live and the level of protection.

Group Rates for the Self-Employed

You never realize just how expensive health insurance is until you have to pay for it out of your own pocket at individual rates. If you're self-employed, you can save up to 25 percent on your health premiums by joining organizations that offer their members group rates on health insurance.

One such group is the Council of Smaller Enterprises in Cleveland, Ohio. This group, composed of self-employed or small-businessmen, negotiated with the local Blue Cross Society to provide health insurance for its members at a group rate. To find such an organization in your community, check with the local chamber of commerce.

Save $495 through AAA

Anybody whose car has broken down in the desert wilds of Nevada or the asphalt wilds of Brooklyn (or anywhere else for that matter) knows that membership in the American Automobile Association (AAA) often saves a lot of time, money, and hassle. But few people realize that AAA can also help save on medical bills. For an added fee of only $5 a year, AAA members are also eligible for a $500 payment toward almost any medical bill stemming from injuries suffered in a car, bus, train, boat, or other "common carrier." This insurance covers emergency room costs, surgery, skilled nursing care, wheelchair rental, oxygen therapy, and many other therapies. If you are already an AAA member, this small investment can pay rich dividends.

Buy Basic Coverage

If you must pay for your health insurance, check to see if you can buy core coverage—basic hospitalization and major medical, but not eye or dental care. This could save you $50 a month or more in premiums. Buying just basic coverage *or* major medical would save you more.

Basic coverage covers you up to a limited number of days, and major medical takes over after that. Although it would be cheaper to buy major medical only, it's unlikely you could handle anything other than the simplest of medical emergencies out of pocket. Even if you have a $6,000 self-insurance fund, hospital rooms can cost $400 a day or more. The fund won't last until your major medical kicks in.

Accept a Higher Deductible

If you are forced to purchase individual health insurance at high rates, you can reduce your annual premiums substantially by paying a higher deductible. For instance, a comprehensive policy with a deductible of $250 might cost thousands of dollars a year in premiums, but a policy with a deductible of $5,000 might cost only $200 or so a year. For the person who is willing to gamble that he or she won't need to see a doctor all year, high-deductible insurance can be a bargain.

Pay Premiums in One Lump

It's almost always cheaper to pay cash than to make time payments, and that's as true for health insurance as it is for automobiles. According to one insurance company, a young family of three with an individual health insurance policy can save about $90 a year by paying their premium in one lump sum rather than paying quarterly. In this case, a 36-year-old man with a 30-year-old wife and 1-year-old child would pay $2,384 per year in quarterly payments, but only $2,292 in a single annual payment. The exact savings may vary from carrier to carrier, but as a rule, lump sum payments are lower.

Don't Overinsure

It's the age of the working couple, and increasingly, both workers in a family have the option to take health insurance. It may not pay for both of you to do so if you expect to jockey back and forth between plans, depending on which has better coverage for a particular medical problem. That's not allowed. You will have to use your plan, and your spouse his or her plan. The children will have to use one plan or the other, depending on their birthdates and yours. The primary plan will pay the bulk of the costs, and the secondary plan may pay all or part of the deductible. You may be making a lot of paperwork in the process, and the double coverage is probably not worth it. Pick the stronger of the two plans, and pocket the monthly premium of the weaker plan.

Or it may not pay for both workers to take health insurance if one of you has a benefits menu offered by your employer, which includes child care, hospitalization and major medical, eye and dental care, and elder care. If one spouse has two of these four programs at little or no cost, skip the health care and go for something else—such as child care, which may cost as much as $500 or more a month when purchased individually—and use the other spouse's health coverage for the whole family.

Choose "Service Benefits"

The costs of catastrophic illness or injury can be as devastating as the disease or injury itself. Therefore it's smart to insure yourself against them by buying the major medical plan with the highest possible coverage per year or per episode of illness, or by enrolling in a Health Maintenance Organization (HMO) that pays unlimited benefits for catastrophic illness.

When examining a major medical policy, look for a plan with an affordable deductible (usually $100 or $250 per year); a copayment of 20 percent or less (the amount you contribute toward your hospital bills); and a reasonable "stop-loss" amount (a stop-loss of $5,000 means that you will not have to pay more than $5,000 toward your medical bills).

Consider the Deductible

If you and your spouse both have health insurance and you've decided to choose between plans, you must consider more than the monthly premium. Consider the deductible—the best plans have $100 per person, $200 per family. On other costs, such as surgery, the best plans limit per-family out-of-pocket expenses to $1,000 per year.

Compare your plans closely. As employers try to cut their soaring benefits costs, company-supplied plans increasingly have $250 individual deductibles and require you to pay up to 20 percent of the first $10,000 in other medical costs. This means you could pay as much as $5,000 out of pocket if two of you need surgery in the same year.

Don't Overlook Maternity Coverage

Couples who are planning to have children must compare covered maternity and child care costs. On plans with nearly complete maternity coverage, having a baby should cost no more than $100 to $250 out of pocket. Under less desirable plans, you can have to pay well over $1,000 for the same services. If you're planning to have, say, two children, it makes no sense to pass up the better of two health plans to save even $40 a month in premiums over four years.

Be Cautious of Cancer Coverage

Most health policies cover cancer treatment as they would any other. The problem is that cancer treatment can be long and so expensive that it exhausts benefits. Cancer insurance for most people is unnecessary; consider it only if your coverage excludes or limits cancer treatment, or if your limits for hospitalization and treatment are low.

The Advantages of an HMO

Most large companies now offer their employees two kinds of health insurance: a traditional "fee-for-service" plan like Blue Cross and Blue Shield, or a "prepaid" plan such as a health maintenance organization (HMO). The question for the individual wage-earner is: Which plan will cost me less?

That depends. If your family joins an HMO, you might pay several hundred dollars more in annual premiums than the co-worker whose family joins Blue Cross. But you won't have to pay the $100 or $250 deductible that Blue Cross subscribers pay, and your medical checkups, immunizations, well-baby visits, and other forms of preventive care (and prescriptions, in many plans) will cost only $2 to $5 each. Preventive services are generally not covered by Blue Cross.

If you have several small children and plan to use a lot of preventive care, or if you're elderly and have chronic medical problems, the HMO might well be cheaper in the long run. In the only major study of HMO costs to date, the state of New Jersey conducted a survey in 1985 and found that annual out-of-pocket expenditures for medical care were consistently lower for HMO subscribers than for those in Blue Cross and Blue Shield.

There is a catch: HMOs will pay bills only if submitted by a member doctor. And in some plans, if you must seek a specialist or surgeon, your choice may be limited—or even eliminated.

Only you know whether you can be comfortable with your loss of choice.

Doctors often talk against HMOs. Be aware that doctors make less by having you as an HMO patient than as a regular patient. Base your decision on your needs.

The Advantages
of Blue Cross and Blue Shield

If you must buy hospitalization on your own, consider the Blue Cross and Blue Shield policies. Be aware that in some states, open enrollment may be limited to only a couple of months a year. Plan for that if you can. And compare with other plans, which can be cheaper.

Unlike insurance from commercial companies, Blue Cross and Blue Shield are offered by a nonprofit organization. This tends to keep premiums down. Blue Cross and Blue Shield usually waive preexisting conditions and offer complete maternity coverage. The biggest benefit of all may be their national reach. It costs much more for medical care in the Northeast than, say, in Iowa. But the Iowa policyholder will find that his bills are covered in New York or Washington under Blue Cross/Blue Shield reciprocal agreements among states.

Choose a Doctor Who Accepts
UCR Reimbursements

Most group health insurance plans provide 100 percent coverage of "usual, customary, and reasonable" doctor's fees, or UCR. There's no guarantee, however, that you won't have to dip into your own wallet to pay your doctor. If your group insurance covers only $175 for a broken leg, and your orthopedist charges $250, you could be billed for the extra $75.

How can you avoid getting stuck with the check? Find out whether your doctor accepts your insurance payments as payment in full. If he charges more, he may have a good reason for it. He may have extra schooling, or more advanced equipment than his competitors. It's just as likely, however, that he charges more simply because his office rent is higher or his outstanding medical school debts are larger. In that case, it might pay to find a doctor who charges less.

Physicians' fees do vary widely. A study conducted in Baltimore a few years ago showed that surgeons charged anywhere from $220 to $1,500 to remove a gallbladder, while orthopedists charged $1,070 to $2,500 to treat a hip fracture. Eye doctors in Baltimore removed cataracts for as little as $300 and as much as $2,500, and cardiologists billed their patients between $63 to $225 for the identical stress test.

Alternative Treatments May Be Covered

If acupuncture is your idea of sound medicine, find an insurance company that agrees with you. Usually therapies such as acupuncture, biofeedback, and massage are often less expensive than orthodox medical therapies. Unfortunately, large insurance companies still shy away from covering these so-called alternative forms of treatment. Your acupuncturist might charge $20 less than your orthopedist for treating back pain, but the M.D. will still be cheaper for you if your health plan doesn't cover acupuncture.

Where does that leave the patient who favors alternative or holistic health care? Such a patient might have to shop for an insurance carrier that accepts claims for alternative medicine. We know of at least one, the Consumers United Insurance Company, 2100 M Street NW, Washington, DC 20037 (202) 872-5390. Ask your insurance broker if he or she knows of others.

Buckle Up

When you wear a seat belt, you not only protect yourself from bodily injury but also protect yourself from paying higher medical bills. According to a study funded by the Massachusetts Seat Belt Coalition, the medical costs incurred for injured motorists who don't wear seat belts are, on average, more than double the costs for motorists who are wearing seat belts at the time of a crash.

Because of this, some insurance companies offer special bonuses to their seat belt-wearing policyholders. One company in Massachusetts waives the usual deductible on medical claims from injured motorists who wear seat belts. This can mean a savings of anywhere from $100 to $1,000. If you're a habitual seat belt wearer, shop around for an insurer who will pay you for buckling up.

The Hidden Costs of Motorcycling

Riding on a motorcycle can be great fun. And, under certain ideal conditions, it is probably quite safe. But your risk of being injured or killed in a traffic accident while on a motorcycle is much greater than it is if you are riding in an automobile. To add insult to injury, you could end up paying for these injuries yourself, because many insurers don't even sell medical insurance to motorcyclists. Riding a motorcycle is financially as well as medically risky.

Tips for Filing Insurance Claims

Insurance claims, like income tax returns, tend to generate so many piles of confusing paperwork and are written in such technical language that many people give up trying to file them at all. Some people are simply embarrassed to file an insurance claim. But file you must, or risk losing hundreds of dollars that are rightfully yours. Here are some hints on how to make filing a claim less painful:

■ Know what services your health insurance policy covers, and know what it doesn't. If you're in doubt, file a claim anyway. The worst that can happen is that it will be rejected.

■ Save every single document that pertains to your health care. This includes all of your receipts from doctors, hospitals, and pharmacies, and all of the correspondence sent to you by your employer or insurance company. One missing document can rob you of your benefits, or force you to waste valuable time trying to replace it. Keep photocopies of every bill you submit with a claim.

■ Keep a separate record of all your visits to a doctor, hospital, or pharmacy, including the date and nature of the visit and the amount of money you paid.

■ Don't be embarrassed to ask for help in filing a claim. If you are incapacitated in any way and are unable to prepare the paperwork yourself, ask a friend or relative to lend a hand. If you have a question about Medicare coverage, call your local Social Security Administration office.

Help for Denied Insurance Claims

If you think your health insurance claim has been denied unfairly, write to your state insurance commissioner. Every state in the Union maintains a department or bureau of insurance that acts as a watchdog over the insurance industry. If you clash with your insurance carrier over a claim, you should complain in writing to the state insurance commissioner. Send him or her your name, address, and telephone number, along with the name, address, and telephone number of your insurance company. Also include your policy number, the type of policy you hold, and the nature of your complaint. Make copies of your complaint, and keep a duplicate for yourself. The department will investigate your complaint and try to resolve the problem.

Elder Care

Medicare

The new Medicare benefits are better than they were before, but you'll still have out-of-pocket expenses. One way to keep these costs down is to use a doctor who charges no more than the Medicare-approved rates. For bills over that amount, you must pay not only your 20 percent copayment but also the difference between the Medicare-approved rate and the doctor's rate.

Don't be fooled into thinking the Medicare law means no more health care bills. It merely reduces the most anyone will have to pay. Even with this new version of the federal insurance, serious illness could cost you thousands of dollars yearly. For details on the new Medicare benefits, contact your local Social Security Administration office (listed under U.S. Government in the

white pages or in the blue pages of your telephone directory).
Your local office will mail you free information on the Medicare
law. You can also contact: Health Care Financing Administration,
Department of Health and Human Services, 6325 Security Boulevard, Baltimore, MD 21207, 1-800-451-2482 or (301) 594-9086.

Medigap

Another way to reduce Medicare costs is to buy insurance that
pays your out-of-pocket costs, or some of them. This is commonly
called "Medigap," or supplemental, insurance because it fills in
the gaps of the Medicare federal health insurance. To know what
coverage you need, you must know what your out-of-pocket Medicare costs are. The lowest copayments, which may be just a few
dollars, are 20 percent copayments on medical services, including
visits to your doctor. The most expensive are 20 percent
copayments on the national average daily charge for a skilled
nursing facility for the first eight days you use it—a charge that
could be in the hundreds. There are also deductibles—amounts
that you must pay before the Medicare insurance kicks in. They
range from $75 for medical services to $564 for hospital costs in
1990. You'll pay more in some categories after 1990. For example,
there is no deductible for outpatient prescriptions in 1990, but
there will be a $600 deductible in 1991. When shopping for a
Medigap policy, make sure it covers all the possible costs—
including established increases and any increases that may
occur.

Shop Smart
for Supplemental Insurance

While shopping for supplemental insurance, look for a company
that guarantees your right to renew the policy. Avoid companies
that reserve the right to cancel your policy if your claims are too
high. Before buying a policy, ask for a 10- to 30-day "free look" so
that you can return your policy and get a full refund if you're dis-
satisfied. If you have an existing health condition, such as diabetes, look for a policy that will cover preexisting conditions.

Beware of door-to-door insurance salespeople, celebrity en-
dorsements, slick mail-order plans that look like official government documents, and one-disease policies, like cancer insurance.

Always check with your state insurance department to see if the insurance company is licensed in your state.

Nursing Care

Look for an increase in nursing care insurance as an employee benefit in the 1990s. If it becomes available to you or a member of your family, examine the benefits carefully to determine if you need additional coverage. The group rates should be lower than individual rates. Make sure you can convert to an individual policy if employment ends.

Disability Insurance

Should You Buy It?

Most people who have disability insurance obtain it through their employers. If it's offered, take it, even though the chances are that you'll never collect on it. But if you do collect on employer-supplied policies, you'll have to pay income tax on the benefits you collect. If you buy your own policy, you won't pay tax on your benefits. Still, the premiums you would have to pay for your own policy far outweigh the taxes you would pay if you collect on an employer-paid policy.

If you must buy your own policy, get one that pays benefits if you are disabled from performing the type of work you do now—not one that pays only if you are unable to work at all.

Self-Employed, Uninsured

If you are self-employed, you probably won't be able to get disability insurance. That's because an insurance carrier will find it hard to accept your proof of lost income.

You may be able to get some insurance to help pay nonmedical bills if you are hospitalized. Almost any time you obtain credit, you can buy insurance that will pay your credit bill while you are hospitalized. On a car purchase, for instance, your insurance premium will become part of the monthly payment. The same can be done for a mortgage. Or, if you want to pay a lower premium, you can pay the entire premium up front or yearly. You can also find insurance that will pay you cash for each day, week, or month you are hospitalized. Warning: These policies will be more expensive than normal disability insurance.

Establish a Self-Insurance Fund

If you are self-employed, try to establish a self-insurance fund: an account that you feed regularly in lieu of disability insurance payments. Don't touch this money unless you are unable to work.

Where to stash these funds? Look for an intermediate or long-term savings instrument, such as a certificate of deposit, that will pay you a higher interest rate. As the account grows, put increasing parts of it into long-term accounts, keeping some of the money liquid. That way, even if you must withdraw some of the savings, you won't have to pay a penalty by cashing in one large certificate.

Tapping IRAs

Disabled persons can tap Individual Retirement Accounts or, if self-employed, Keogh Plans, without paying a penalty. This should be done as a last resort.

Life Insurance

Start While You're Young

Plan for lifelong insurance while you're young by purchasing renewable term policies. These policies can be extended as each term expires, without the need for a physical examination.

Psst . . . Save a Bundle!

Avoid Celebrity Specials

No physicals! No rejections! And no bargain!

The mail-order life insurance that is hawked on late-night television—often by yesterday's faded television and movie stars—is one of the worst insurance buys you'll find. Rates are high, and the fine print demonstrates why nobody is rejected for the insurance: Such policies often require the insured to live a specified amount of time—as much as three years.

Three years of very high premiums will make the policy—even if your benefactors can collect—a poor value. The vast majority of people can get life insurance, although unhealthy and older buyers will pay higher premiums. Shop around for the best rates from a legitimate insurance company.

Who Gets Life Insurance?

When it comes time to buy life insurance, should you buy coverage for your entire family? Not necessarily. First, insure the working spouse or spouses in proportion to their incomes. Next, insure the nonworking spouse whose nonmonetary contributions would have to be paid for, thus adding to your cost of living, after his or her death. For example, if your wife stays home to take care of a small child and does all the cooking and cleaning, figure what it would cost you to hire a nanny, cook, and cleaning person to get these jobs done in the event of her death.

Should You Insure Your Children?

Some people insure their children, mainly as a painless way of accruing some savings for the future. While this isn't the best way to save, it *is* a low-cost way to do so and may be attractive to young parents who don't have extra income to set aside in CDs or other savings vehicles for their children. It's also not a bad idea to insure your child if he or she has an illness that may later cause him or her to be an insurance risk. A convertible policy bought for a child will carry over into adulthood.

Stay Healthy and Earn Rate Breaks

Men pay the most for insurance and women the least. That's because insurance industry studies have shown that men are likely to die earlier. They also, traditionally, have smoked and drunk more. But even a woman who smokes will pay less than a man who doesn't.

If, however, you are physically active (in nondangerous activities), maintain proper weight, work in a nonstressful job, don't smoke, and have no history of heart trouble, high blood pressure, cancer, AIDS, or other major diseases, you may qualify as a preferred risk. This can save you about 5 percent a year on premiums. (At one insurance company, a nonsmoker would save over $19,000 over the course of 30 years, compared to a smoker.) If you get yourself into shape and/or quit smoking after buying a policy, try to get yourself reclassified; your premium savings may offset some of what it costs to join the fitness club or keep that bicycle properly maintained.

Don't Put It in Your Name

Putting insurance in the name of a spouse can ease collection upon the insured's death. There would be no contention that it is part of an estate (although it's usually not considered such). In some states, taxes must be paid on inherited property—such as on a policy that is made a gift upon your death. But insurance benefits are untaxed.

Life Insurance Options

Term

Term insurance is the best buy for young couples. It costs the least per $1,000 in benefits. You get so many thousands of dollars in insurance coverage for a certain term—1 year, 5 years, 10, or even 20 years, for instance. As you age, your premium will increase, but so will your income to help pay for it. Make sure the policy is renewable, meaning that you won't need a physical when the term expires.

Whole Life

This single-premium insurance buys more tax breaks than protection for your family. A one-time $20,000 payment, for example, will buy about $100,000 in benefits for a 35-year-old man. The accumulated interest is deferred from current-year income, thus saving money at tax time. You may also borrow against its cash value at competitive rates.

Universal Life

Universal life combines savings and death benefits. It's not the bargain that term life is, but it's about 30 percent cheaper than whole life. It allows withdrawing about 10 percent of the cash value per year if you need it, and it allows borrowing. It also allows yearly, quarterly, or monthly premium payments.

16

ESTATE PLANNING: A WILL TO SAVE

Dying isn't cheap. There's the unexpected medical bill to contend with. Then there's the funeral director. And the lawyer. Even the tax collector wants to get into the act.

Careful planning can cut the costs of all these things. Your estate, especially in this age of spiraling salaries and real estate values, could be sizable. The bottom line is, give everything away. The catch, of course, is that you want it to go to the right people—not to the state, not to Uncle Sam, and not to the funeral director.

By drawing up a will, planning gifts to your family, establishing trusts, buying adequate insurance, timing the sale of your home, and preplanning your funeral, you can save thousands—even tens of thousands—of dollars to pass on to your family. Here's how.

Estates and Estate Taxes

Giving Money Away

Why give your money away? That's the whole object of estate planning: to retain as much of your wealth as possible for your heirs, and to pass it on to them with the least trouble. Don't give away anything that you'll miss. Your own security is important. But keep in mind that when you die, it could take a year or longer to probate your will, which means get it through the legal process. Until that's done, and until all your debts are paid, the executor will not be able to distribute anything to your heirs.

You no longer have to give large sums of money away so that you pay a lower gift tax than estate tax. That's because the two rates are now the same. And any gift tax you pay now will discount any estate tax you'll owe after death. The federal government and many states that follow federal guidelines allow you to give away these amounts without paying any taxes:

$10,000 per person per year
$600,000 over your lifetime

Gifts to spouses during your lifetime are not taxed (some states require you to give at least part of your estate to your spouse). Gifts to charities are not taxed either.

Know When to Give

When you give gifts may make a difference in estate taxes. Some states retain a law that the IRS has abandoned: If gifts are given within three years of death, they remain subject to estate taxes.

Who Must Pay Estate Taxes?

Federal estate taxes must be paid on estates larger than $600,000. If your estate is smaller, it will pass essentially intact, except for debt settlement and legal fees, to the heirs you name in your will.

Sell Your Home to Your Kids

As you grow older, your belongings may become as much a liability as an asset. This becomes especially true if you should require nursing care. Often, a parent intends to leave a house to children but has to sell the home to cover the costs of nursing care.

Here's something to consider, especially if you're a sole surviving spouse in retirement: Don't own your home. Instead, sell it to your children and rent it from them. By investing the proceeds from the sale, you should be able to pay a reasonable rent to your children—enough to cover their mortgage and taxes. You escape capital gains (income) taxes on your residence up to $125,000 if you are past age 55. If the children cannot afford a down payment, consider making the down payment a gift (up to $20,000 if both parents are living).

This arrangement has the same effect as a reverse mortgage, except that your children will realize the profit from selling your home years later, when you are gone. With a reverse mortgage, the lending bank reaps all that profit.

Plan Your Estate

Will

Maintain
Your Family's Lifestyle

If you are a breadwinner, how will your family's lifestyle be maintained without your income? Plan for family income by having adequate savings and insurance—life insurance to provide income after you're gone, and adequate health insurance so that your estate is not plundered by soaring medical costs before you die.

Take Care of College Costs

How will your children afford college? You should have adequate savings or a trust fund that will take care of college costs. The College Savings Bank of Princeton, New Jersey, has a plan that helps you gauge the cost of a particular school and through savings and investment, meet these costs. You may also want to consider paying tuition now with a guarantee that costs will be covered when your children attend college. Beware: Your child will have to make the grade and want to attend the school where you prepaid. Many states and Congress are considering such plans to allow the tuition to be spent at any school.

Cut Back
on Pension Payments

Consider taking a smaller monthly pension payment if it ensures that your spouse will continue to receive the payment upon your death. Remember, a nonworking spouse who is suddenly thrown into the job market will have fewer years to accumulate retirement credits or savings. Most nonworking spouses are women, and they likely will earn less upon returning to a job, since women as a whole continue to earn less than men, even for similar work. Make sure your spouse is the beneficiary of your Individual Retirement Account (IRA), Keogh Plan, 401(k) account, and company pension plan should you die before retirement.

Watch What You Will

Don't will more than you have—your estate may not be big enough to satisfy the bequests in your will. In some states, specific property bequests take precedence over nonspecific property bequests and cash. Let's say your intention is to leave $5,000 to your brother, your car to your sister, and $1,000 to a charity, but you have only $1,000 in cash at death. Your sister gets the car (that was specifically named), but your other possessions will be sold to raise cash, which your brother and the charity will split proportionately.

Funerals

Be Wary of Funeral Insurance

One way to preplan your funeral is through funeral insurance, but you can accomplish the same thing on your own, and at lower cost. All the insurance does is set up your funeral with a specific funeral director. Generally, you and the director agree on the services, and you pay now or in installments. This prearrangement is set up as insurance so that the benefits will be tax-free.

Be aware that when you buy funeral insurance you are limiting your funeral choices. If the director holding your "policy" goes out of business, you're left with nothing—unless the money you paid was in a trust, which guarantees that it won't be used until it is released for your funeral.

Set Up a Trust

You can set up a trust for funeral expenses through a bank. The bank will pay the proceeds of the trust upon your death to the funeral director with whom you have arranged burial or cremation. You can also prearrange with the funeral director to pay for the funeral minus the $250 burial allowance from Social Security. The Social Security check then can go to him.

Psst . . . Save a Bundle!

Plan Ahead

By preplanning your funeral—everything from readings to the type of coffin to whether or not you want cremation—you can save your family a lot of hassle. You may also save them $2,000 to $3,000.

Funeral Services

Funeral directors are in business to make money. The more they sell, the more they profit, and the less you'll leave your heirs. Remember, too, that the decisions you don't make now will be made by your family at a most stressful time.

Funeral services, for the most part, aren't fixed. (State laws may require some services—embalming, for instance.) As for the frills, you can go all the way or use the money for something else—your family, possibly. Compare prices on these services:

■ Burial. This is the most expensive part of dying. It involves not only a coffin but also a cemetery plot.

■ Embalming. Your state may require this, or it may not. In states where embalming is optional, it may be required if the person died of certain communicable diseases, if the body is to be viewed after a certain period, or if the body is to be moved to another state. If you don't want full embalming but want an open coffin for viewing, you may be able to buy minimal preparation at a fraction of the cost.

■ Coffins. Cardboard and wood are cheapest (as low as $150 to $250), and metal costs more ($1,200 to $2,000 or more). The most expensive coffins have seals, supposedly to preserve the body. Don't believe it. They may keep water out, but nothing will keep the body from decomposing. Often, the difference between a

$2,000 funeral and a $3,000 funeral is the deluxe coffin. Think seriously about whether you would rather give an extra $1,000 or $2,000 to a funeral director or to your family.

■ Cremation. This is the money-saving alternative to burial, but funeral directors have ways of making it costly, too. Scattering ashes is cheaper than placing them in an urn.

■ Visitation or viewing. If you use the funeral home for this service you will pay extra. More viewings mean more costs. You may be able to have a viewing at home or at a church to cut costs. (If you want the body present, however, you'll have to pay the funeral director to move it.) Home or church visitation will cut down not only on use of the funeral home but also on use of funeral home employees. Reducing both should save you money.

Psst . . . Save a Bundle!

Forgo the Urn

If placement of ashes in an urn is desired, don't think it's necessary to pay $1,000 or even $2,000. Urns are available for as little as $50. Scattering the ashes remains the cheapest disposition.

Where There's a Will

Do You Need One?

Your will is your last chance to call the shots. How important is it? If you leave no will, your state government will decide where your money goes. The state will give the money to your closest heirs: your spouse and children. But even that can be open to dispute, and the chances of an estate being contested increase when no will is left. With the increasing number of marriages that end in divorce, wills become especially important, particularly if the relationship of ex-spouses and noncustodial children was marked with acrimony.

Hire an Attorney

While it is not necessary to have a will drawn by an attorney, be aware that any self-help book is unlikely to contain all the rules for drawing a legal will in every state. The rules vary; in many states, three witnesses are necessary for a will to be legal. In others, fewer are allowed. The chances of a self-drawn will being challenged are high.

Consider finding an attorney. Having her or him draw the will for you will probably cost you $75 to $200. That's not pocket change, but it's far cheaper than not having a will drawn, because an estate left without a will requires more legal work—and more expense—after your death.

Filing a will is not one of the most complicated things you'll ever have an attorney do. You don't need a high-powered $250-an-hour attorney for a simple will—or even for a complicated one. It is, as far as legal work goes, routine.

Other Legal Services

Some auto clubs and other organizations offer legal insurance. These policies offer legal services from participating attorneys for a fee that is smaller than the normal one. Often, these policies include the drawing of a will. If you have such a policy, and drawing of wills is included, using the service could save you money. But if you're not going to use the attorney to handle matters if you die, dig a little deeper into your pocket and get an attorney your heirs will use again.

Name Your Executor

When naming an executor, keep in mind two qualifications: You need someone who can get a lot of work done at a time of stress, and someone you trust. You can name a relative, a friend, or an attorney. Your executor will have to:

■ Probate your will. That means taking it through the legal process, with the help of an attorney, to make it official.

■ File insurance forms. This is the money that will keep your family when you're gone. Make sure your executor knows where to get all the forms, such as insurance policies or applications for death benefits from labor or fraternal organizations.

■ Settle your debts. If things are jointly owned—and jointly financed—with a spouse, the spouse remains liable for the loans. But a single or widowed person's debts must be settled, and that means using insurance proceeds to do so, or selling assets to settle the claims against your estate.

Name a Guardian: 6 Points to Consider

Many parents overlook the need to name a legal guardian should they both die. Usually, one parent will precede the other in death. But the purpose of a will is to arrange for things as you want them after you're gone. It's a tough job finding someone you believe in so thoroughly that they could substitute for you as parents after you're gone. And you have to find someone who could handle the responsibility of child rearing.

Here are things to consider when naming a legal guardian for your children:

■ Do they know the children and love them? You can't place a value on that. These people, whether relatives or friends, should be very close to your family.

■ Will the children love and respect them?

■ Are they stable enough to handle the responsibilities?

■ Are they experienced parents? If not, are they close enough to the children that they would be willing to serve as parents if need be?

■ Can they afford it? Are they financially responsible enough that they will use the money you leave them in the best interests of your children? Have you discussed your expectations and how much you will have to leave to assure that your plans are completed without financial hardship to the guardians?

■ Will they agree to do it and prepare for it as well as possible? That may mean spending extra time with the kids now, while you're still around.

Living Wills

A living will is your stated intent to die when you feel the time has come. Even people with a strong will to live may choose this alternative. It can spare survivors a great deal of agony. It can also cut medical costs.

The living will is a legal document that states your predetermined intention to prevent doctors from unnecessarily prolonging your life. In some states, the legality of living wills has been established in the courts. In others, it has yet to be established. A living will should be drawn by an attorney.

Along similar lines, you may become incapacitated but in no danger of dying imminently. You may want to draw a document that names a guardian or conservator who would have power of attorney the moment you become incapacitated. This would allow decisions to be made regarding your medical care, debts, and legal matters. Again, it could save a great deal of anguish among the people who care for you if you have unequivocally stated your wishes under these circumstances. Talk these things over with your family as rationally and unemotionally as possible.

For details on living wills, contact: Concern for Dying, 250 West 57th Street, Room 831, New York, NY 10107 (212) 246-6962.

Index

Page numbers for entire chapters are indicated in **boldface** type. Page numbers for tables are indicated in *italic* type.

A

AAA. *See* American Automobile Association
AARP. *See* American Association of Retired Persons
Accountant, for filing taxes, 347
Acupuncture, 361
Advertisements, food, 4–5
Air bags, for automobiles, 47–49, *48*
Air conditioners, energy ratings of, 189–90
Air conditioning, 175, 176, 189–93
Airfares, 272
Airport hotel, 273
Airport parking, 273
Alarm systems, for automobiles, 69–70
Alcohol, 320–21
American Association of Retired Persons (AARP), 311
American Automobile Association (AAA), 49, 356
American Youth Hostels (AYH), 277
Amtrak, 273, 274
Annual Fuel Utilization Efficiency (AFUE), 187–88
Antique furniture reproductions, 104–5
Appliances
  electric, information on, 149
  energy-efficient, 143–47, *144, 145*
  gas, information on, 149
  installation of, 124
  last year's models of, 152
  purchase of, 148–52, *149*
    brochures on, 148
  comparative information for, 149–50
  discounts on, 150
  seasonal, 148, *149*
  service contracts for, 151–52
  store-brand, 152
  timers for, 154
  used, rebuilt, or reconditioned, 152–53
  warranty on, 150–51
Aquastat, 185–86
Architects, 119, 130–31
Army College Fund, 263
Army-Navy stores, 77
Army ROTC, 264
Artichokes, wild Jerusalem, 216
Attic, radiant heat barrier in, 192
Attic fans, 191
Attorney, for preparing will, 377
Auctions, furniture purchased at, 101
Audio equipment, 290–91
Automobile clubs, 49–50
Automobile insurance discounts, *48*
Automobile safety, 47–49, *48*, 65
  health insurance and, 361–62
Automobiles, **46–70**
  airport parking for, 273
  big, 62–63
  for business, depreciation of, 345
  carrying spare parts for, 66
  cleaning, 67–68
  dealers of, 56–57, 58–59
  deterring theft of, 69–70
  discount repairs of, 53
  do-it-yourself preventive maintenance of, 66, 67
  extending life of, 65–68, 67
  flashy accessories for, theft of, 70
  gas for, 55–56
  government-ordered recall of, 65
  heated garages for, 67

interior care of, 68
keys for, 69
lease of, 61–62
maintenance and repair of,
    49–56, 52
  choosing mechanic for, 51
  do-it-yourself, 50
  rates for, 51–53
  tools for, 51, 52
oil for, 56, 65–66
option packages for, 59, 60–61
parking attendants for, tipping,
    286
purchase of, 56–63
  bargaining and, 57–59
  borrowing for, 58, 59–60, 60
  from dealer's lot, 60–61
  versus leasing, 61–62
  manufacturers' incentives and,
    59–60
  place and time for, 56–57
  rental prior to, 62
  research prior to, 57
  size considerations and, 62–63
rebates on, 59–60
rental of when traveling, 275
repair manuals for, 57
seats in, for children, 249
small, 62–63
tires for, 53–55, 66
towing of, 49, 50
underside of, 68
used, 63–65

B
Baby food, 29–30, 248
Baby-sitters, 252, 253
Back injuries, 321
Bargaining
  for automobiles, 57–59
  for entertainment items, 293
  for health care, 305
Basement cold frame, 233
Bed and breakfast establishments,
    276–77
Bedroom furniture, 106
Beef, 22

Birth, 308–9. See also Pregnancy
Blood donations, 327
Blue Cross, 300, 301, 303, 309,
    359, 360
Blueprints, for house, 118–20
Blue Shield, 301, 309, 359, 360
Boiler, water, 173, 185–86
Bonds
  to finance higher education,
    262–63
  United States Savings, 262, 352
Bone meal, 203
Book clubs, 295
Books, 294–95
  for college students, 267
  medical information in, 315–16,
    324–25
Booster heater, on dishwasher,
    157, 170
Box stores, food shopping at, 12
Brand names, food shopping and, 17
Bread, homemade, 41
Breast-feeding, 247
Bulbs, flower, 224, 225
Burglary. See Home, safety of
Business owners, tax advice for,
    344–46

C
Cabinets, installation of, 124
Cable TV, 290
Cancer insurance, 359
Cardiopulmonary resuscitation
    (CPR), 327
Carpeting, 95–97, 207
Cars. See Automobiles
Catalogs
  clothing purchased from, 77–78
  furniture purchased from, 104–5
Caulking, 180, 181
Ceiling fan, 187
Cesarean delivery, 309
Chain stores, for clothing, 76
Charitable contributions, 343
Chicken, quartering, 35
Children, 246–55
  baby food for, 248

Children (continued)
  breast-feeding, 247
  care of, 252–55
  car seats for, 249
  clothing for, 81–82, 249–50
  furniture for, 250
  legal guardian for, 378
  life insurance for, 368
  medical care for, 251
  shoes for, 87
  snacks for, 247–48
  taxes and, 352–53
Chimney, cleaning, 184
Circumcision, 309
Cleaning
  of automobiles, 67–68
  of chimney, 184
  of clothing, 84
  of home, 132–33
Cloches, 235
Clothes dryers, 147, 159–61
Clothing, 71–89. See also Shoes
  accessories for, 73
  care and repair of, 74–75, 83–85
  for children, 81–82, 249–50
  cleaning, 84
  fads in, 73
  hand-me-down, 81
  higher quality, 81
  labels on, 80
  mix-and-match separates, 73
  pantyhose, 82
  personal selection of, 80
  purchase of, 76–83
    from catalog or by mail order,
      77–78
    for children, 81–82
    at factory outlets, 77
    planning prior to, 72
    types of stores for, 76–77, 79
  returns of, to store, 80–81
  seasonal sales of, 74
  signs of quality in, 78–79
  storage of, 85
  sweaters, 79
  underwear, 79
  versatile, 72

  washing, 84–85
Cold frames, 232–33
College(s). See also Education,
    higher
  community, 269
  cutting costs in, 266–67
  reputation of, 268
  selection of, 258
College work-study, 260
Comparison shopping, in
    supermarket, 6
Compost, 201–3
ConSern. See Consortium for
    Supplemental Educational
    Resource Needs
Consignment stores, 78, 102
Consortium for Supplemental
    Educational Resource
    Needs (ConSern), 266
Consumer Reports, 57, 149–150
Consumer Reports Buying Guide,
    291
Contraceptive services, free, 307-8
Contractor, for home construction,
    122–23
Convenience stores, for food, 14
Cooking, cutting electricity costs
    and, 161–64
Coolers, evaporative, 191
Cooling system(s), 188, 189–93
Cosmetics, 88–89
Cosmetics substitutes, 88, 89
Coupons, for food purchases, 7, 8, 9
CPR. See Cardiopulmonary
    resuscitation
Credit cards, 281–82, 343
C-section, 309
Custodial accounts, 261–62

D
Day care centers, 252–53
Death, financial planning for. See
    Estate planning; Life
    insurance
Decorating, interior, 99–100
Dental care, 319
Dental x-rays, 306

Department stores, for clothing, 76
Detergent gas, 55–56
Detergents, 158, 159
Diet, low-fat, 320
Dining, 284–85
    tipping and, 285, *286–87*
Direct Mail Marketing Association,
    104
Disability insurance, 365–66
Discount stores, 13, 76
Dishwashers, 154–55
    booster heater on, 157, 170
Doctors
    fees charged by, health
        insurance and, 360–61
    hospitals and, 299–300
    Medicare accepted by, 313
    second opinions from, 304–6
    specialized, 306
Doors
    fitting and hanging, 124
    home safety and, 136–39
    sliding glass, 138–39
    storm, 181
Dressings. *See* Salad dressings
Drugs
    for the elderly, 311
    free, 323
    generic, 316
Dryers, clothes, 147, 159–61
Drywall work, 123
Ductwork, leaks in, 184

E
Earthstar Graywater Heat
    Reclaimer, 171–72
Education. *See also* College;
    Schools
    higher, **256–70**
        employer contribution to, 269
        estate planning and, 373
        federal support for, 263–64
        financial aid from federal
            government for, 259–60
        financial aid needs for, 257–59
        loans for, 260–61
        loan sources for, 265–66

maximizing savings for, 261–63
prepaid tuition plans for,
    264–65
smart strategies for, 268–70
Elderly
    day care for, 312
    dining discounts for, 284
    health care for, 310–15
        AARP-affiliated pharmacies
            and, 311
        cooperatives and, 310–11
        medical equipment and,
            314–15
        Medicare and, 312–15, 363–64
    health insurance for, 363–65
    nursing care for, 365
    shared housing for, 311–12
    sports for, 295
    travel by, 281
    wheelchairs for, 314
Electrical outlets, sealing of, to
    prevent heat loss, 179
Electrical work, for new home, 125
Electricians, for home remodeling,
    131, 132
Electricity
    cutting costs of, 153–61, *155*
        cooking and, 161–64
        through energy-efficient use of
            appliances, 154–57
        lighting and, 164–67
        by off-peak period use, 153–54
    versus gas, for cooking, 163
    water heaters and, 172–73
Emergencies, medical, 299
Employment, child care and, 252,
    254–55
Energy. *See also* Appliances
    electricity, 153–67
    home cooling, 189–93
    home heating, 183–89
    home insulation, 178–82
    water heating, 167–75
Energy audit, of home, 178
Energy Guide Labels, on
    appliances, 143–44
Energy savings, **142–93**

Entertainment, **283–96**
    bargains in, 292–94
    books, 294–95
    cable TV, 290
    dining, 284–85
    movie theaters, 288–89
    music, 290–91
    rental items for, 292–93
    sports, 295–96
    theater, 289–90
    tipping and, 285, *286–87*
    VCRs, 287–88
Estate planning, **370–79**
    college costs and, 373
    funerals and, 374–76
    pension payments and, 373
    by selling home to children, 372
    wills and, 374, 376–79
Executor, of estate, 377–78
Eyeglasses, over-the-counter,
    317–18

F
Fabric clubs, 75
Fabrics, for upholstered furniture,
    98
Factory outlets, for clothing, 77
Fans
    attic, 191
    ceiling, 187
    kitchen and bathroom, 175–76
Farmers' markets, 15
Faucets, leaky, 168
Federal government
    health care information from,
        318
    higher education and, 259–60,
        263–64
Federal Nutrition Education
    Program (FNEP), 44
Fertilizers, 201–5, *204*
Financial aid, for higher education,
    257–61
Fireplaces, 186–87
Fish, 25, 34
    determining servings of, *31–32*
    preserving freshness of, *19–20*
Fixtures

home, installation of, 124
    water-saving, 169
Flower garden, 222–24
Fluorescent lighting, compact,
    164–65
Flying. *See* Travel, air
Food, **3–45**
    advertisements for, 4–5
    brown-bag lunches, 29
    for college students, 267
    consumption of, 29–36
    cooking of, electricity costs of,
        162, 164
    delivered to elderly, 312, 314
    frozen, 36
    gardening for, 36
    for infants, 29–30
    leftovers, 30, *31*
    milk, 18
    preparation of, do-it-yourself,
        37–38
    preserving freshness of, *19–21*
        cost of, 217–19, *218–19*
    purchase of
        brand names and, 17
        through buying clubs and
            co-ops, 15
        convenience and, 14, 16,
            37–38
        coupons and, 7, 8, 9
        direct from source, 15
        freshness and, 17–18
        in large quantities, 8–9, 15
        from manufacturers' outlets,
            15
        at nonfood outlets, 14
        strategies for, 9–11
        in supermarkets, 4–9
        types of stores for, 11–14, 16
        from wholesale outlets, 15
    quality of, 22, 25
    recipes
        for basic bread, 41
        herb and spice substitutes in,
            22, *24*
        ingredient substitutes in, 22,
            23–24
        for muffins, 39–40

for pudding, 39
for salad dressings and
    seasonings, 41–43
selecting right amount of, 30,
    31–33
storage of, 18, 19–21, 37
Food co-ops, 15
Food mixes, 38–40
Food programs, government, 44–45
Food servings, determining
    number of, 31–33
Food stamps, 45
401(k) plan, 350, 351, 373
Freezer(s), 146–47, 154
Fruit(s)
    best time to buy, 26–28
    determining servings of, 33
    gardening for, 228–29
    preserving freshness of, 20
    selecting quality, 25, 26–28
Fruit trees, easy picking from, 237
Funeral(s), 374–76
    insurance for, 374
    services, 375–76
Fungi, in plants, 209–10
Furnace. See Heating systems
Furniture, 90–106
    bedroom, 106
    carpeting, 95–97
    case goods, 93
    for child's room, 250
    designer showrooms for, 100
    discounted, by phone, 93–94
    frugal, 101–3
    futon, 101
    galleries, 99
    home office, 106
    kit, 102–3
    long-lasting, 92
    multifunction, 101
    outdoor, 106
    price of, 91–92
    purchase of, 91–95
        at auction, 101
        from catalogs and by mail
            order, 104–5
        at consignment stores, 102
        free accessories with, 94

at garage sales, 102
    seasons for, 91
    tips for, 99–100
    at thrift shops, 101
rental of, 105–6
reproductions, antique, by mail,
    104–5
self-assembly of, 102–3
suites of, 92–93
unexpected sources for, 105–6
upholstered, 97–99
used, 102

G
Garage sales, 292
    furniture purchased at, 102
Garden. See also Plants
    best buys for, 224–25
    companions and allies in, 214–16
    drip irrigation systems for,
        235–36
    fertilizers for, 201–5
    flower, cutting costs in, 222–24
    mulches for, 205–8
    pest controls for, 208–17, 214–16
    plant propagation in, 220–222,
        220, 221
    rationing plan for, 197
    weed killers for, 213, 216
Garden beds, 219
Garden care, 194–237. See also
        Landscaping; Lawn
Garden cover crops, 195–96
Garden trading, 221
Gardening
    back comfort while, 237
    economical equipment for,
        232–37
    for food, 36
    for fruit, 228–29
    home food preservation and,
        217–19, 218–19
    knee comfort while, 236–37
    plant supports and 231–32
    seeds and seedlings for, 226–28
    seed sources for, 196
    soil care and, 195–200, 196, 198
    tools and equipment for, 229–31

Garments. *See* Clothing
Gas
  for automobiles, 55–56
  versus electricity, for cooking,
    163
Gas lamps, 165
Gas range, 162–63
Generic brands, food shopping
  and, 17
Generic drugs, 316
G.I. Bill, 263
Gift tax, 268
Glasses, over-the-counter, 317–18
Goodwill (agency), 78, 101
Government, federal
  food programs, 44–45
  health care information from,
    318
  higher education and, 259–60,
    263–64
Grains, determining servings of, *33*
Grants, for higher education, 258,
  259
Grasses, 196, *196*, 245
Grass seed, 243
Groceries. *See* Food
Grocery stores, 12
Grooming, 87–89
Ground covers, 242–43, *243*
Guardian, legal, 378

H
Haircuts, 87–88
Handyman special, 109
Health, life insurance and, 368
Health care, **297–328**
  alcohol and, 320–21
  back injuries and, 321
  bartering for, 324
  blood donations and, 327
  body weight and, 319–20
  for children, 251
  CPR and, 327
  doctors and, 304–7
  for the elderly, 310–15
  eyeglasses and, 317–18
  free checkup and, 317
  free drugs and, 323

  free government advice on, 318
  generic drugs and, 316
  hearing aids and, 323
  at home, 300–301
  home safety and, 325–26
  hospital bills and, 298–304
  information on, 315–16, 324–25
  low- and no-cost, 315–28
  Medicaid for, 327–28
  medical guides to, 315–16
  mental, 307, 322
  periodontal disease and, 319
  by phone, 318–19
  poison control and, 326
  pregnancy and birth and, 307–10
  records of, 324
  research and, 322–23
  self-help groups for, 321–22
  self-testing and, 317
  at Shriners' hospitals, 326
Health Care U.S.A., 324–25
Health insurance. *See* Insurance,
  health
Health Maintenance Organization
  (HMO), 358, 359–60
Hearing aids, 323
Heart attack, body weight and,
  319
Heat, cheap, 183–89
Heat barriers, radiant, 192
Heater, booster, on dishwashers,
  157, 170
Heating
  of water, 167–75
  of water beds, 158
Heating system(s)
  efficiency of, 188
  forced-air, 183
  integrated, 189
  modifications for, *186*
  replacement of, 187
  tune-ups of, 183
  upgrading, 185
  utilization efficiency of, 187–88
Heat pumps, 188–89
Heat pump water heaters, 173
Heat recovery, from used hot
  water, 171

Herb and spice substitutes, in
      recipes, *24*
Herb dressings, recipes for, 42
Hill-Burton program, 303
HMO. *See* Health Maintenance
      Organization
Hobbies, taxes and, 344–45
Home(s), **107–41**
   architect's fees to design, 119
   assessed value of, 133–35
   building of
      being your own contractor for,
         120–21
      blueprints for, 118–20
      doors and cabinets and, 124
      drywall work and, 123
      electrical work and, 125
      installation of fixtures and, 124
      finish work and, 122, *122*
      hiring contractor for, 123
      installation of appliances and,
         124
      negotiations with contractor
         and, 122–23
      owner contribution to, 122–25
      permits for, 123
      plumbing and, 125
      roof work and, 124
      shelving and, 124
   business office in, taxation and,
      345
   cleaning, 132–33
   cooling of, 189–93
   energy audit of, 178
   exchange of, for vacation, 275–76
   heating of, 183–89
   humidity in, 177–78
   improvements versus repairs to,
      129
   kit, 125
   lowering taxes on, 133–35
   mortgage on. *See* Mortgage
   moving from, 117–18
   purchase of
      directly from owner, 112
      by handyman, 109
      importance of location for, 108
      seasons for, 111–12

      zoning and, 108
   radon tests for, 139–40
   rehabilitation of, 109
   remodeling of, 126–35
      appropriateness of, 128
      architect hired for, 130–31
      contract for, 130
      do-it-yourself, 126, *127*
      duration of residence after,
         128
      electricians hired for, 131,
         132
      hiring help for, 129–33
      home-equity loan for, 126–28
      plumber hired for, 131–32
      resale value after, 128–29
      taxes affected by, 129
   safety of, 135–39
      doors and, 136–39
      landscaping and, 136
      locks for, 135–36
      Neighborhood Watch program
         for, 137
      when vacant, 135
      windows and, 138
   saving energy costs in, 175–77
   seller's market for, 111, 112
   temperature in, 177
   value appreciation of, 109
   water tests for, 140–41
   weatherization of, 178–82
Home equity, higher education
      payments and, 262
Home-equity loan 126–28
Home food preservation, cost of,
      217–19, *218–19*
Home health care, 300–301
Hospice care, 301–2
Hospitals
   appropriateness of admission to,
      304
   auditing bills from, 298–99
   check-in days for, 299
   comparative costs of, 302
   emergencies and, 299
   free care in, 303
   versus home care, 300–301
   versus hospices, 301–2

Hospitals *(continued)*
    medical consultation and,
        299–300
    versus outpatient clinics, 300
    rooms in, 303–4
    terminal illness and, 302
Hostels, 277
Hotels, 277–78
    tipping in, *286*
Hot Water Saver, 171
Humidity, in home, 177–78

I
Illness, terminal, 302
Illumination. *See* Lighting
Immunizations, for children, 251
Impulse buying, in supermarkets, 7
Individual Retirement Account
        (IRA), 373
    disability and, 366
    financial aid for higher education
        and, 257, 259
    taxes and, 347–48
Infants, feeding, 247–48
Insects. *See also* Pests
    beneficial, in garden, 213
    fruit and vegetables damaged by,
        25
Insulation
    of ductwork, 175
    in home, 178–82
    for hot water pipes, 171
    for water heaters, 170
Insurance, **354–69**
    disability, 365–66
    funeral, 374
    health, 298, 355–63. *See also*
        Blue Cross; Blue Shield;
        Medicaid; Medicare
    for alternative treatments, 361
    from American Automobile
        Association, 356
    basic coverage of, 356
    from Blue Cross and Blue
        Shield, 360
    for cancer, 359
    claims for, 362–63

deductible on, 358
    doctors' fees and, 360–61
    for the elderly, 363–65
    excessive, 357–58
    group rates for, 355–56
    higher deductibles on, 357
    by HMOs, 358, 359–60
    lump-sum premium payment
        for, 357
    maternity coverage and,
        358–59
    motorcycling and, 362
    seat belts and, 361–62
    for self-employed, 345
    landscape, 239
    legal, 377
    life, 367–69
    moving, 118
Interest
    on automobile loan, 59, *60*
    paid, tax-deductible, 342
    prepaying, 343
Interior decorating, 99–100
IRA. *See* Individual Retirement
        Account

K
Keogh Plans, 348–49, 366, 373
Kit furniture, 102–3
Kit homes, 125

L
Lamb, 22
Lamps, 165, 167
Landscape trees, worst, 241, *241*
Landscaping, **237–45.** *See also*
        Gardening; Lawn
    construction materials for, 242
    do-it-yourself, 238–39
    double-duty, 239
    home safety and, 136
    insurance for, 239
    low-maintenance and low-cost,
        237–38
    nursery savings and, 240–41
    sun-powered lights for, 165, 167
Laundry costs, 158, *159*

Lawn(s), **237–45.** *See also*
        Gardening; Landscaping
    grass seed for, 243
    versus ground cover, 242
    low-maintenance grasses for, 245
    mowing of, 244, *244*
    weed-free, 245
Leftovers, 30, *31*
Legal insurance, 377
Legume cover crops, 196, *196*, 202
Letter writing, as alternative to
        phoning, 340
Libraries, 289, 294
Life insurance, 367–69
Light bulbs, 164–65, 166
Lighting
    compact fluorescent, 164–65
    cutting electric bills and, 164–67
    by gas lamps, 165
    for home safety, 136
    outdoor, 167
    sun-powered, for landscaping,
        165, 167
    supply stores for, 94–95
Lights, for seedlings, 227–28
Lipsticks, 88–89
Living will, 302, 379
Loans
    for automobiles, 59, *60*
    for higher education, 260–61,
        265–66
    home-equity, 126–28
    for home purchase. *See*
        Mortgage
Locks, for home safety, 135–36
Loss leaders, 5, 148
Lunch, brown bag, 29

M
Mail order
    clothing purchased by, 77–78
    furniture purchased by, 104–5
Manures, green, 202
Maps, 49
Maternity (insurance) coverage,
        358–59
Meals on Wheels, 312, 314

Meat
    boneless, 34
    butchering of, 34
    determining servings of, *31*
    less-tender cuts of, 30
    preserving freshness of, *19*
    selecting quality, 22
    stretching portions of, 34
Mechanics' lien, 121, 130
Medicaid, 301, 327–28
Medical care. *See* Health care
Medical equipment, for elderly,
        314–15
Medical examinations, free, 317
Medical expenses, as tax
        deduction, 344
Medical information, in books,
        351–16, 324–25
Medical records, 324
Medical tests, 317
Medicare, 300, 301, 311, 312–15,
        363–64
Medigap, 364
Membership stores, for food, 14
Mental health, 307, 322
Microwave ovens, 164
Midwives, 308
Milk, shopping for, 18
Mortgage(s), 113–17, *114–15*
    adjustable convertible, 114
    adjustable rate, 113–14
    bimonthly payment of, 116
    conventional, 114–15, *115*
    handyman special and, 116
    options for, 113
    points and, 113, *114–15*
    prepaying, 116–17
Motorcycling, 362
Movie theaters, 288–89
Moving, 117–18
Muffins, 39–40
Mulches, 205–8
Music, 290–91

N
National Institutes of Health (NIH)
        322–23

Neighborhoods, 108, 109
  schools near, 110-11
Neighborhood Watch program, 137
Nellie Mae. *See* New England
      Education Loan Marketing
      Association
New England Education Loan
      Marketing Association
      (Nellie Mae), 265
Nursing care, for elderly, 365
Nursing homes, shared housing as
      alternative to, 311–12
Nutrition, government programs
      and, 44

O

Office, home, taxation and, 346
Office furniture, 106
Oil, for automobiles, 56,65–66
Outdoor furniture, 106
Outdoor lighting, 167
Outpatient surgery, 300
Ovens, 161, 162
  microwave, 164

P

Pachysandra, 222
Pantyhose, 82
Parent Loans for Undergraduate
      Students (PLUS), 260–61
Parking, at airports, 273
Pasta, *33*
Pea trellis, 232
Pell grants, 259
Pension payments, estate planning
      and, 373
Pensions, 349
People's Medical Society (PMS),
      324
Periodontal disease, 319
Perkins loans, 260
Pests, garden
  control of, 208–17, *214–16*
  companion planting for, 213,
      214–16
  homemade sprays for, 208–9
  natural, 212–13, *214–16*
  types of, 209–12, *214–16*
Pharmaceuticals. *See* Drugs

Plant bulbs, compost for, 203
Plants. *See also* Garden
  companions and allies of, for pest
      control, *214–16*
  equipment to protect, 232–36
  low-maintenance, 25
  propagation of, 220–22, *220, 221*
  pruning and caring for, 229
  supports for, 231–32
  transplanting, 221, *221*
Plumber, for home remodeling,
      131–32
Plumbing, for new home, 125
PLUS. *See* Parent Loans for
      Undergraduate Students
Poison control centers, 326
Poison ivy, 217
Pollution, water, in home, 140–41
Possessions, selling of, 293–94
Poultry
  determining servings of, *31*
  quartering, 35
  selecting quality, 22, 25
  stretching portions of, 34
Pregnancy, 307–8. *See also* Birth
Price scanners, 13
Proof of purchase (POP), 8
Property. *See* Home; Possessions
Pruning equipment, 230–31
Psychiatric care, 307, 322
Pudding mix, 39

Q

Quackgrass, 217
Quantity purchases, of food, 8–9

R

Radiators, bleeding, 185
Radon test, for home, 139–40
Real estate. *See* Home
Recipes. *See* Food, recipes
Recreational vehicles, (RVs),
      274–75
Refrigerators, 146–47, 156
Refunding, from food purchases,
      7–8
Rental, of entertainment items,
      292–93
Repair shops, 292

Reproductions, of antique
    furniture, 104–5
Restaurants, 284–85
    tipping in, 285, *286–87*
Retirement account(s)
    financial aid for higher education
        and, 257, 259
    individual. *See* Individual
        Retirement Account
Retirement plans
    estate planning and, 373
    taxes and, 347–49, 350
Retreads, 54–55
Road hazard warranty, against tire
        damage, 54
Roof, installation of gutters and
        downspouts on, 124
Rose bush, 225
ROTC, Army, 264
RVs. *See* Recreational vehicles

S
Safety, home, 325–26
Salad dressings, 41–42
Sallie Mae. *See* Student Loan
        Marketing Association
Salvage stores, food shopping at, 16
Salvation Army, 78, 101
Scanners, price, 13
Scholarships, 258
School, child care after, 254
Schools, local, evaluation of,
        110–11
Seasonings, 41–42, 43
Seat belts, 361–62
Security, home, 135–39
Seed flats, 227
Seedling containers, 226–27
Seedling lights, 227–28
Seeds
    for gardening, 226
    for grass, 243
    growing flowers from, 223
    sources for, 196
Senior citizens. *See* Elderly
Service contracts, for appliances,
        151–52
SHARE, 265

Shellfish, *20, 25*
Shelving, installation of, 124
Shoes
    care of, 85–87
    for children, 87
    purchase of, 82–83
    soles of, 86
Shower heads, 169
Shriners of North America, 326
Shrubs, choosing, 225
Sickness. *See* Health care
Sidewalk, for yard, 242
Slugs, 212
Smoking
    during pregnancy, 308
    insurance rates and, 368
Snacks, for children, 247–48
Snails, 212
Soil
    care of, 195–200, *196, 198*
    free conditioners, for, 197, *198*
    potting, making your own,
        199–200
    rock powders or minerals to
        improve, 197
    testing of, 197, 199
Soil mixes, homemade, 200
Solar-electric lamps, 165, 167
Solar water heating, 174–75
Specialty shops, 13, 76
Sperm banks, 309–10
Sports, 295–96
Steam boiler, 185
Stocks, for children, 352
Storm-and-screen windows, 182
Storm windows and doors, 181
Stress, 322
Student Loan Marketing
        Association (Sallie Mae), 266
Sun-blocking window treatments,
        192, *193*
Sunflower Tepee, 231
Supermarket shopping, 4–9, 11–12
    bulk buying and, 8–9
    by comparison, 6
    impulse buying and, 7
    list for, 7
    for nonfood items, 6

Supermarket shopping *(continued)*
  refunds versus coupons for, 7–8
  unit pricing and, 8
Superstores, food shopping at, 14
Supplemental Educational
        Opportunity Grants
        (SEOGs), 259
Supplemental Loans for Students
        (SLS), 261
Surgeons, negotiating with, 305–6
Surgery, 300, 304–6
Sweaters, 79
Swimming pool, filter pump for,
        157

T
Taxes, **341–53**
  business owners and, 344–46
  children and, 352–53
  on custodial account interest,
        261–62
  deductions from, 342–44
  estate, 351, 371–72
  filing forms for, 346–47
  401(k) plans and, 350, *351*
  on gifts to students from
        grandparents, 268
  giving money away and, 349,
        351
  home remodeling and, 129
  IRAs and, 347–48
  Keogh Plans, and, 348–49
  pensions and, 349
  property, 133–35
Taxi drivers, tipping, *286*
Telephones, 337–38
  extension cord for, 340
Telephone service(s), **329–40**
  800 numbers, 334
  equipment decisions and, 337–38
  local calls, 337
  long-distance, 333–34
  choosing company for, 335–36
  900 numbers, 332
  special, 330–32
  wiring installation for, 339
  wiring maintenance agreements
        and, 332

Television, cable, 290
Temperature, radiant, in home,
        177
Testing/Tests
  medical, 251, 317
  for radon in home, 139–40
  of soil, 197, 199
  of water in home, 140–41
Textbooks, 267
Theater, 289–90
Thermostat(s), 154
  clock, 184
  fan, for warm air furnace, 183
  faulty, 183
Thrifty shops, 292
  clothing purchased at, 78
  food shopping at, 13
  furniture purchased at, 101
Tipping, 285, *286–87*
Tires, for automobiles, 53–55, 66
Tools
  for automobile maintenance and
        repair, 51, 52
  gardening, 229–31
Tooth loss, 319
Trains, 273–74
Travel, **271–82**
  air, 272–73
  auto clubs and, 49–50
  bed and breakfast bargains and,
        276–77
  car rental for, 275
  clubs for, 278–79
  credit cards for, 281–82
  free overnight stops and, 276
  home exchange and, 275–76
  hostels for, 277
  hotels for, 273, 277–78
  planning by phone for, 279
  rail, 273–74
  in recreational vehicle, 274–75
  by senior citizens, 281
  on short notice, 278
  for short periods, 280
  to Washington, D.C., 280
Trees, 225, 228, 240–41, *241*
Tree shoots, cutting back, 216
Trellis, 231–32

Trust
  for funeral expenses, 374
  irrevocable, 351
  minor's, 352–53
Tuition, **256–70**
  as fringe benefit, 268
  installment plan for, 270
  waivers of, 269
Tuition plans, prepaid, 264–65

U
Underwear, 79
Uniform Gifts to Minors Act, 261
United States Savings Bonds, 262, 352
Unit pricing, in supermarkets, 8
Upholstered furniture, 97–99
Used automobile, 63–65
Utility companies, free items from, 161

V
Vacationing, *See* Travel
Vasectomy, 309–10
VCRs. *See* Videocassette recorders
Veal, 22
Vegetable garden, 234
Vegetables
  best time to buy, *26–28*
  determining servings of, *32–33*
  preserving freshness of, *21*
  selecting quality, 25, *26–28*
Vegetarian meals, 36
Vents, clogged, in steam radiator system 185
Videocassette recorders (VCRs), 287–88

W
Wardrobe. *See* Clothing
Warehouse stores, for food, 12
Warranty, on appliances, 150–51
Washing machine, cost of operating, 158, *159*
Washington, D.C., travel to, 280
Water beds, 158

Water heater(s)
  adjusting thermostat on, 170
  choosing new, 172
  draining, 168
  electricity and, 172–73
  heat pump, 173
  insulation wrap for, 170
  one-way valves on, 168
  options for, 175
  timer on, 169
Water heating, 167–75
  electric, 169
  solar, 174–75
Water pipes, hot, insulation for, 171
Water Saver, Hot, 171
Water-saving fixtures, 169
Water tests, for home, 140–41
Weatherization, of home, 178–82
Weather-stripping, 180, 181
Weed killers, 213, 216, 245
Weight control, 319–20
Wheelchairs, 314
WIC. *See* Women, Infants, and Children
Wills, 374, 376–77
  determining need for, 376–77
  executor for, 377–78
  legal guardian specified in, 378
  living, 302, 379
  prepared by attorney, 377
Windows, 138, 181, 182
Window treatments, 182, 192, *193*
Women, Infants, and Children (WIC), 44

X
X-rays, dental, 306

Y
Yard, 242
YMCA/YWCA, 296

Z
Zero-coupons, 262–63
Zoning, for properties, 108

Rodale Press, Inc., publishes PREVENTION, America's leading health magazine.
For information on how to order your subscription,
write to PREVENTION, Emmaus, PA 18098.